Symbolization and Creativity

Symbolization and Creativity

SUSAN K. DERI

INTERNATIONAL UNIVERSITIES PRESS, INC.
New York

Library of Congress Cataloging in Publication Data

Deri, Susan K.
Symbolization and creativity.

Bibliography: p.
Includes index.
I. Title. 1. Creative ability. 2. Symbolism (Psychology)
BF408.D48 1983 153.3′5 83-26482
ISBN 0-8236-6292-6

Manufactured in the United States of America

Contents

Foreword *by Peter Deri* vii

Part I

1. Form Creation as a Life-Patterning Process 3
2. Time, Dual Instinct Theory, and Creativity 9
3. The Case of Paul 19

Part II

4. The Bridging-Over Function of Symbols 29
5. The Organizing Function of Symbolization 61
6. Centrifugal or Internal Symbolization 77
7. Desymbolization and Missymbolization 153

Part III

8. Winnicott's Creativity 241
9. The Psychic Structure of the Creating Artist: A Theoretical Construction 281
10. Impairment in the Capacity for Authentic Dialogue 297
11. The Significance for Psychoanalysis of the Symbolizing Nature of Verbal Language 313
12. Using the Psychoanalytic Situation to Foster Good Symbolization 323

References 349

Index 357

Foreword

In Chapter 6 of this work, Susan Deri quotes from Wilhelm Stekel's "The Polyphony of Thought." There Stekel describes the "struggle of expressing thoughts in language. . . . we never have single thoughts but always many, an entire polyphony, of which speech expresses but one melody." I have struggled with this problem of the inadequacy of words for some time now while writing this foreword, for it is from three very different points of view that I write the words you are now reading. I write as a neophyte analyst commenting on the work of a senior training analyst; I write as the author's son; and, most painfully, I write as someone still suffering from her sudden death shortly after completing the manuscript of this book.

The thoughts and ideas to be found here are traceable through her papers, an earlier book, and lectures written over the past thirty-five years. Very generally, her interest was always to enlarge psychoanalytic theory in such a way as to accommodate a theory of creativity broader and more basic than the view that would equate it with sublimation; the theory she offers places greater emphasis on instincts and drives than is usually seen in analytic accounts of creativity. The first thing, then, that makes this book so unusual is that a question typically posed by those identifying themselves with an ego psychological point of view is answered here in a most biopsychological way. Susan Deri argues that creativity is an innate force or drive that should be viewed as similar, perhaps analogous, to the organizing gestalt principles of visual perception whereby incomplete stimuli are made into better gestalts by processes of closure, figure-ground organization, etc.

The essence of her argument here runs as a red thread through much of her earlier writing and is born of her association with her earliest mentor, Dr. Lipót Szondi. This essence is her strong belief that drives and instincts, powerful as she believes them to be, are not to be counterposed to ego function, control mechanisms, or anything of the sort; rather, she theorizes, the forces that will eventually transform the drives and instincts into more friendly and usable attributes are present from the very beginning. She feels that one reason such a conception of the unconscious is not more popular is that the topographic theory fell into disfavor with the advent of structural theory.

Another reason this book is unusual is that the various disciplines contributing to a theory are not typically dealt with in such depth by a single author. Not only does she integrate different psychoanalytic orientations, but she weaves into her psychoanalytic thinking strands from various areas of academic psychology. Finally she couches her entire thinking within the philosophical framework of Ernst Cassirer and Susanne K. Langer. Her theory, then, can be seen as "out-biologizing" Freud; as giving more centrality to Winnicott than many object relations theorists do; and as using gestalt principles of visual perception as an analog for internal mental perception. In addition, she relies on concepts from the topological field theory of Kurt Lewin, the Piagetian notions of assimilation and accommodation, and various biological and physical metaphors to conceptualize the most basic processes of communication among the various layers and structures of the mind.

It is tempting to speculate on how a person remains so open to ostensibly unrelated or even counterposed ways of thinking. In my mother's case, I suspect the trait had a lot to do with her early training in psychology and psychoanalysis in Hungary. She was fortunate to have been taught, simultaneously and almost communally, by Szondi, who was already developing his ideas about the insufficient emphasis on the role of genetic constitution in Freudian psychology, and by the two earliest spokesmen of what was later to become object relations theory—Imre Hermann and Michael Balint. An unusual result of her model of mental life is that in spite of (or perhaps because of) her heavy grounding in biology, she ends up being more optimistic regarding the possibility of therapeutic change than one might expect.

Though perhaps I should attempt here to summarize the powerful and elaborately developed theory presented in Chapter 6, I suspect there is little I could make clearer or more lucid than she did. After finishing the chapter's first section, I felt the subsequent parts—one on clinical applications, the other on the role of the mother as catalyst in symbol formation and creativity—were ample reward for having stayed with the more difficult theory building that preceded them. Regarding the relationship between Winnicott's concepts and the question of symbolization and creativity, suffice it to say that Susan Deri views the preconscious as an intrapsychic meeting ground or bridging area, and Winnicott's "transitional space" as having similar functions interpersonally.

The word "symbol," she points out, has a Greek root meaning "to connect." Appropriately enough, few books will trigger as many connections in the reader's mind as this one will. For me, the book has had a telling effect on how I view my patients, on what I view as curative in my work, and on my view of the meaning of a patient's personal biography. Speaking as an analyst of the younger generation, I think it safe to assume that many of us will find the book both inspiring and a little frightening. We are not used to hearing that the structural theory does not add all that much to metapsychology, and might actually close off certain fruitful lines of thought. We are not used to hearing about the serious difficulties in explaining consciousness, but rather about the vicissitudes of the unconscious. (The author reminds us that Freud knew that consciousness was in fact more problematic than the unconscious.) And we certainly are not used to thinking about the unavoidable relativity of psychoanalytic reconstructions. We think in terms of symptoms, not missymbolizations, and we are far more enamored of language than the author is.

As for analysts of the older generation, I can only guess at their reactions. My hunch is that many will think, "I always had a similar thought in the back of my mind." Some of the author's peers, I suspect, will feel she has so redefined the notion of conflict, so changed its locale, that she has in fact abandoned a central tenet of psychoanalytic thought. Some might feel she has painted with too broad a brush in relegating the idea of "neutralized energy" to the status of an unfortunate state of affairs, rather than viewing it as the necessary prelude to creativity.

I suspect that many readers will be vaguely troubled by something about this book that is rather difficult to pinpoint. Perhaps a principle of Gestalt psychology has been violated: too much is covered and all of it seems important. The book seems a forest of forests rather than a forest of trees. All I can say is that I have myself had to read many sections many times over—though not, I should add, without benefit. The reader experiencing particular difficulty with Chapter 6 might profitably read the author's long footnote to the chapter she contributed to *Between Reality and Fantasy: Transitional Objects and Phenomena*, edited by Simon A. Grolnick, Leonard Barkin, and Werner Muensterberger (New York: Jason Aronson, 1978). It was there that she originally, and of course more succinctly, presented the concepts elaborated here.

While I was going over the manuscript, another uncomfortable feeling came to my mind and then left only to reappear. The thought was that there might really be no need for a new metapsychology; that the distinction between the "transformation" and the "harnessing" of instincts might really be a matter of semantics. Then, recalling my mother's modification of a "horse and rider" figure to that of the centaur, an idea she originally presented about ten years ago, I started to think in very concrete, phenomenological terms: were I to meet a horse and rider, I suspect I would look alternately at one *and then* the other, perhaps sometimes trying to see them as a whole; were I to meet a centaur, I know my gaze would be riveted on the section where the two parts blend or bridge, one *into* the other. It was then that I could see the connection between this slight reformulation of a theoretical construct and a significant new attitude toward the clinical situation. Although I might be using words that would not be my mother's, this book is a plea against making subtle and continuous concepts over into neatly discrete discontinuities; to her way of thinking, the data require the former mode of thought if they are to be meaningfully understood. She was most taken with Winnicott's respect for the paradoxical. The preconscious, the "transitional space," and the centaur are to me all a bit paradoxical.

I would like to end on a somewhat personal note which I think fits with the rather personal style of my mother's writing. It was not easy being her son. Often she would say or do things that would pull me in several directions at once: I would want simultaneously to apologize for her, to disown her, and—most problematically—to be just like her. Don't expect to be spared these troublesome sentiments as you read this book.

Although she did not write the dedication for her book, she wished to dedicate it to her grandchildren, Christopher and Sarah.

PETER DERI

PART I

CHAPTER 1

Form Creation as a Life-Patterning Process

The creative principle underlies human life, but nowhere is it systematically treated in the Freudian psychoanalytic literature. Creativity is generally treated under the heading of sublimation, as one method of instinctual aim displacement. Yet creativity is an organismic urge, reflected in the development of form both in and around us. We are apt to forget this overriding drive toward creativity, without which life in any *form* would be inconceivable. We tend to assign to the word "creativity" the narrow meaning of human beings' conscious effort to shape raw material into expressive, communicative form.

In contrast, I use the concept of creativity in its widest sense, as form creation of any kind, as the shaping of what I shall call a good gestalt.[1] In this sense, creativity refers to the innumerable ongoing actions, reactions, decisions, and choices—unconscious, preconscious, and conscious—which

[1] Certain dynamic principles of Gestalt psychology, based on the work of Wertheimer, Koffka, and Köhler, are useful in explaining the functioning of the human mind. In particular, I shall refer to the pressure toward closure in incomplete gestalts, well or poorly equilibrated dynamic fields, and the rules of symmetry and asymmetry in structure formation.

give form and texture to an individual life. Within this continuous life-shaping activity, we find the better-known specific creative act, when a person purposefully shapes raw material—be it words, sounds, clay, wood, or lines and colors—to express and communicate through some artistic work.

In the wide sense, each individual biography is the sum total of a person's creative activities; it is his or her personal "work of art." All these life-shaping activities add up to a good or a bad gestalt or, rather, to something someplace in between. "Good" here refers to the quality of the *fit* one is able to create between oneself and one's surrounding environment (Goldstein, 1939). An indicator of "goodness" is the subjective experience of "feeling at home in one's skin," as well as in the world. In this case, interactions between the self and outside objects are experienced as meaningful. Some objects light up as having positive valences (Lewin, 1935, 1936), i.e. they seem desirable. Corresponding to this is the motivation to find a path leading toward the desirable object. The effort needed to traverse that path is weighed against the resistance and friction inherent in the objective situation. A healthy person feels neither omnipotent nor impotent vis-à-vis the desired goals in his or her life. Some goals seem reachable, some not. At times it may be necessary to substitute one aim for another. A good substitute implies that the wish-tension directed toward the original aim will be released, at least to a considerable degree, when the alternative goal is reached. Here the subjective feeling is one of enjoyment. This capacity to accept and use substitutes lends flexibility to a person's life; it greatly enhances the possibility of molding self and environment into a well-functioning, organically connected gestalt.

A key factor in the creation of a viable lifespace is the quality of symbol formation. Symbol formation is the specifically human way of creating order and connectedness within the person's psychic organization, as well as the means of bridging from the inside to the outside. A person's capacity for symbolization defines his or her creativity (or lack of it). To my mind, only through a generic theory of symbolization will we be able to understand the possibilities for success or failure in the development of a personally meaningful life-space.

Before taking up in detail the all-important issue of symbol formation, however, I would like to pursue my schematic description of the dynamics of healthy life a little further. Whether or not our life acquires good form depends on many factors, including our constitutional endowment and the quality of life in the world into which we are born. Some of these factors are totally outside our individual ability to change, but they nevertheless influence the state of our personal lifespace. Both genetic and environmental "givens" are matters of *chance* from the point of view of the newborn. They have nothing to do with personal choice. They are the outer limits, the frame into which the growing person has to create his or her life.

Of all the environmentally given "chance factors" it is the mother's personality that contributes most to the growing infant's experience of his or her life. It is primarily the mother who hands over the objects of the world to her child (Winnicott, 1965). As we shall see in more detail in Part III, the way in which the mother performs this act determines to a large extent the key in which children will experience themselves and the whole environment. A child may come to feel that "the outside can give what I want and the outside wants what I can give." On the other hand, the outside may appear unyielding and unreceptive. Which of these alternatives will characterize the child's attitude to the world and to him- or herself depends to a large extent on the early interplay between mother and child.

The intuitively empathic mother offers gratifications that synchronize well with the infant's biological rhythms. The quality of *her* motions while handling the child, the tactile-kinesthetic quality of her touch and holding, must flow with and into the child's own rhythms and vague wishful expectations. The infant's own universe then feels unified, without jagged disruptions. This feeling of unity at first probably includes mother. Soon, it will be experienced as a feeling of harmony *with* mother, as well as *within* the infant's own skin. The sense of a natural psychosomatic unity of life processes is the outcome of an early good fit between mother and child, of an optimal dual-union.[2]

If the infant's constitutional givens are adequate, then the mother's empathic care lays the foundation for good integration within the child—between body and mind, between diverse and antithetical instinctual drives (Deri, 1966), and between self and environment. In ideal terms, in the beginning of life, wish, act, and fulfillment should coincide for just the right amount of time. Although there is no phase of early development when such perfect harmony exists, sharp discontinuities can be avoided by a good mother. If gratification occurs within a reasonable time period, the infant's mounting need-tensions will not lead to disruptive rage. In other words, if gratification occurs within the time period before unfulfilled wish turns into trauma, the baby will not experience a dis-

[2] I prefer Hermann's (1936) concept of "dual-union" to refer to the primary relationship between the mother and the infant, instead of the now-fashionable term "symbiosis" (Mahler, 1968). Borrowed from biology, the term "symbiosis" describes the mutually dependent, even parasitic, existence of two dissimilar organisms. Too many semantic acrobatics are needed to apply this biological term to the earliest mother-infant relationship. In contrast, Hermann's concept of dual-union allows for the objective twoness of the relationship, as well as implying a unity. We do not know, but rather assume, that young infants experience absolutely no boundary (no twoness) between themselves and their mothers. The paradox implicit in the concept of "dual-union" thus seems quite apposite to designate the infant's hazy awareness of closeness to the mother.

junctive break within the flow of his or her life. At first hazy, and then clearer, memories of previous gratifications establish basic trust (Erikson, 1950) and hope. Hope, as we shall see in the next chapter, underlies the creative process.

CHAPTER 2

Time, Dual Instinct Theory, and Creativity

In the previous chapter creativity in its widest sense was defined as meaningful form creation of any kind. Meaningful form creation is symbol creation. A symbol is a formed gestalt that carries meaning. What fundamental attitudes or proclivities are the prerequisites for the capacity to create good, meaningful form? Two such fundamental prerequisites are the attitude to time and the proportional relation between Eros and Thanatos. Let us start by discussing the role of time, specifically the role of a trusting attitude toward the future.

The Role of Hope

Without hope, without trust in the future, there can be no creativity. The reality of the ongoing nature of time, as well as of the limits imposed by time, must be accepted to create a meaningful life. Acceptance of time is the crux of ego formation. In psychoanalytic terms, there must be a transition from primary-process to secondary-process functioning.

As we know, primary processes ignore the reality of time;

they push toward immediate tension discharge. This "timeless" functioning is guided by what we call the "pleasure principle." Yet, without consideration for time, a person may be led to heedless, instinct-driven acting out. To establish and maintain a viable life pattern, the person must be able to function on the secondary-process level. The essence of ego development is the increasing role given to secondary-process functioning, and the essence of secondary-process functioning is the introduction of *time* into mental operations. As the saying goes, mature adults "think before they act." By evaluating the external and internal situation, they can anticipate consequences and ensure the success of their actions.

Underlying such reality-oriented functioning is the hope or belief that actions *can* be successful. Without this hope, why would one invest time in planning and carefully executing some act? Confidence in the outcome of one's actions depends on the memory of previous successes; it is for this reason that the earliest well-timed gratifications mean so much for the child's later action patterns. If the earliest mental operation of *wish* regularly meets with success, i.e., with gratification within an optimal time limit, then time becomes a friendly dimension along which good things are expected to happen. An optimistic, expectant attitude toward the future implies libidinal cathexis of both the self and time.

If the child's wishes are consistently frustrated, then the dimension of time will be equated with painful waiting. Time becomes "the enemy" to rebel against. Here we find people who, although they operate to some degree on a secondary-process level, show limited patience and a short attention span. They may be bright and potentially talented, yet unsuccessful in schoolwork; they cannot produce term papers on time or abandon projects altogether if they are too time-consuming. It seems impossible for these people to stick to a distant goal, nor do they function well within limits set by time. In analysis, they consistently come late or very early, and may resist ending the sessions. For instance, they may keep their eyes on their watches to be sure *they* end the session instead of the analyst's announcing that "time is up."

How much this attitude of impatience and fighting time grows out of the mother's poorly synchronized care, and how much stems from the child's innate constitutional characteristics, is an unanswerable question. Frustration tolerance, the acceptance of waiting, can be assumed to have a wide range of constitutional variability, depending on the innate pace of neural conductivity and inborn peculiarities of the endocrine system. Some children are frustration-prone by nature and harmonizing with their internal rhythms demands an exceptionally empathic mother, far beyond the "average expectable, good-enough mother." Whether, or to what extent, early therapeutic infant care can result in "resetting" a constitutionally impatient child's racing "internal clock" has not yet been demonstrated.

To reiterate: Reality-adapted and long-range self-fulfilling activities cannot take place without a positive attitude toward time. The creation and completion of anything need time and trust in the outcome. The creation of complex forms, in particular, requires extended time, and here one must consider even the strictly biological maturation of body and mind. Whether and in what way a person's libidinized attitude toward these "nonvoluntary" maturational processes will influence their outcome remains an open question. Yet, without resorting to mysticism, many physicians and psychologists would agree that trust and hope in recovery, for instance, can influence the healing process. Certainly psychosomatic interrelationships are well documented. In a similar vein, we might assume that the child's total physical and mental development is influenced by the child's earliest experiences of habitual gratification or frustration. These early experiences might not only determine the child's mood, but also "tune up" the functioning of various physiological systems, especially with regard to muscle tension and movement patterns. What I am arguing is that *hope*, an optimistic attitude to the future, influences *all* creative form development—from physiological maturation, to the defining of one's lifespace, to the making of specific art objects.

Eros, Thanatos, and Creativity

The creativity-enhancing attitudes of hope and confidence in oneself and the world could also be described in terms of libidinal cathexis. That libido is intrinsically connected with creativity becomes clear if we reconsider Freud's dual instinct theory, presented in *Beyond the Pleasure Principle* (1920). Here Eros, the "life instinct," and Thanatos, the "death instinct," represent the basic instinctual dialectic of organic life. The specific force through which Eros manifests itself is libido. Libido, in Freud's formulation, represents the primal urge to live; its function is to bind separate parts into larger units. It is through the force of libido that Eros, the life instinct, counteracts the destructiveness of Thanatos, the death instinct.

Thanatos works toward the dissolution of the organic forms that sustain life. Freud hypothesized that by breaking up living forms, Thanatos aims to eliminate the tension state implicit in life processes, and thereby "reestablish" the tensionless state of inorganic matter. Thus, Thanatos is considered to be the instinctual base of the repetition compulsion and the tendencies to inertia that work against the creative principle of Eros. Thanatos is the great "equalizer" by way of destroying the unique configurations of life. Of course, in the long run Thanatos wins out over Eros, as living forms disintegrate with death. Yet, during life, libido is the binding force that forms and holds together the configurations of life processes into cohesive gestalts. Libido is the counterweight to the principle of inertia. Without libido, life stagnates or disintegrates. There is no energy to build or maintain viable life structures.

We do not know where this gestalt-forming life energy originates. But we do know that the mother's dependable loving care can do much to elicit the free flow of libido from the baby's reservoir of undifferentiated "energy" (Deri, 1966). The baby must come to experience a love of life and the desire to exert the effort needed to create an ever-expanding lifespace. Since exertion per se is unpleasurable, only a trusting, libidinous attitude toward the outcome of this effort will outweigh the pull of inertia.

Oddly enough, Freud, in defining his reality principle, does not spell out this specific role of libido in overriding the pleasure principle. According to his "Formulations on the Two Principles of Mental Functioning" (1911), "necessity" and the avoidance of greater pain are the motive forces that compel the growing child to abandon the pleasure principle and undertake the longer, more effortful but more realistic route toward his or her goals.

My point here is that embarking on this effortful journey also implies trust in the real world, in the future, and in one's own capacities to reach what one wants. This trusting attitude is based on a reservoir of pro-life "energy" or libido, in terms of the instinct dialectics of Eros and Thanatos. The creation of life-enhancing good gestalts always implies a considerable plus on the side of Eros, of libido, which counteracts inertia and disintegration.

In terms of the structural theory, a well-structured, well-functioning ego is the psychic instance that facilitates the creation of a good lifespace. A good ego is a life-enhancing gestalt. The ego is characterized by its coherent organization (Freud, 1923). Therefore, we can assume that ego development, too, requires a preponderance of the forces of Eros over Thanatos. And once formed, the healthy ego performs a linking or "synthesizing" function (Nunberg, 1931), similar to that ascribed to libido. This synthesizing function protects the ego's cohesive organization against disruptive impingements (within limits). We can also understand that such a stable psychic core as a healthy ego will continue to order incoming contents, whether from the inside or the outside.

The ego is an organized and organizing gestalt. It organizes our perceptions of the inside and the outside; the increasing ordering of each realm reinforces that of the other in a circular way. The more "orderly" the psychic processes, the better the person's organization of the outside world (projective techniques are based on this principle) and consequently the better his or her chances to create a personally satisfying lifespace.

But how does this circular organizing process begin? How can one account for the origin, the creation of that organized psychic core? Questions pertaining to the original creation of anything can never be answered in a satisfactory causal way (unless one resorts to theology or to the fact that they were biologically-genetically predetermined gestalts). So let us leave the question of the origin of biopsychological gestalt formation aside, and continue with an example from Wertheimer's (1923) perception experiments, to illustrate what I mean by the organizing power of a gestalt and the function of the cohesive gestalt forces.

If a series of dots is presented in the basic form of a triangle, even if the dots are gradually spaced quite widely apart, they will still be perceived as "belonging together" in the shape of a triangle. In contrast, with a random cluster of dots, when the spaces between them are increased to the same extent, they are no longer perceived as "belonging together" but as separate entities. The original gestalt of a triangle exerted its organizing power by overcoming the dispersing effect of increased distance. Such experiments document the principle of gestalt cohesion. Some prove how much gradual distortion a well-delineated picture of, for example, a person, can withstand. If, in a picture series presented consecutively, the first image shows a woman with a hat and a fur cape, a great number of the following pictures will still be perceived as a woman, even though they gradually change more and more into an animal shape. If the highly distorted versions are shown, not in a gradually changing series, but by themselves, then they are never perceived as a woman but as some strange animal. Again, the original gestalt (the woman), due to the cohesive gestalt force, upholds its unified pattern in the face of considerable distortion.

It is this tendency to uphold a unified pattern that seems particularly relevant to any consideration of the ego's order-creating functions. Drawing on our analogy to perception experiments, we can surmise that once the organized psychic gestalt of an ego exists, it will maintain itself by means of its own cohesive gestalt forces. This does not answer the question of origins, but it does answer the question of how the developed ego performs its order-making functions. (Symbol formation always aims at order-making.)

We must compromise with partial answers since we have to remain within the sphere of biopsychology. Even here, many of our so-called explanatory concepts seem to beg the question, "explaining" the phenomenon under question merely by "deriving" it from a concept that describes the very same phenomenon. The reader might well criticize my own use of Freud's derivation of life processes from the "life instinct" and disintegration processes from the "death instinct." What is important, however, is that even such descriptive concepts group events and things together in a new way, thereby changing our way of perceiving and thinking about the world.

Freud's dual instinct theory was a great creative innovation, even though it "only" gave names to existing phenomena, and despite the fact that the meaning of his term "instinct" remains hazy. (The meaning of "instinct" when applied to humans is always vague.) What Freud's theory does provide is a heuristic tool, by grouping all organismic processes (psychological ones included) into two main categories: those which are "pro-life" and those which are "anti-life." Freud chose the names Eros and Thanatos to denote the two antithetical tendencies, and he specified the forces through which they manifest themselves. He assigned libido as the mediating force to Eros, and sadism or aggression to Thanatos.

As we have seen, libido links parts together into larger, life-enhancing wholes, while sadism and aggression tend to break down the living configurations into inert, dead matter. Libido, then, is the propelling force toward the formation of organic gestalts, toward the functioning human being. Aggression has the opposite goal: to split up the unity of "good" gestalts, annihilating life.

By contrasting Eros and libido with Thanatos, sadism, and aggression, Freud implied his belief that love and hate are, respectively, the basic life-organizing and life-disorganizing forces in the universe. This extension of Freud's Eros versus Thanatos concept underlies the theory of creativity elaborated in this book.

Without denying the ever-present dialectic opposition between the forces of Eros and Thanatos in all creative acts, the forces of Eros have to override those of Thanatos for the achievement of a good gestalt. A good gestalt which expresses meaning is a symbol in the generic sense of that term. Symbols connect separate entities, they bridge over a distance, they heal splits, they bring unity into the person's total life-space. These functions need the ascendancy of Eros over Thanatos. A good mother is likely to bring about this situation in her child. However, such a favorable beginning is often not the case. Growing children often falter in the task of building an enjoyable, well-connected lifespace for themselves. The forces of Thanatos are ruining their gestalt-building processes. If the ensuing pain leads such a person into psychoanalysis, then the aim of treatment is to redress the relative weight of the pro-life versus anti-life forces. After successful treatment the analysand becomes "libidinized"; Eros is in lead over the forces of Thanatos; stable, loving relationships to people, to projects, to life in general become possible. Splits are overcome by way of good symbolization.

CHAPTER 3

The Case of Paul

Before leaving this first part, I wish to add a "coda" in the form of a case history. This is in tribute to the patient who, many years ago, started me on the road to organizing my thoughts on the interconnections of hope, libido, and creativity.

In spite of his unhappy life, Paul was very much a noncomplainer. His one repetitive plaint was: "I have nothing to look forward to." His life was stagnating. Nothing of interest ever happened. But like a good soldier of life, he kept on living his uneventful days and years without making any fuss. His quiet, disciplined endurance of life was impressive—so different from the noisy self-pity of hysteroid borderline patients.

Paul was the only child of exceptionally talented parents. He was brought up in two foreign countries and came to the United States as a young engineer. He was close to forty and unmarried when treatment began. It lasted for approximately three and a half years, with thrice-weekly sessions.

Paul lived his life mostly in solitude—not because he disliked people, but because he was too socially awkward to establish human contacts. At his job he got along well with his colleagues and other workers. After well over ten years, he was still at his first job in this country. He certainly had endurance and stability. These positive characteristics lay on the other side of his lack of initiative and lack of hope that anything could be better.

Paul described his job as "okay." He earned enough to live modestly, without having to worry about where the next month's rent for his one-room efficiency apartment would come from—or how to afford his simple but respectable clothes. He had very few extra expenses since he had neither a social life nor any particular desires for himself. His one great wish was to get married and have a family, with a circle of friends. But these were "theoretical" wishes, since he was totally unable to realize them through any act. It was not that he was unfriendly by nature, or schizoid or aggressive. He simply lacked the basic technique of social intercourse. He had no trust whatsoever in his own attractiveness, and consequently no hope that anybody would enjoy his company. He did trust, and with good reason, his intellectual abilities. He knew he could be more than a "routine' engineer. But he saw no point in trying harder—for what purpose and for whose sake? He lacked the healthy narcissism of finding satisfaction and interest in his own achievements. All this would change, he felt, if he had a wife and family. Yet he avoided going any place where he might meet a girlfriend or friends of any kind. During his yearly two-week vacations, for instance, he drove around in his car and slept in a different motel each night. In this way he didn't have to face the perplexing task of socializing with people in summer resorts.

Where did this considerable mistrust in his own likableness come from?

As a child, Paul grew up in a large apartment in a big city, but mainly he stayed in his own room, which was filled with toys. Innumerable blocks, construction sets, and science toys were his company. His successful parents were on the road most of the time, pursuing their glamorous careers. When they were home, they had no time for their child. If Paul ventured out of his room, he was quickly sent back and told to play with his toys. So he did. A maid was supposed to take care of him, but the maids changed frequently and none of them seemed to take a special interest in Paul. Thus, the inanimate toys became his constant companions. His only other "friends" were his grandparents, who were quite old, as Paul had been born to his parents in their middle-age. Since these grandparents lived in the same city, Paul visited them every week. These visits were the highlight of his childhood; they were something "to look forward to."

Then, due to political pressures, Paul and his parents had to move to a faraway country. The parents' careers were interrupted and in order to make ends meet they ran a boarding house. This activity was most unsuited for both parents' temperaments, and they became depressed and irritable. Paul tried his best to be helpful. In school he was an excellent student, and after doing his homework he cleaned the house, took out the garbage, and did everything he could think of to ease his parents' lives. But all this was to no avail in terms of receiving love and appreciation. His parents remained morose and full of self-pity. Apparently, the father, after a while, could have picked up his old career, but by that time he had become almost a recluse and hardly talked, even to his wife and son.

Paul, by now a teenager, developed some vague oedipal fantasies of proving to his mother how much more useful and caring he was than his father. Yet his mother's self-involvement precluded any reciprocation of Paul's efforts; she could not show any signs of warmth toward her son. Indeed, she seemed unconcerned that Paul had no friends and never pursued any activities for his own sake. He was a "male Cinderella"—simply there to do the work. The same pattern continued while Paul was in engineering school. (Obviously, all those construction toys did fulfill a purpose.)

Both parents died when Paul was in his twenties. After their death, he saw no reason why he should stay in a country he disliked politically and he came to the United States, although he knew nobody there. He trusted his professional abilities and was sure he would find a job—which he did. Once settled, work was all he did.

After more than ten years he found his way into psychoanalysis. Reading books on psychology gave him the idea that psychoanalysis might help him overcome his social and sexual inadequacies. He had attempted intercourse a few times with prostitutes but had been impotent each time.

Treatment went on in a regular, somewhat monotonous fashion. Much time was taken up with details of his daily work, but Paul knew from his reading that he should tell me about his childhood. It was not exactly "free" association, but quite informative. Interpretations were acknowledged with some interest, but without emotionally intense insights. He did recover some memories in the course of analytic work. He recalled his anger and loneliness when playing alone as a child. He also remembered his excitement at the news that his parents were returning home and how expectantly he dashed out of his room to be with them. Most startling for him was the recovery of the memory of the temper tantrums he threw when his parents sent him back to his room and how often, on such occasions, his father beat him up and had to remove him physically from the living room. And he had believed he was such a good, obedient child. Eventually, Paul's hopeful expectations were crushed enough times that he did become a "good, obedient" child.

Paul appeared for his sessions on the dot. Each time, unfailingly, he greeted me with a broad smile and the comment: "And how *are* you today?" After several months I asked him why he thought he had to greet me in this stereotyped manner. He was surprised at my question. He said he did not *have* to greet me that way, but that he was always genuinely happy to come to his sessions—the only three hours of the week he "looked forward to." He was also interested in how I felt; I was practically the only person he talked to outside of his job. After this answer I never brought up the topic again. I certainly did not want to crush his good feelings toward the treatment and me. It was part of his awkwardness that he had no way other than this stereotyped one to show his positive feelings. Yet I never attempted to interpret this as "positive transference." I was happy that he had something "to look forward to."

Paul frequently brought dreams to his sessions. Mostly they dealt with constructions and machines, or clocks (time!), breaking down. All these broken things, however, somehow got "fixed up again" by the end of the dream. Sometimes he dreamt of natural disasters, "but nobody got hurt." Of course these dreams reflected a great deal of denial, but they also showed a core of healthy hope that in the long run things would turn out all right.

What was amazing about Paul was precisely his ability to keep a sense of hope and trust in the future—indicated by the very fact that he undertook psychoanalysis and firmly expected help from it. An equally favorable prognostic sign was his unhating nature and lack of self-dramatization. He was a stoic who accepted life's untoward happenings sadly but without great *Sturm und Drang*. What he wanted from life was nothing grandiose—just a warm family life and some friends.

His experiences in treatment slowly melted his anxious defenses. Some valences in his lifespace started to light up. Undoubtedly under the aegis of a positive transference, he began to develop satisfaction and pride in his work. He proudly reported on his extra achievements, including innovative inventions. Gradually he became more and more a creative inventor, far from a "routine" engineer. Several of his inventions benefited handicapped people, which gave him a great deal of satisfaction. His evening hours and weekends were filled with challenging and enjoyable projects. His apartment became a busy workshop. The dimension of time took on a positive cast; he always had something to look forward to—solving a problem or finishing a project. And once a project was done, there were still so many legal steps to perform to get the invention patented.

With all these improvements, I dared to make a suggestion when the next summer vacation approached. I suggested he stay in one resort instead of his usual motel-to-motel vacation. He agreed and chose a church-connected resort. There he met a divorced woman somewhat his junior, whom—to make a long story short—he married within a year. They genuinely cared about each other—two people who had both endured much pain and loneliness in their lives. They knew how to appreciate human warmth and concern.

The beginning of sex life, of course, threw Paul into a panic. A whole series of dreams expressed his fears of intercourse. Uncontrollable floods destroyed dams and every other construction in sight. Also, various machines kept breaking down. Expectably, Paul was impotent for a while. His wife's honest solicitude with regard to this problem helped a great deal. She convinced him that he made her happy whether or not he performed the full sex act. At the same time, in his analysis he worked in crescendo on his oedipal guilt and his adolescent fantasies about seducing his mother away from her husband by proving how much more caring he, the son, was than his morose, irritable father.

All this led to success. Paul and his wife were sharing life happily, sex life included. Soon Paul found a much more rewarding job for himself, one in which he was expected to function as a creative inventor. It took him to another city, where they bought their own house. All these new steps in life were now worthwhile because he had what he wanted most: an understanding wife and a family on the way.

For years I received Christmas cards, always with one more child on the picture—three children in three years. Life for Paul certainly was not stagnating anymore; interesting events were happening; he was full of initiative and had lots to look forward to. The forces of Eros were never quite destroyed in him; they were just inhibited from functioning freely. Now they dominated his creative life activities.

PART II

CHAPTER 4

The Bridging-Over Function of Symbols

The Concepts of Lifespace and Gestalt

In the first chapter I characterized a healthy life as a good gestalt. In a good gestalt the parts connect to each other in a good fit, as well as to the whole in which they are embedded; there is coherence and unity. A healthy life, then, implies fitting connectedness between the regions of one's lifespace, including the different areas within oneself. The bridges that fittingly join these areas are created by symbol formation. Symbols both link the person to the environment and provide the basis for communication within the self. It is through symbols that we become "in touch" with ourselves.

I have already indicated that gestalt principles are important to my theory of symbolization and creativity. Of particular relevance are certain of Kurt Lewin's (1935, 1936) ideas. He advanced the concept of "lifespace" to denote the intrinsic unity of "the Person in his Environment" as one dynamic gestalt system. In his theory the person comprises numerous intrapsychic regions, just as the environment consists of various environmental regions. These regions are separated by boundaries with different degrees of permeability, or rigidity. Boundaries that do not allow for connecting pathways between adjacent regions are barriers.

Lewin called his theoretical system "topological and vector psychology." "Topological," because processes are mapped out in terms of regions and boundary relations.[1] "Vector," because "process" always means that something is in motion and motion implies the existence of one or several directional forces, i.e., vectors. According to Lewin, a person in his or her lifespace is impelled by forces toward or away from environmental objects (including people). Because Lewin presented an "ahistorical" analysis of events, he chose the neutral term "force" to designate the moving agent, in preference to "libido" or "aggression," or any other term implying a particular locus of origin or specific quality of force. Forces (vectors) move the person toward objects that are "positive valences" and away from objects that are "negative valences." Objects change their function in the lifespace depending on the person's needs. Every time a need is in a "state of tension," an outside object becomes a "valence" toward (or away from) which the person is impelled by a directed force (vector). Needs and valences are correlated concepts. The valence aspect of the physical environment constantly undergoes change in correlation to changes in the need-tension system. "Personally meaningful milieu or lifespace" refers to that segment of the environment that contains personally relevant valences.

The aim of psychotherapy is to enable the patient to carve out a personally meaningful, fitting lifespace. Psychoanalysis attempts to achieve this goal by resolving intrapsychic con-

[1] Lewin borrowed the term "topology" from mathematics. Topology is a nonquantitative branch of mathematics that deals with relations among bound regions, such as inclusion or exclusion of regions in relation to each other, the relation between the whole and its parts, as well as the possible communications between various regions.

flicts. It deals primarily with ordering and connecting the inside regions, trusting that once this task is accomplished, the person's motivational system will take care of organizing the environment into a meaningful lifespace. This assumption sets obvious limits to the population psychoanalysis can help. It is a population for whom establishing a meaningful connection to environmental objects is the problem and not the availability of the material things necessary for a satisfying life.

By themselves, the physical objects surrounding a person tell us nothing. A person may be isolated in the midst of meaningless things if no felt forces connect him or her with those objects. Objects that are not valences are just dead filling of the physical environment. "Corpses, just corpses piling up," an anhedonic patient used to say whenever he bought a new gadget, the latest tape recorder or movie camera.

If mental health is defined as a well-articulated and well-connected lifespace, containing many positive valences and pathways leading to those valences, then, conversely, mental ill health is a poorly articulated and inadequately connected lifespace, with few, if any, objects "lighting up" as desirable and available positive valences.

Some people find everything boring and uninteresting. Others believe their happiness depends on one particular object, whether a person, a house, or a mink coat—only, that particular object happens to be unavailable. No alternative or substitute will do. Both types of people are equally unhappy, though in different emotional keys. Their lifespaces are experienced as arid and unfulfilling. Following Lewin's topological description, we can say that these unfulfillable lifespaces are poorly articulated. The boundaries between their inner personal regions may be confused and overlapping, where separate articulation would be appropriate, or the areas may be cut off by barriers, where good communication would be desirable. In either case, the inadequately articulated need systems (the inner personal regions) lead to a lack of usable, meaningful valences in the environment. Again, needs and valences are intrinsically correlated.

Gestalt Characteristics

A creatively lived life implies a lifespace with the characteristics of a good gestalt. But what are these characteristics? What is a good gestalt?

Gestalt psychology was developed in the first third of the twentieth century by Wertheimer (1923), Köhler (1929), and Koffka (1935). In contrast to the previous theoretical approach in psychology, referred to by Gestalt theorists as "psychic atomism," the key concept in Gestalt psychology is *organization*. "Organized unit," "schema," "system," all could be used more or less synonymously with "gestalt." This is an inclusive concept which bridges over all realms of psychology and the physical sciences.

The basic laws of Gestalt psychology were arrived at through perception experiments. Basic questions were: How does the organization of our perceptual field occur? Why do we see segregated "things"? What are the laws governing the order of our visual world? Under what conditions are "things" perceived as a cohesive, unified "group"? Though Gestalt psychology started with perception experiments, the same principles were later applied to investigations of memory, recall, thinking, and motivation.

This is not the place to go into the description of single Gestalt psychology experiments. They are easily available to the interested reader in the works cited above. Koffka's (1935) *Principles of Gestalt Psychology* is the best comprehensive sourcebook for all experimental work as well as for theoretical considerations. Its 720 pages are densely informative, yet the immediacy of its style and the intellectual excitement emanating from it make the reading of every page a pleasure. Trying to condense the content of that book would make no sense. I shall quote some of those salient thoughts which are most relevant for the theory of symbolization and mental organization presented later in this book, particularly in Chapter 6.

To start with Köhler's answer to the question about the organization of our visual field: "objects appear in the visual field only if their boundaries are visually preserved. . . . Processes which make visual objects emerge in the field are . . . processes which establish certain separations, separations of visual units, as they are processes which make objects unitary entities" (1969, p. 53). Closed figures emerge in the visual field more readily than linear patterns. Numerous perceptual "illusions" are based on this principle. The difficulty in perceiving familiar linear patterns, such as letters, written words, or numbers, when they are embedded in closed figures is experimental proof of the perceptual preference for closed, unitary patterns that are "strong gestalts" (Gottschaldt, 1926, 1929).

More recently Witkin et al. (1954) have shown a correlation between the capacity for perceptually lifting out embedded figures from their cohesive gestalt context and the person's degree of psychological differentiation. Apparently the early vicissitudes of the separation-individuation process (Mahler, 1968) are reflected in patterns of perceiving.

Gestalts are segregated or detached wholes. The perceptual field, if articulated and not chaotic, is organized from the beginning into figure-ground structure. (Lack of organized figure-ground structure will be discussed later, in connection with psychotic art.) The figure is the focus of perception; it is the closed gestalt segregated from and enclosed by the ground. The figure is perceived literally as "standing out" from the ground, almost as if in relief. Grouping always occurs between figures upon the ground; never is the segregated figure grouped together with the surrounding ground. Koffka calls the ground a "not-thing," like "the space-filling fog which arises from completely homogeneous stimulation" (1935, p. 177). In contrast to "not-things," the main characteristic of "things" is "shaped boundedness." A figure, i.e., the stimulation perceived as a gestalt, is usually smaller than, and enclosed by, the ground. Under conditions of area equality, those parts which have greater internal articulation will become figures. Experiments have shown that the figures, in contrast to the ground, become the objects of the viewer's interest, "and conversely: where the center of our interest lies, there, 'ceteris paribus,' a figure is likely to arise. This interchangeability of cause and effect is quite general. . . . Forces in the ego can take effect in the field and codetermine its articulation" (Koffka, 1935, p. 197).

The above conclusions of Gestalt psychology perception experiments have profound relevance for a theoretical account of the therapeutic effect of psychoanalysis. If viewed from the point of view of perception psychology, the aim of psychoanalysis can be described as an order-making, organizing process that attempts to transform the internal, and consequently the external, visual world of the analysand. Freud's topographic model of the mind (I try to avoid the term "psychic apparatus") will be explicated later in terms of the effect of gestalt formation on internal perception and consequently on consciousness. Internal symbol formation is a gestalt-forming process, and the construction of the preconscious is predicated on this organizing process. Internal representations are delineated gestalts that can be perceived by internal perception. They are internal mental symbols with "shaped boundedness" which constitute the preconscious. The level of their gestalt quality determines the capacity for knowing the content of one's mind. The unconscious, on the other hand, is not constituted by perceivable, delineated symbol-gestalts. It harbors the more chaotic urges without delineating contours, without figure-ground organization, and is consequently beyond reach for perception. To make the unconscious conscious means to establish contours that make new perceptions possible. Koffka's dictum that "where the center of our interest lies, there . . . a figure is likely to arise," assumes special significance in the course of therapeutic reorganization. Without contour and consequently without a bounded figure, no specific meaning or significance can arise. The undifferentiated ground is capable only of conveying hazy, undefined and undefinable feeling-tones. They can be intense in their driving quality, yet hazy as to their meaning.

The function of psychoanalysis is not only to delineate new figures on a given ground, but occasionally also to reverse the figure-ground relation. What was taken for granted as background "stuff" (in contradistinction to "thing"—Koffka's expression), under the impact of new attention or interest cathexis, can become a "thing." The reverse can also happen—namely, some events that loom up in the patient's inner perceptual field as framed, traumatic "things," on closer inspection can lose their outstanding significance and recede into the background, where the ordinary necessities of life are stored, and serve as the backdrop for events with truly specific significance. All these reorganizations of the inner perceptual field depend on the position and function of contours.

Thus, the principle of the potential dual function of contours, as illustrated in Rubin's (1915) experiments with ambiguous figures, finds direct application in the therapeutic principles of psychoanalysis. At one given time, contours give shape only to one part of the field, while the other part remains unshaped ground. A contour performs the function of asymmetrical segregation of the field into a figure and its ground. However, it is possible, as Rubin has experimentally proved, to construct figures in which the same contour line alternates its asymmetrical function, delineating first one part of the field as the figure and then the other part. Rubin's reversible figure, in which one can see either a white vase on black background or the silhouettes of two black profiles facing each other on white background, is well known from psychology textbooks. The figure-ground relation reverses itself spontaneously, or this can be brought about by the viewer's conscious perceptual effort to change the function of the contour. Analogously, in psychoanalysis, patients can experience that an up-to-then frozen image suddenly undergoes figure-ground reversal; in other words, what are materially the very same elements can be seen as constituting very different gestalts with completely new meaning. In this way psychoanalysis can actually change the past.

Reorganization of the same elements into different gestalts can occur because there are several gestalt-forming principles which, depending on other coexisting factors, can alternate in their leading role of organizing a coherent gestalt. Some of these organizing principles have to do with the constellation of the external stimuli, such as proximity, likeness, succession, position; some, with the inner dynamic state of the perceiving person or organism. Wertheimer's (1923) experiments prove that the spatial or temporal *interaction* of stimuli is the decisive factor for visual processes. The perception of local facts depends on conditions in their environment. One has only to think of such simple but profound experiments as the different hue perception of the "same" gray on white versus black background. Analogously, the meaning of a memory can change if the patient succeeds in understanding the total background of that one event in a new way (though this shift is a more complex phenomenon than different hue perception). The fact that memory images are mental symbols makes them particularly conducive for change of meaning, since the meaning-structure of symbols (in contradistinction to signs) is always "one to many" (one symbol carries multiple potential meanings). That is one reason why treatment can work. With the help of the analyst's interventions and the analysand's free associations, the outlines of a new symbol-gestalt are drawn, into which the old symptomatic symbol fits in as a part. This new whole-part configuration implies new meaning. More often than not, it is not that *a* specific repressed unconscious content becomes conscious, but that the analysand's perceptual processes are helped along to form new gestalts out of the old and known elements. The patient learns to see old things in a new way. This rearrangement of old elements into new gestalts is the essence of all productive, creative thinking, as described by Wertheimer in his remarkable little book *Productive Thinking* (1945).

We have seen that productive, creative gestalt formation involves the capacity to break up an existing gestalt into its elements and to use these for the organization of a new one. This reorganization is often a difficult task exactly because it involves mental acts that go against the forces associated with the principles of "natural" gestalt formation. Of these, the most inclusive concept expressing the basic law of gestalt formation is the principle of *Prägnanz* (used in this German form). It means that perception by its nature tends to see forms in terms of maximum possible completeness, closure, simplicity, regularity, and symmetry. Symmetry implies the perceptual tendency toward "pair formation"—if the stimulus distribution allows for it at all.

These gestalt-forming tendencies are considered "givens"

of human perception. They harbor psychological dangers as well as the seeds for creativity. All the well-known perceptual "illusions" are based on the laws of gestalt perception. The preference for closed figures, regularity, and symmetry makes us see an unclosed C-shape as a closed circle; the "law for good continuation" accounts for our "overlooking" some "unfitting" change of direction or gap in a line. Since a straight line is a more stable structure than a broken one, gestalt perception—within limits—will tend to perceive it as if continued in its straightness: "any curve will proceed in its own natural way, a circle [more correctly, the beginning of a circle] as a circle, an ellipse as an ellipse and so forth" (Koffka, 1935, p. 153). These simplifying perceptual tendencies are also evident in experiments on recall of visual patterns by way of repeated drawings (Gibson, 1929) and in the figural aftereffects of focused perception (Köhler, 1969).

In the value-free universe of perception experiments, these are just interesting lawful phenomena. Not so in the real world of human perception. There, the tendency for simplification and *Prägnanz* can cause grave distortions of reality, leading to inappropriate and harmful responses. Gestalt principles refer to perceptual organization of form without content. A "good" gestalt, obeying the principles of simplicity, regularity, "good" continuation, and symmetry, might stand for very bad, dangerous content. Real-life phenomena are complex, containing contradictory features within one gestalt. "Smoothing" out these realities can lead to a "neatly" but dangerously simplified view of the world, which in turn can lead to extreme, unmodulated emotions and actions—possibly including atomic holocaust. The laws of simplifying gestalt perception are utilized in political propaganda by feeding the public unambiguous, easily perceptible symbol-gestalts. The correction of these dangers of gestalt formation lies outside the scope of psychoanalysis. Within the scope of psychoanalysis lies the correction of early childhood perceptions which, due to the perceptual tendency for simplification and *Prägnanz*, result in one-sided, oversimplified representations of reality.

Serious emotional disturbances, up to and including paranoia, can be connected with the fixation of such early "perceptual illusions." Psychoanalytic work has to conquer and dissolve the cohesiveness of these primitive but "strong" gestalts and change them into more complex and more comprehensive configurations. These new gestalts, as structures by themselves, are less "strong," less cohesive, because they contain contradictory tendencies. In a larger framework, however, the new gestalts are not only more complex but also "better" in terms of their formal gestalt qualities. They are "better" because they are more symmetrical with the structure of reality they are supposed to represent. In a larger framework, the symbol and the symbolized are two relatively symmetrical parts of the same gestalt. Percepts and memory images are representational symbols; their function is dependably to represent in the "inner world" the situation in the "outer world." Therefore the gestalt quality of a representational symbol cannot be judged by itself. By itself it can be "strong," well-delineated, symmetrical, and cohesive; yet, if considered in relation to its other half, to the "raw material" it is supposed to "mirror" to some extent, this *total* symbolic form can turn out to be lopsided, not symmetrical, defective in structure.

The gestalt concept of *isomorphism* fits the proper relation between symbol and symbolized. It does not denote total symmetry in terms of a mirror-image, but it designates a structural correspondence between two sets of phenomena. Wertheimer and Köhler applied the concept of isomorphism to the assumed resemblance of cortical and perceptual gestalt processes. In the theory of symbolization presented in this book, isomorphic relation between the internal, or visible, image-symbol and the "raw material" to be symbolized is considered the earmark of "true," valid, and consequently psychologically whole-some, symbol formation.

This much discussion of the basic principles of gestalt theory was needed as a ground for later theoretical comments on symbolization. The integration of psychoanalytic theory with concepts of Gestalt psychology seems to me highly desirable since the basic laws of organization hold equally for physical, physiological, or psychological phenomena. The external, as well as the psychic, universe consists of patterned or structured processes that follow the laws of gestalt formation. Psychoanalytic theorizing at this point in time would benefit and gain in clarity from being viewed *sub specie* a generic theory of structure development and a dynamic field theory. The latter refers to the ever-active field forces that tend toward alleviating the stresses (imbalances) within the field and aim at a state of equilibrium by improving the gestalt quality of either the total or a part of the field. According to this view, psychoanalysis should strengthen the driving forces that work in the direction of improving the gestalt quality of the person's total lifespace. Psychoanalysis aims at bringing about psychic changes that will make the total gestalt of the analysand's lifespace a more harmoniously organized configuration.

The Lifespace as a Gestalt

A gestalt can be an organically developed system or one organized, created, by human acts. By an organically developed gestalt, I mean a biological unit or system such as the whole body or a subsystem within the body, like the cardiovascular or the central nervous system. In the sphere of psychological phenomena, the distinction between organic and organized gestalts is blurred, as is the distinction between purely biological versus psychological events. We do not know where biology ends and psychology starts.

As psychologists, we focus on the psychological determinants that contribute to the creation of a person's lifespace, while being fully aware that this view is one-sided and incomplete. A person's total lifespace—which includes his or her past, present, and expected or projected future—is both an organic and an organized gestalt. Its creation, as we shall see, is predicated on the capacity for expressive symbol formation.

Each person's total lifespace, or biography, is a unique pattern. A good gestalt implies that the pattern is well ordered, with a coherent unity. "Unity" refers to the mutual interdependence of parts—it does not mean simplicity. A good gestalt can be a complex system consisting of numerous subsidiary gestalts, which may function with considerable autonomy. Yet all the subsidiary parts are connected to each other and all contribute to the smooth functioning of the whole. There is thus some limit to the autonomy of the subsystems.

The importance of the unifying principle of a gestalt can be seen in cases of its failure. Cancer cells, for instance, proliferate without consideration for the laws governing the whole organism. Similarly, neurotic symptoms function according to their own subsystem laws, which disrupt the total psychic organization. In other words, cancerous tumors and neurotic symptoms do not fit well into the pattern of the whole, leading to a malfunctioning, bad gestalt, i.e., a sick organism.

As I indicated in Chapter 1, the media for the creation of a lifespace are our given potentials plus the world around us, with all its infinite possibilities for choice. Out of this we carve certain configurations and make them part of our own life. The world into which we are born serves as a vast Rorschach card. It is in part structured by its own nature, but we imprint it with our own meanings (the process of symbolization) and select out certain elements as significant. Through this process, a personally meaningful milieu emerges from the impersonal raw material of the background environment.

Obviously for such a meaningful milieu to come about there must be good communication between the two main constituents of the lifespace: "the Person and the Environment," in Kurt Lewin's terms. Good communication implies a well-equilibrated balance, a kind of symmetry. Content must pass freely both from the outside to the inside of the person and vice versa. We might picture this two-way flow of information as a *balanced dialogue* between person and environment, between inside and outside.

The intrapsychic regions, too, must be in good communication with each other in order for an unimpeded inside-outside dialogue to take place. The boundaries separating the intrapsychic regions, or at the interface with the environment, can be of different degrees of permeability, but none should function as an impermeable barrier. A barrier creates a split within the total system, and inevitably distorts the dialogue between inside and outside. Information gets sidetracked and missymbolization occurs. Specific communication disturbances due to splits at different boundary lines will be discussed later. They underlie the formation of symptoms.

Psychoanalysis and a Generic Theory of Symbolization

Since the specifically human mode of communication is symbolic, I believe symbolization to be *the* central issue in human psychology. So far I have simply stated that symbols build bridges connecting different regions and thereby establish the necessary conditions for good communication within the person's lifespace. Now we need to explore more precisely the nature of symbols and how they foster unity.

In psychoanalysis, at least until very recently, the concepts of symbol and symbolization were restricted to a specific pathological modality. Freud's field of investigation was the irrational component of human behavior. His discovery of the symbolic meaning of neurotic symptoms and dream imagery emphasized the hidden, disguised content *behind* the manifest appearance of the symbol. He thus showed that these seemingly freak phenomena fit into the generally unified context of human behavior. Yet he never considered symbol formation as the means by which this unified context comes about.

Psychoanalysts have thus concentrated on decoding the hidden, unconscious elements in the manifest verbalizations and imagery offered by their patients. Freud conceptualized this process in terms of a dichotomy: The concealing surface was the symbol; behind it lay a totally different thing—the *real* meaning. This opposition between symbol and meaning led to neglect of the manifest dream content. Nor did Freud differentiate between the different meanings conveyed by symbols referring to the "same" object. In his *Interpretation of Dreams* (1900), Freud lists objects as representing the same thing. For instance, all hollow receptacles symbolize the vagina, while all long pointed objects are phallic symbols. The analyst's task, then, was to substitute for the symbol its *real* meaning and discard the symbol itself. The manifest dream imagery did not warrant further scrutiny, since its only function was concealment. Much important information was thrown away in this split view of symbolization.

A case example will illustrate what I feel is missing here.

At the beginning of her analysis, a patient of mine kept dreaming about garbage cans and dirty laundry bags, while toward the end of her treatment she dreamt about beautiful flower vases and, once, about a delicate, pink, painted sugar bowl. In Freudian terms, all these objects represented her vagina. But what a difference they portray with regard to her feelings about her female sex organ! It took five years of hard analytic work for her feelings about her vagina to progress from a garbage pail to a delicately painted sugar bowl. Progress in analysis is often reflected in similar changes in the choice of symbols. Only by considering symbols as *revealing and communicating as well as concealing* can their full meaning be understood.

Freud, Jones, and psychoanalysts in general see symbol formation purely as the outcome of repression.[2] In his famous essay on "The Theory of Symbolism," Jones (1912) states that "only what is repressed can be symbolized, only what is repressed needs to be symbolized" (p. 116). He points out that symbol formation entails noting resemblances rather than differences; he therefore considers symbolization to represent "the tendency of the primitive mind as observed in children, in savages . . . [and] insanity" (p. 105). He gives numerous examples to prove that scientific progress is based on noting differences, in contrast to a "lazy" emphasis on similarities.

Jones obviously believed that the particularizing aspect of perception and thinking is a higher-caliber mental operation than the grouping of similarities. This view seems myopic. For, if we did not pay attention to the essential resemblances, rather than focusing on the manifold details of differences, how could concept formation take place? Without generic

[2] When I read my first paper on symbolization at the Amsterdam Congress in 1965, the situation was still the same. Jones's (1912) study on symbolization was still much quoted during the discussion as an argument against what I called the "generic" function of symbolization.

concepts (mental symbols), thought processes would be chaotic. Concept formation is itself an instance of symbolization in the generic sense, which belies pathological connotations.

Indeed, Arieti, in his book *Creativity: The Magic Synthesis* (1976), considers that the observation of similarities is the basis for creative thinking in science. As he puts it: "Similarity indicates that there is some kind of recurrence and, therefore, regularity in the universe. It is from these segments of regularity that the human mind plunges into the understanding of the cosmos and into the making of its own inner reality" (p. 410). He notes that there are numerous instances "in which great discoveries were made by the act of perceiving an identity among two or more things that had been thought dissimilar or unrelated" (p. 270). Arieti does not ignore that a certain kind of categorizing by similarities is also characteristic of schizophrenic thinking. What he singles out, however, is the generic process; the creative and the pathological application of the same mental operation must then be differentiated.

The fact of course is that both abstracting, generalizing and discriminating, particularizing mental operations participate equally in scientific thinking and in establishing order in the object world around us. Jones's way of presenting the issue is an example of the either-or, dichotomized thinking that has characterized psychoanalytic concept formation for a long time. Although this mode of thinking may have served some useful purpose in establishing a new discipline, it has also limited psychoanalytic theory's ability to deal with certain subjects. In particular, such Aristotelian, divisive, either-or definition does disservice to symbolization, because the *essence of a symbol is that it unites opposing categories within one gestalt.* A good definition of a symbol is a French aphorism—I forget where I read it—*le symbole, c'est la présence d'une absence.* This paradox clearly conveys the Janus-face of a symbol. Resolution of the paradox runs counter to the essential bridging-over function of a symbol.

The Definition of a Symbol

For the ancient Greeks, the word *symbolon* denoted a broken ring or coin. Half of it was kept by the host and the other half handed to the departing friend, so that their descendants would know they had met a friend if the two broken halves matched exactly to form a whole. More specifically, the Greek word *symballein* means to unite, to connect, to bring separate parts together. And this is the function of symbols wherever and in whatever form they appear. Symbols arise from the wish to bridge over to something or somebody in another realm; *to reach what is directly unreachable.* Symbols point beyond themselves and furnish apprehension of another region beyond the one where the symbol itself is located. Symbols in any form convey a sense of transcendence. This function of transcendence holds for everyday language as well as for art and religious symbols.

The magic rites of the primitives, as well as the sacraments of present-day religions, are symbolic in their nature. Both kinds of symbolism originate in the wish to reach across a boundary to some invisible power believed to exist in another realm. These symbols have nothing to do with repression (though they do have something to do with denial). They grow out of faith and hope.

The wishful nature of symbols is also illustrated by Paleolithic man, who covered the walls of his cave with images in order to ensure fertility and successful hunting. As Gideon indicates: "In primitive times . . . the symbol was identical with the wish . . . it was believed to possess the power of working magic" (1962, p. 91). Bachofen places the origin of the symbol in the tomb (Gideon, 1962, p. 79). And indeed, the symbolism of early burial ceremonies clearly expressed the wish to reach over to existence *beyond* the sharp dividing line of death; the wish to communicate with the dead one as someone invisible but still alive in another realm.

Symbol formation, then, always takes place in the context of longing. The symbol provides a means of connecting separated regions, of crossing over boundaries. As I shall discuss in the next chapter, a symbol binds different categories together, making for unity. In terms of Lewin's topological and vector psychology, symbol formation comes about under the pressure of a force originating in one region and striving toward communication with another, not directly reachable, region. The symbol bridges over the boundary separating the two regions.

Ontogenetic Origins of Symbolization

In line with the above, we can assume that the first attempts at symbolization take place when the infant longs for something that is not available. Winnicott's theory of transitional objects and transitional phenomena deals with the young child's ways of bridging the gap to the absent mother. Winnicott's theory will be dealt with in Part III. Here I wish to discuss some of Freud's (1895, 1900) early concepts, which are relevant to a theory of symbolization, even though Freud himself did not consider them in this light.

Freud postulated that the first mental act is the *wish* and the first product of the infant's mind, the *primary hallucinatory wish fulfillment*. Although this is only a theoretical construct (since there is no way to test what goes on in the infant's mind), it shows that Freud considered what I would call "protosymbolization" the first act of the human mind.

The hallucinatory appearance of the absent need-gratifying object is the first instance of *la présence d'une absence*. It is the first bridge to an unavailable positive valence.

Freud based his concept of the infant's hallucinatory wish fulfillment on Helmholtz's "Constancy Principle." According to this principle, the nervous system functions to rid itself of excitation. Freud applied this neurological principle to motivation in general. The primary motivation of newborns is to divest themselves of tension in the fastest possible way. This is the direct-discharge mode of primary-process functioning. Hunger in the absence of the gratifying breast results in high need-tension. The intensity of the wish cathects the memory image of the gratifying breast with hallucinatory power. Hallucination of the absent breast offers the fastest relief of need-tension; it is the fastest symbol-bridge to the unreachable desired object.

Freud's ontogenetic hypothesis is analogous to Gideon's (1962) phylogenetic one: "In primitive times . . . the symbol was identical with the wish." Both conceive of the symbol image as an immediate connection to the desired but absent object. Both assume the memory image constitutes the symbol. Memory images are products of the ever-present symbolically transforming activity of the human mind (brain) (Langer, 1942).

The Intervention of Secondary Process

Highly cathected memory images, however, do not satisfy. One cannot eat hallucinated food. Primary-process functioning, though aimed at immediate relief from tension, in actuality leads to total frustration. The *timeless* primary-process mode of direct discharge has to change into the *time-consuming* secondary-process search for the needed object for the person to survive. For *practical* purposes, the mental world of imaginary representations must be differentiated from the outer world of concrete objects. The memory image of the object must be treated as what it really is: a symbol. As such, it now serves as a beacon to direct attention to its matching counterpart among the things in the outside world.

Freud (1895, 1900) called this process *the search for perceptual identity*. Freud (1895) in fact described the search for perceptual identity as if infants actually went through the discriminating act of discarding different shapes until they finally found the round thing they remembered gave satisfying milk—and proceeded to suck on it. This description has to be considered a theoretical paradigm, since developmental psychology does not offer factual support for this search. My point here, however, is that the concept of a search for "perceptual identity" is crucial in normal as well as pathological perception.

Once the memory image is treated as a directing token, as a symbol leading to the wished-for object, secondary-process functioning has set in. This implies waiting, the ability to delay gratification, and the mental operations of comparison and discrimination. All these are ego functions. *Symbol formation, cognitive development, and ego development coincide and reinforce each other*. Any attempt to establish causal priority here boils down to an arbitrary juggling of these concepts.

Search for Perceptual Identity: The Guiding Function of the Symbol

The search for perceptual identity can be likened to the lotto game of children. The child holds up the picture of one object and has to find its duplicate on a board. Similarly, we wander around with images of wished-for objects in our preconscious mind and survey the environment for their matching counterparts, even though we are not consciously aware of all the steps in this process. Under normal circumstances, the lotto game between memory images and outside objects is played in a flexible manner. Memory images are not *point-by-point replicas* of the objects they represent; they are *schematized symbolic representations* of them. Yet, if the internal representations are *isomorphic* with the essential features of the object, then these internal symbolic representations will serve as dependable guides to the outside world. Their function is analogous to the ancient Greeks' *symbolon*. Just as the two matching halves of the broken ring lead to old friends, so do the memory-symbols lead to their corresponding counterparts in the outside world. Perception of things we know is always recognition, and recognition is always based on perceptual identity.

Gestalt-forming principles, in particular those of pair formation based on symmetry, underlie this process of perceptual identity. Incomplete gestalts carry an autonomous pressure toward completion, toward closure. At times an incomplete gestalt may act like a magnet, pulling to itself (and sometimes creating) the missing part that will balance its configuration. In fact, certain perceptual illusions are based on this effect of the law of closure. In any case, a pattern consisting of two symmetrical halves is better equilibrated than one of the halves. Indeed, symmetry is the crucial ordering principle in the biological universe.[3]

[3] The significance of symmetry in the organization of living form is clearly seen in the self-copying capacity of genes. Each gene seems to have an organizing effect on materials surrounding it, whereby a gene identical in its external configuration and lying next to the original gene is formed. This unique capacity makes genes the foundation of development and reproduction. The basic life-unit is *producing* its own mirror-image.

Pair formation on the basis of symmetry is also the crucial organizational principle of chromosomes in the process of meiosis, i.e., reductive cell division.

Plato's *Symposium* offers a different, mythological version of the drive toward closure by way of establishing symmetry. Within this dialogue, Aristophanes explains the power of love as resulting from the gods' decision to divide originally hermaphroditic, four-legged and four-armed, perfectly spherical creatures into two haves. This division was called for because the perfectly symmetrical creatures were so complete and self-sufficient that they defied the gods' orders to perform human tasks. They lacked nothing, and thus did not seek to do anything. But after they were split, they had something to look for: They strove to find their split-off half and thereby achieve symmetrical completion. What Plato tells us is that Homo sapiens is an essentially split organism; we are human exactly because we are incomplete. This wish to experience total unity with the physically separate "other" remains an ever-present human desire. We, then, search for union and completeness not only through physical contact, but also through various symbolic forms in the worlds of ideas, art, and religion.

To reiterate: The symbol is a guide toward the missing half that will complete a gestalt. In the act of perception, recognition takes place when a memory image, matching the

---

Gametes, the sperm and egg cells, are produced by reductive division. In meiosis the double chromosome set of the parent cell separates into two single sets. Each of these goes into one of the two daughter cells, or gametes. Just preceding meiosis, the homologous chromosomes deriving from the two parents line up side by side in an ordered pattern of pairs. It is due to this pattern of symmetrical pairs that reductive division results in gametes containing only one parental set of chromosomes, for meiosis divides the homologous pairs along the middle axis. With fertilization, however, comes the unification of two gametes, one from each parent, and the reestablishment of the double set of chromosomes. (All body cells have double set.)

Thus, the very process of reproduction can be seen as an instance of the gestalt law of closure, whereby the "incomplete" gametes with their half-set of chromosomes find their symmetrical completion by uniting with their counterpart half-set of chromosomes. The pairing of the chromosomes, the double set, is once again complete. Pair formation on the basis of symmetry underlies the unfolding of our biological existence.

present perception, separates itself out of the mass of existing internal representations exactly because it is symmetrical with the outside pattern. This gestalt-forming process by pair formation *is* the act of recognition. It manifests itself in the experience of knowing, for example, that "this is a table." This feeling of "clicking" is the moment when the internal lotto picture, i.e., the image-symbol, finds its matching "other half" in the outside world.

Pathology in the Search for Perceptual Identity: The Misguiding Symbol

Normal perception needs a certain degree of emotional calmness—the capacity to contemplate the object as it really is. Some people cathect their internal representations with such intensity that they continue playing the lotto game with them, even if there is no matching counterpart in reality. In fact, if there is none, then they "create" one. They distort their present perception and perceive the closest person (in the analytic situation, the analyst) as if he or she were a duplicate of the person whose image dominates their internal world. These perceptual distortions are one kind of transference manifestation.

A sensitive, articulate patient of mine, who had never read any psychology, expressed his own experience of this phenomenon in the following way: "Hilda is a wonderful girl, better than any of the 'crazies' I've met lately and not like Barbara, who was cold and ungiving [the one woman with whom he had had a long relationship]. Hilda is just the opposite. She lets me know how much she enjoys me and, in contrast to Barbara, Hilda is ready for sex always. And yet, when I make love to her, I can feel *my compulsion to force Barbara's mask on her face* and then I have rejecting thoughts which would fit Barbara but not Hilda. I hope I won't ruin this relationship by trying to force Hilda to become Barbara."

Weeks later his insight went even deeper. By then he was concerned about Hilda's intense desire for love-making, marriage, and children. These were actually his own greatest conscious wishes for years. Yet now that he had found a woman who wanted the same things, he felt anxious, hemmed in, and lost much of his sexual desire. In the past, loneliness had driven him into deep depression. Now he felt claustrophobic from closeness. But at least he had reached the point where he was able to separate his healthy perception from the sick one. He was able to maintain a double perspective. He could see Hilda as she really was and also see his own compulsion to mold her image into somebody else's. As he put it: "I came to realize that there are three people in this relationship—my mother, my father, and me. I pretend to be the adult who plans marriage—buying a house and all that. But actually I am the little boy who tries to repeat what his parents had—have the house in the country where I grew up and a mommy next to me. And I really want to make a mommy out of all the girls . . . and then I get afraid of them . . . they will squelch me, tease me, like my mother did. [He had a most unpredictable mother.] It is not only Barbara's mask I try to force on Hilda, but I already forced mother's mask on Barbara. That's how I ruined all my relationships. The end is always the same; I get frightened."

In perceptually misguided analytic transference, the patient perceives the analyst as if he or she were the replica of a memory image stored long ago in the patient's mind. Such is the strength of the patient's internal beacon, which, like all symbols, can not only lead to the proper object but also mislead.

One of my first patients in this country was an Englishman with snobbish views of most of humanity but a particularly disparaging take on the Irish. In anger he once called me a "typical Irish Catholic dame." This clearly was not meant as a compliment, but what was interesting was that he obviously did not register my Hungarian accent. His remark convinced me forever of the assimilating power of preformed internal image-symbols.

Since memory images are not exact replicas but schematized symbolic representations of objects, there is always a subjective, creative element in their formation. Like all symbols, they unite two opposing categories—in this instance, the outside objective and the inside subjective. Under emotionally calm circumstances, the subjective element does not prevent the formation of memory-symbols that are isomorphically congruent with their referents. But if the schematization takes place under intense emotional pressure, then the symbolic internal representations may distort their supposedly corresponding outside counterparts. These faulty symbolizations become harmful gestalts that disrupt the smooth functioning of the whole psychic organization. Since they are not isomorphic with what they are supposed to represent, they are not dependable bridges to the outside world. Yet the assimilating power of the search for perceptual identity is such that the misformed internal symbol distorts perception to find the matching counterpart where none exists in reality.

To various degrees, we all see the world through the template of our internal symbols. This is the theory underlying the Rorschach test and projective techniques in general. This fact lends a somewhat individualized cast to our perceptions without, however, interfering with their objectively guiding function. Under pathological circumstances, the inner template is seriously distorted and leads to further misperceptions. This phenomenon is loosely called projection, although its dynamics are different from the defense mechanism described by Freud. The latter type of projection is motivated by the unconscious wish to disown an undesirable characteristic of the self, while the former is perceptual illusion, caused by the pressure to match an existing faulty memory-symbol with a symmetrical counterpart.

In his paper "Transference and Reality," Nunberg (1951) differentiates transference caused by perceptual illusion from transference of emotional attitudes without perceptual distortion.[4] The former type represents more severe pathology and is closer to psychotic transference than the latter, which is found in analyzable hysterics. Nunberg describes two cases in which transference was based on perceptual distortion. The first patient "did not 'transfer' her emotions from her father to her analyst, but . . . *attempted* to transform her analyst into her father. . . . Thus transference often breaks down . . . because of . . . frustrated efforts at establishing an identity of present images with past ones" (pp. 118–119). "The second patient *succeeded* in getting an identical picture of her father through the medium of a real person, the analyst, to such an extent that the analyst's voice became her father's voice. She almost had a hallucination of her father. . . . [This woman] experienced the person of the past in the person of the present. Present objects and past images became identical in her mind" (p. 120). In such instances, the lost object is felt to be found by virtue of distorted perception. Nunberg ascribes this process to the synthetic function of the ego. In terms of gestalt perception, it is the effect of a previous mental set that acts as an assimilating framework, making new perceptions fit the pattern of the old. The unconscious dynamics behind this gestalt effect seem linked to an ongoing search for the lost object.

In other words, seriously damaging perceptual illusions can

[4] Elsewhere (Deri, 1967), I have called transference based on perceptual distortion the "gestalt perception model" and transference of emotional attitudes, the "hydraulic model."

be furthered by gestalt forces acting in conjunction with unconscious psychodynamics. The law of closure pushes toward a *formally* better-equilibrated gestalt, irrespective of the value of its content. Pathological content is just as subject to the pull toward closure as healthy content. This moral- and value-blindness of gestalt forces underlies much of the tragic aspect of life. It makes no difference if it is the devil striving to become a complete devil or the angel attempting to be a perfect angel. (We can only hope that in the large scheme of things the angel fits in better than the devil.)

As therapists, we try to harness these formative forces in the service of healthy gestalts. But once a pathological structure reaches a certain point of development, the gestalt forces set in to make it cohesive and durable by producing the best possible equilibrium of its parts. Besides symptoms and character disorders, long-lasting perceptual distortions are enhanced in this way. The question is: What wins out—the autonomous perceptual apparatus or the originally misformed image-symbol? If the perceptual apparatus is able to maintain its autonomous functioning, then the infantile, misformed image-symbols will yield their form and accommodate to new reality perceptions, making for more isomorphic pair formation. The "click" of recognition will then become reality-adapted.

In pathological conditions, however, the process is reversed. The early misformed images, backed up by vehement emotions, take the upper hand and rob the perceptual system of its reality-oriented autonomous functioning. The misformed internal symbols, instead of accommodating to reality, assimilate new perceptions to their distorted shape. In this case, the gestalt forces "defend" and perpetuate the structure of the already-existing misperceptions. Symmetrical percepts are created where there are none in reality. The subjective experience of "recognition" ensues, even though objectively the reality situation is not isomorphic.

In benign transference situations such misperceptions are fleeting and can be utilized therapeutically. On the other hand, psychotic transference, both within and outside of analysis, is characterized by the intransigence of the misperceptions and the person's conviction that his or her faulty "recognitions" are real. Symbols, acting in conjunction with gestalt forces, can acquire dangerous power over reality. Advertising psychology and systematic political propaganda are based on this principle. In times of war, for instance, perception can be manipulated by symbols until the enemy is literally *seen* as malevolent and humanly worthless. Most people have enough frightening early images stacked away in their minds that they can be revived as preformed symbol-tools to "see" with under the bombardment of propaganda.

We assume that subjectively colored misperceptions are developmentally "normal" in very young children, whose emotionality is more intense and diffuse than that of adults. Because of their relatively unstructured psychic "apparatus," children's emotions easily invade their perceptual and cognitive functions. The ability to form and maintain complex symbol-gestalts only develops with maturation.

Very young children, for instance, cannot yet accommodate contradictory features within one gestalt. The picture of one mother, who inevitably alternates between frustrating and satisfying her child, tends to be split into two contrasting internalized images. Under the pressure of intense emotions, the law of closure may operate in an immature and hasty way and produce exaggeratedly unified gestalts. The frustrating mother may give rise to an internal representation that resembles a total witch with no redeeming features, while the gratifying mother is pictured as the diametric opposite. In the course of normal development these primitively unified gestalts lose their excessively one-sided features with accommodation to reality. With the development of the concept of *time*, corollary concepts of change and constancy evolve. Comprehension of object constancy, despite the object's changing pattern of behavior, represents a milestone in the child's intellectual development (Piaget, 1937). With this cognitive achievement, the child's internal symbolization of the mother changes. Her frustrating and gratifying features are grasped as aspects of one and the same person. The previously split, contrasting images yield their fairytale excesses and fuse into a single complex gestalt that is isomorphic with the real, changing yet constant mother.

This maturation in the symbolization process takes place if the level of emotionality is moderate enough to allow the perceptual apparatus to maintain its autonomous functioning. Inordinately strong emotions, mainly hate and fear, may, however, interfere with the maturation of perceptual symbolization. A child may also have an inborn ego defect with regard to symbol formation. Whatever the cause, the fact remains that without isomorphically integrative symbolization, the environment is perceived as populated, on the one hand, by malevolent witchlike creatures and, on the other, by people of unreal perfection. The same person may also be perceived as two different entities, alternating between these two extremes. This is the split world of the borderline patient. If uncorrected by psychotherapy, the process of missymbolization deteriorates, with missymbolization begetting misperception, leading to even more threatening internal symbols in an endless chain reaction . . . until the world becomes so threatening that aggressive acts of "self-defense" ensue.

Melanie Klein (1932) was the first to describe this vicious circle in the young child's internal symbolic world. She saw such missymbolization as originating in the child's constitutionally strong "death instinct," which generates sadistic impulses against the mother. According to Klein, characteristics of the real mother or the real environment are disregarded.

The child's frightening "perceptions" and imagery derive solely from the projection of his or her own aggressive impulses outward. Images stemming from the child's libidinal impulses are then overidealized and kept strictly apart in order not to be "contaminated" by the "monsters," against which they are needed as "protection." A completely misformed set of symbols thus comes to guide reality perception—with disastrous consequences.

Despite Klein's unlikely datings and extremely metaphoric language, she gave us a new way to conceptualize certain confounding phenomena.[5] She described the destructive effect that violent feelings against the mother have on perception and on internal symbolization. And she was the first among analysts to see in the capacity for symbolization the absolute prerequisite for ego development, intellectual curiosity, and creativity (Klein, 1930; Segal, 1957, 1964). Moreover, it was Klein who pointed to the need for patients to synthesize their "all-bad" and "all-good" internal symbols into a complex gestalt containing both positive and negative features. She indicated that without tolerance for ambivalent structures—for good and bad, love and hate, within the representation of the same person, including oneself—one cannot experience humanizing guilt, remorse, or concern for others. Nor can one constructively mourn lost objects—and it is only after people are properly mourned that their images get relegated to memory instead of invading present perception.

I am not making an argument for Klein's contention that the infant's constitutional "death instinct" is the sole, or even main, determinant of misperception and missymbolization. Nevertheless, my clinical work has convinced me that the

[5] The literature on borderline pathology is teeming with Kleinian ideas, such as "split internal objects," without, however, full acknowledgment of her contribution.

patient's sadistic rage has to be mitigated by an admixture of libido in order for the correct reality perception and isomorphic internal symbolization to come about. Sadistic rage can destroy permeable internal boundaries, the prerequisites for good symbol formation. By reducing rage and amalgamating the patient's aggression with sufficient libido, psychoanalytic therapy enables patients to build and maintain good gestalts, both intrapsychically and within their total lifespace. It is in this sense that mental well-being and creativity (in the wide sense) coincide. The process is a circular one. It would be difficult to determine whether well-articulated psychic structure is indeed the *original* prerequisite for symbolization, or whether symbolization itself creates well-articulated mental structure.

Whichever way we look at this process, a certain organismic disposition for sustaining calm states is needed for the time-consuming act of creating good symbols, i.e., complex gestalts. The fusion of the forces of Thanatos with those of Eros enhances the potential for calmness and thus furthers symbolization and gestalt creation in general. We shall now turn to the reciprocal reinforcement between symbolization and psychic structuralization.

CHAPTER 5

The Organizing Function of Symbolization

Any subdivision of the different functions of symbolization is arbitrary, as each aspect of this complex process is intrinsically interwoven with all the other aspects. The connecting and guiding functions of symbols seemed a good starting point, since ontogenetically symbolization is initiated by the infant's wish to bridge over the gap to the absent mother. Yet we can also approach the topic of symbolization in terms of *order, directedness, and form development*.

The end "aim" of symbolization is always the creation of order, and orderliness presupposes directedness. Symbols, by pointing beyond themselves, toward what cannot be directly reached, reflect a need for some explicit connection to what is outside. In other words, symbols are not arbitrary; a directed intentionality underlies the connecting function of symbolization, leading to participation with another region. Even the very first protosymbols—the wishful hallucination and the first transitional object—are born out of a directed intention: the desire to connect with the breast and the mother.

What I wish to stress is that the capacity for symbolization is a necessary condition for human life. At a very basic level, no organic life is possible without some form of interaction across a semipermeable boundary. In biology this boundary is an actual membrane, across which biochemical exchange processes take place. These membrane-crossing transactions result in structural and energic changes within the membrane itself, as well as in the regions on either side. The end-result is morphological and physiological pattern development.

Symbol formation can also be conceptualized as a boundary-crossing process. To reiterate: In Lewin's (1936) topological and vector psychology, a boundary is defined as the force-field separating two qualitatively different regions, i.e., two regions with contents of an essentially different nature and with different laws governing their intraregional events. A permeable boundary is not an obstacle to communication. Symbols communicate across these boundaries, making for some kind of interchange between the contents of the two regions. As in biochemical exchanges, symbol formation leads to transformations in both the structure and the energy within the regions on either side of the boundary. It also changes the energy-cathecting conditions within the force-field, or "boundary" itself.

My point is that symbol formation is not a random but a *directed* process. It results in increased articulation of form and in binding of energy, thereby lending orderliness to the total organism and to its perceived environment. The development of ordered patterns is the prerequisite of organismic existence, be these patterns visible morphological forms or not directly visible psychological events. Thus symbolization, in its widest order-creating sense, turns out to be the basic condition for human life. Cassirer's (1944, p. 26) definition of man as an "*animal symbolicum*" can be paraphrased: "If not an *animal symbolicum*, man would not be an animal at all."

The Role of Choice and Directedness in Animals and in Humans

To put the matter quite simply: Human beings need to rely on symbols because they lack the coherent instinctive directedness found in animals. Animals are equipped with complex inborn action patterns that connect them unambiguously to their relevant milieu. Specifically, Uexküll (1921) has demonstrated that animals, by virtue of their inherent "structural plan," find for themselves their perfectly fitting and ordered environment. Each animal *seeks* to communicate with only those aspects of the environment which fit its particular structural plan. Uexküll calls this phenomenon the "lock and key" principle. Only those environmental stimuli become "keys" for which the organism possesses the "fitting lock." Tinbergen (1951), in conjunction with Konrad Lorenz, offers similar conclusions about the instinctive mechanisms underlying animals' ordered, directed behavior. A "highly specialized nervous mechanism" is responsible for the match between situation and response, so that in the end the animal always "does the right thing at the right time" (more than we can say about humans). A selective reflex mechanism blocks the inner excitations until the "fitting sign stimulus" is encountered. Thus, each reaction is controlled by its own "innate releasing mechanism," keyed to its own "fitting" environmental sign stimulus.

What these theories state is that environmental valences are organically and unambiguously given for animals. Instinctive forces direct them to lay their eggs in a particular place, to choose a certain mate, or to migrate from one location to another. In contrast, humans are not endowed with such clear-cut directions. We are neither as instinct-bound nor as stimulus-bound as animals are. Emotionally and intellectually, we can transcend the immediacy of a given situation.

Actually we do not know to what extent human choices, too, are distant derivatives of genetic endowment (Szondi, 1947). It is decidedly more difficult to determine the contribution of heredity to behavior in human beings than in animals. In general, animal behavior patterns are well developed from the start, almost immediately after birth. Yet even the most basic human behavior patterns are established only gradually, during the first two years of life, and thus come under social (mostly parental) influence. This fact precludes any neat separation of the role of genetic or constitutional givens versus environmental factors in steering human choices.

Human infants' uniquely early birth (compared with the developmental level of other mammals at birth), their naked skin, and their lack of clear-cut instinctive orientation make for extreme helplessness and vulnerability. As if to compensate for this lack of organismic directedness and external protective covering, humans have developed considerably more brain-cortical substance than any other species. In addition, there is the human brain's specifically human psychic correlate: the ego with its symbolizing capacity. One might well picture the capacity for symbolization as a kind of mental "protective covering." It makes up for our lack of an instinctive preadaptedness which would lead us to our niche in a complex environment. Only over hundreds of thousands of years has the human brain evolved to its present form. This form gives us a special ability—the capacity to create symbols, whether in thought, language, or perceptible external forms.

The essential difference between animals and humans, then, hinges on the coherent instinctive directedness found in animals in contrast to the *relative freedom of choice among alternatives* available to humans. The capacity for symbolization underlies this relative freedom of choice. The specifically human freedom means that the relation between the organism and the valence-character of the environment is flexible or, rather, multivalent. It is the symbolizing process that imbues objects with meaning and valence. Moreover, this process is not unidirectional. The meaning and valence of the same object can change with shifts in the individual's psychic tension systems.

This potential multivalence in the meaning and value of environmental objects endows human life with a particular richness, but it can also give rise to conflict situations and pathological choices. The complexity of the human nervous system *demands* continuous symbolizing activity. Symbols may lead to the proper object, but they may also mislead. The very same complex central nervous system that accounts for human thinking or for the building of the Chartres Cathedral also sows the seeds for human psychopathology. Character neurosis and schizophrenia are just as much specifically human potentials as artistic or intellectual creativity. Animals are not consciously creative, but neither do they become borderline characters or schizophrenics (although humans have devised experiments to make animals confused and unhappy, even self-destructive). Animals, for the most part, follow a single route. Symbolization, on the other hand, opens up the path to human creativity, as well as to specifically human psychic disturbances and to uncertainty, or doubt.

In line with this, Binswanger (1958) has described the most specifically human characteristic as the freedom to consciously choose one's own form of existence. It must be added, however, that this freedom is always a relative or qualified one. Humans, both as individuals and as a species, do have some sort of "structural plan," which—combined with environmental restrictions—sets limits to our choices.[1] One need

[1] Szondi's experimental method aims at discovering this individual "structural plan" (Szondi, 1947; Deri, 1949). The Szondi Test is based on choices of "most liked" and "most disliked" faces from forty-eight photographs of mental patients. The pictures are presented consecutively in six groups, with eight different mental

only think of Icarus' fate to see what happens if we disregard the realistic constraints of our inborn "structural plan." Nor can we humans choose a form of existence in which we relate as unambiguously to our environment as do animals with their unobstructed instinctive directedness (the advice of presently fashionable oriental philosophies notwithstanding). What guides us, what connects us, is the very process of symbolization, or how we come to perceive and conceive the world around us.

Unlike birds, humans cannot migrate to distant places without a good map. Many of us feel lost while migrating through the unpredictable, uncharted course of life because we lack a good "cognitive map" to orient us adaptively in the inner and outer worlds. A good cognitive map is the individual's inner storehouse of well-structured symbolic representations, with *isomorphic* likeness—though not identity—to his or her real inner and outer circumstances. Without such a dependable cognitive map, the person may feel overwhelmed, as if thrown into the unsolvable "puzzle" or jungle of life. Bor-

---

illnesses represented in each group. The subject chooses two "most liked" ones and two "most disliked" ones from each group. The final distribution of choices within the eight "factors" is graphically recorded on a scoring sheet. The whole test is repeated with the same subject on ten different days.

It is the series of ten "profiles" that is interpreted as to the pattern of the subject's "instinctual needs" and character. The interpretive meaning of the eight factors in various positions ("like": plus; "dislike": minus; "ambivalent": plus-minus; "not chosen": zero) cannot be discussed here. The "loading," i.e., the number of pictures chosen, within one factor reflects the intensity of the subject's need-tension with regard to the instinctual need represented in extreme form by that particular mental illness, i.e., by that factor. In evaluating the total pattern of ten profiles, factors that change their "loading" are separated from the "root factors" with intense loading that remain constant in the series of profiles. The constant tension within these "root factors" is interpreted as the subject's "structural plan." These factors are the fixed "structural givens" which, to some extent, represent the limits within which therapy can aim for change. I say "to some extent" because the same "root factors" lend themselves to a number (but limited number) of different channelizations. The aim of Szondi's *Schicksalsanalysis* is to find the best possible channelizations for the individual's "structural plan," which, according to Szondi, is laid down genetically. Different types of channelization of an "instinctual need" can be viewed as different forms of symbolization. (For a discussion of Szondi's genetic instinct theory, see Chapter 6.)

derline patients, in particular, often describe such feelings. In some sense, they do not know how or where to choose. What we need to understand is the key role of symbolization in lending directedness to our lives.

Symbol Formation and Homeostatic Tension Regulation

Due to our physical nature, particularly our premature birth, we cannot cope directly—without the mediation of symbols—with the complexity of inner and outer stimulation. The newborn infant, born at a much less developed stage than any other mammal, is helpless and susceptible to painful overstimulation through his or her sensitive skin, as well as from inner sources of instinctual demands. Pain and instinctual needs have an inherently driving quality, causing a high level of tension within the organism. If this tension reaches a critical intensity, then the organism loses its capacity to function coherently in an integrated manner. The degree of order necessary for whole-some organismic functioning then gives way to chaotic disorganization. Thus, striving for some measure of homeostatic equilibrium (the self-regulatory principle) can be seen as the primary motivation and goal of all organismic activity (Bertalanffy, 1952). The level of organismic tension has to be regulated, whether by discharge or transformation of "energy," in order to safeguard the healthy functioning of the individual.

The infant's first mode of tension regulation takes place by way of primary-process direct discharge of unbound energy.[2] We also know that primary-process functioning is not prac-

[2] In the next chapter, I shall present in more detail my argument for this continued use of Freud's concept of psychic energy. I use the term in its phenomenological sense, as the experience of an inner force (or forces) driving toward movement or action. Dynamic psychology needs the concept, recent attempts to eliminate it notwithstanding.

ticable in the long run; gradual modification of energy discharge into complex secondary-process modes must take place if the individual is to survive. Whatever the form of energy discharge, be it according to the pleasure principle, the reality principle, or "beyond the pleasure principle," its organismic goal remains the same: to keep the total excitation or tension level from rising above a point where it would disrupt the functioning of the organism. With increasing differentiation of the mind, the methods employed to guard the wholeness of the organism change in form and content. Yet the opposite also holds: With changes in the means of reducing energic pressure, the human mind becomes more structured and increasingly differentiated.

It is symbolization that is par excellence the human mode of energy regulation. The importance of symbolization stems from its energy-binding and transforming power (a point that will be spelled out in the next chapter). To put it simply: The symbolic world of ideas, concepts, and language mediates between the action-prone human being and his or her surrounding object world. Through symbolization, the push toward immediate tension release can be delayed, allowing for secondary-process, more orderly direction of energy discharge. In this way the symbolic process safeguards the wholeness of the individual by distancing in space and time the impulse-ridden subject from the world of real objects. A symbol is a representation; it is not the object. Thus, while symbols serve to *connect* the subject with his or her intended chosen object, at the same time they vouchsafe the *separateness* indispensable for the integrity of the individual. This is one aspect of the Janus-face of symbols: the unification of opposing functions within one gestalt.

Earlier I emphasized that symbolization is a gestalt-forming process. Symbols are more gestalted, more delineated forms than the symbolized "things" they represent. Symbolic representation always implies a measure of condensation, a bringing together toward an articulated whole. Symbolization leads away from internal and external chaos toward articulated order. It is precisely through this gestalting, ordering function that symbolization promotes homeostatic equilibrium within the energy household of the organism. And so does the symbolizing function of perception bring order into our perceptual world.

Perception Is Already Symbolic Representation

The gestalt-forming, organizing function of symbolization is built right into human perception. Were it not for the automatic symbolizing, schematizing activity of perception, we would be lost in the "big, blooming, buzzing confusion" William James (1902) describes. Perception selectively organizes what we see; it is *not* simply a passive, point-by-point registration of external stimuli. Experiments by Gestalt psychologists have clearly demonstrated this fact. They questioned what up to then was taken for granted.

Why do we see delineated, meaningful things instead of a chaos of intermingling lines and surfaces? This seemingly simple question ushered in a new epoch in our conception of the working of the human mind. This scientifically truly "generative" question led to perception experiments that threw light on the "how" of human perception, even though much of the causal "why" remains unknown. Answers might be forthcoming from the work of neuropsychologists, for example, the work of Pribram (1971). In any case, what Gestalt psychology experiments do prove is that human perception cannot be separated from organizational processes and cognition and, in the broad sense of the term, interpretation.

Symbolization originates in perception. But the reverse is

also true. Our storehouse of existing internal symbols bestows order and meaning on our perception of the external world. The theory of projective techniques is based on this principle. Gombrich, in *Art and Illusion* (1960) and "Meditations on a Hobby Horse or the Roots of Artistic Form" (1951) irradiates this circular interaction in tracing the effect of art works on our perception. We first perceive an art work with our existing symbolic schemata, but as we enter into the visual experience of a great work of art, these schemata change. Van Gogh's *Chair* or *Shoes* imbues forever the way we see a chair or a pair of old shoes; Constable's clouds permeate our vision of the sky. The possibilities of seeing are expanded.

I characterized symbols with the metaphor of a bridge connecting two qualitatively different realms. This bridge is built by the process of symbolization, which transposes or translates phenomena from one realm into another. Perception and memory-image formation, in particular, carry out a transforming function of symbolization. They re-present the three-dimensional, concrete terrain of the outer world in the nonmaterial, abstract realm of our inner world. Ordinarily we take this process for granted; we don't stop to wonder at how this almost magical transformation takes place. Yet the "mysterious" symbolizing power of perception is *the* basic problem of epistemology, the systematic search for the grounds of human knowledge, for the basis of its validity and its limits. In order to understand epistemology, we need to study the laws governing perceptual symbol transformation. (As I shall later indicate, these laws have special implications for the psychoanalytic process, for they compel us to reevaluate the meaning of verbal exchange between patient and analyst.)

The ontogenetic motivation for symbolization derives from the wish to bridge over, to reach what is not directly reachable. Neither the "real" outer world nor our unconscious inner world is totally within the grasp of our perceiving or cognizing ego. We rely on isomorphically congruent symbolic representations of these realms. Both Plato and Kant have in fact stated that we cannot apprehend objects as they *really* are; we can never know the *Ding an sich* ("thing in itself"); we receive only transformed notions of it.

Kant also conceived of perception as an active, ordering process (by way of the *a priori* categories of time, space, and causality) and not as a passive registration. In this sense, Kant links up with the Gestalt theorists' view of perception as an *a priori*, actively organizing process. And Freud is Kantian in his contention that neither the unconscious inner world nor the intensity and complexity of outside stimulation can be perceived in its original form. His concept of a "stimulus barrier" that transforms outside stimuli is relevant to the generic theory of symbolization.

The "Stimulus Barrier" and the Need for Symbolizing Perception

Freud clearly indicated that we cannot deal with the *full* complexity and intensity of impinging stimuli. As early as his *Project for a Scientific Psychology* (1895), Freud described this limitation in neurophysiological terms. Following Fechner, he spoke of the minimum and maximum thresholds for receiving external stimuli. In Freud's opinion, "the effectiveness of stimuli is restricted more or less to *medium* quantities. At the same time the nature of the nerve-coverings acts as a sieve, so that not every kind of stimulus can be effective. . . . The stimuli which actually reach the Ø [perception] neurones have a quantity and a qualitative characteristic" (p. 374). Freud then referred to the "particular period of neuronic motion which is certainly not the same as that of the stimulus but has some relation to it, determined according to a reduction formula that is unknown to us" (p. 375).[3] The two schematic pictures Freud used to illustrate these ideas show the difference between the real external stimuli and the abbreviated pattern of stimulation received by the sense organ (p. 375). A key point here is Freud's citing not only a quantitative reduction but also some qualitative abstraction of the stimulus pattern. This view is congruent with the concept of "symbolizing perception."

Twenty-five years later, Freud's thoughts on this topic remain much the same. In *Beyond the Pleasure Principle* (1920), the concept of "protective shield," or stimulus barrier, is used to denote these perceptual phenomena. The "protective shield" guards the organism against "an external world charged with the most powerful energies. . . . [The sense organ] would be killed by the stimulation emanating from these if it were not provided with a protective shield against stimuli. . . . *Protection against* stimuli is an almost more important function for the living organism than *reception of* stimuli. . . . The main purpose of the *reception* of stimuli is to discover the direction and nature of the external stimuli; and for that it is enough to take small specimens of the external world" (p. 27).

Despite Freud's scientific commitment to derive sensations and perceptions from "quantities" of energy and excitation, one finds here references to a qualitatively transforming function of perception. "Protection against stimuli" entails both quantitative reduction and qualitative change (the move from chaos to order). Freud's depiction of the protective shield as preserving "special modes of transformation of energy" and his emphasis on sampling the "direction and nature of the external stimuli" attest to a belief that perception involves some kind of transforming function, similar to what I call isomorphically congruent symbolic transformation.

[3] Freud indeed came close to specifying this relation as "isomorphic."

Nevertheless, Freud did not view perceptual "abbreviation" as a symbolizing function—most probably because perception is primarily informative of outside conditions. We know that for Freud, and consequently for psychoanalysis, the concept of symbolization was limited to the concealing tactics of repression. That the same process might serve contradictory purposes was unacceptable. Or, rather, in line with Freud's categorical thinking, the coexistence of opposites was deemed a sign of primary-process functioning. Such a possibility was not compatible with the laws of secondary process. For Freud, symbolization meant disguise and had to be separate from an activity like perception that functioned to disclose reality. And here we come to the crux of Freud's blind spot: that perception intrinsically has a *dual* function. In constructing *isomorphically* abbreviated schemata, perception *reveals* the features and meaning of outside reality. Yet at the same time *it keeps parts of this reality hidden*, given the filtering function of the "protective shield" (to use Freud's concept).

What Freud, and many others, have pointed out is that we cannot possibly take in all the stimuli around us. Perception, then, must be both selective and condensing. Susanne Langer clearly articulates the symbolizing nature of this process: "The material furnished by the senses is constantly wrought into *symbols*, which are our elementary ideas" (1942, p. 46). Or: "The human brain is constantly carrying on a process of symbolic transformation of the experiential data that come to it" (p. 47).

The Translating Function of Symbolization

In essence, we have been saying that symbolization functions to *give meaning* to phenomena in one region by registering or translating them into the "language" of another region. A good translation has to be *isomorphic* with the original text or it will not convey the meaning. Yet even the best translations, to some extent, alter the flavor and meaning of the original. Bad translations definitely distort the text's meaning and may lead us to misjudge its intent. Symptoms, for example, can be seen as misinforming, "bad translations." Good isomorphic symbolization truly *communicates*, while inadequate symbolization distorts meaning.

One question to consider is whether symbolically schematized percepts furnish information that primarily reveals reality, or whether they tend more to hide it. The first instance will be referred to as *true or isomorphic* symbolization. Borrowing a term from Piaget (1945), I shall call the second trend "cryptosymbolization." To follow Piaget's thinking: The ratio between the existing intrapsychic schemata's accommodation *to* the external stimulus pattern, versus the preponderance of assimilative tendencies, differentiates between these two modes of perceptual symbolization. An optimal balance between accommodation and assimilation allows for both aspects of the newly formed schemata: the necessary extent of influence of outer reality that guarantees realistic appreciation of the outside world, as well as some input from the subjective inner world that connects the newly formed perceptual schemata to the perceiving subject's past. Piaget derives the cryptosymbols of dreams and maladaptive symptoms from the preponderance of assimilation over accommodation. This means that existing mental schemata are not allowed to change in accordance with the realistic nature of new impressions, but rather the opposite takes place: Perception becomes distorted due to the assimilative impact of the old percepts, the existing "mental schemata."

In my conceptualization, "mental schemata" are mental symbols, "tools" with which we perceive and think. If they overrepresent past subjective ingredients at the expense of the realistic features of new stimulation, then they are not true or isomorphic symbols but misinforming cryptosymbols.

As we have seen, symbols are intrinsically bound up with *communication* across a boundary, be it interpersonal or intrapsychic communication. Besides the intensity of emotional states leading to overassimilative cryptosymbolization, it is the nature and locus of the boundary to be crossed that decide whether the symbol primarily communicates truth (an isomorphic symbol) or acts to conceal truth (a cryptosymbol). Freud (1900) and psychoanalysts after him viewed symbols as disguises, hiding true content, because they only considered *crossing the repression barrier* as symbol-producing. In other words, they limited their definition to the cryptosymbol.

Isomorphic symbols, however, cross permeable boundaries that allow for true communication by symbolic means. Normal perception, memory-image formation, and emotionally unobstructed communication by verbal or pictorial language are examples of this informative function of isomorphic, true symbols. This revealing function of isomorphic symbolization was not considered by Freud and his followers—with damaging effects on dream interpretation and other aspects of the theory of treatment. Recognition of the symbolizing aspect of language, perception, and "normal" memory would have changed the evaluation of the verbal exchange between analysand and analyst.

To summarize: Symbolization is an ongoing gestalt-forming process, leading to increasing order and connectedness. Specifically, the "translating" or form- and meaning-giving function of symbolization works in two directions: (1) in a *centripetal* direction, from the outside to the inside, as in perception and memory-image formation, and (2) in a *cen-*

trifugal direction, from the "depth" of the inside upward and outward. In this chapter we have followed the first direction. In the next chapter we will explore the second. Briefly, "upward"-directed symbolization starts by unfolding and articulating the fluid content of the id (Freud's original *Ucs.*, not the repressed unconscious). Through successive "translations," the original id content comes to pass through the "preconscious" and the "conscious" regions (both of which form part of the ego), and finally gains symbolized expression in the outside world. In any case, whether centripetal or centrifugal, symbolization results in transforming chaos into order. This process entails *both* excluding some features of the original raw material and selectively articulating others.

CHAPTER 6

Centrifugal or Internal Symbolization

What I call centrifugal or internal symbolization falls under the psychoanalytic heading of instinct derivatives. Just as overpowering external stimuli are transformed into symbols via perception and memory-image formation, instinct derivatives give meaning and structure to "unbound," more purely discharge-oriented id strivings. In other words, instinct derivatives can be considered symbolized translations of unformed impulses. As I have already noted, this shaping of unformed impulses into meaningfully structured gestalts takes place as the instinctual raw material crosses the permeable boundary between the unconscious (id) and the preconscious storehouse of memory traces. By crossing this boundary, the unbound passions of the id are bound into "tamed," usable intentions, affects, aim-directed wishes, thoughts, and images. These are the instinct derivatives that bestow specific aims and meanings on the more purely discharge-oriented id strivings. The latter correspond to the "unbound state of energy," while "energy" in the instinct derivatives is in a "bound" state (Breuer and Freud, 1893 –1895; Freud, 1895). Primary and secondary processes are the corollary to this distinction.

The content of the unconscious itself is not communicable;

it is not directly knowable without first traveling through the depository of symbolic forms in the preconscious. Perception, whether internal or external, can make out only "things" with an edge, i.e., delineated forms—not an unbounded medley or chaos. Only the storehouse of delineated symbolic structures in the preconscious can be perceived. The deeper levels of the preconscious serve as the halfway-house through which the unbound raw material of the id has to pass in order to come out on the ego side as formed structures carrying specific meaning. It is these structures that serve as connecting bridges between the motivated person and his or her environment. The richer the preconscious storehouse of symbolic structures, the better-connected and more articulated the person's total lifespace will be, with an increased dialogue between person and environment. Symbols are the tools that help to carve out the meaningfully fitting personal milieu. A rich and well-functioning preconscious is the prerequisite for such a satisfying lifespace. The aim of psychoanalytic treatment becomes the enhancement of the analysand's capacity for correct symbolization, centrifugal (inner) as well as centripetal (perceptual).

I view internal symbolization as the one manifestation of the organismic propensity for form development, or gestalt formation. The fluid id content is gradually structured into meaningful preconscious gestalts. Intimately interwoven with this process is the transformation of energy (from an unbound to a bound state), as well as the evolution of meaning. In human psychology, energy concepts, gestalt-forming processes, and symbolic-meaning functions are inseparably intertwined.[1] The fact that the interrelation of these three realms of phenomena—forces, symbolic forms, and mean-

[1] It would be desirable to coordinate these thoughts with the findings of brain neurologists. Penfield's (1975) discovery of the interpretive cortex, for instance, seems particularly relevant to a consideration of symbolization and consciousness.

ing—is as yet beyond clear conceptualization (and may well forever remain so due to the essential incongruence between the nature of the transformation processes and the nature of discursive verbal language) is not enough reason to excise one of these realms from theorizing, in order to come up with a more clear-cut theory.

There is a strong movement among a group of psychoanalytic theoreticians to reformulate psychoanalytic metapsychology in a way that excludes energy concepts (see G. Klein, 1970; Gill and Holzman, 1976; Schafer, 1976). They aim to construct a self-consistent, purely psychological theory, concerned with values and meanings. To accomplish this, they have discarded Freud's neurologically based energy concepts, which they regard as "mechanistic." The cleaned-up theoretical package is quite attractive because of its consistency and seemingly humanistic stance. But is it *really* humanistic? Can the functioning of the human mind indeed be understood without due consideration of biology and concepts denoting force? The human being is not a neatly constructed product of "creation." Why, then, should we expect a homogeneous explanatory theory? Biological, physiochemical, energic, and symbolic processes all determine what we call human psychology. True, concepts such as "psychic energy" or "instinctual force" do not have clear-cut objectifiable referents, but leaving these terms out of a theory of human action does not further our understanding of human motivation. Words can be deleted from sentences, but their omission will not change the complexity of the phenomena under consideration. Should physicists drop the concept of energy from their theorizing because it is not *fully* understood or neatly definable? Science would stagnate. Clamoring for precise definitions *before* any theorizing is scientifically sterile.

Kovel, in his article "Things and Words" (1978), expresses doubts similar to mine about the clean-up campaign of the anti-energy theorists. While he acknowledges the never-resolved tension in Freud's theoretical writings between "force" and "meaning," and admits that Freud's contradictory statements may engender confusion, he appreciates the heuristic stimulation of such a lack of closure in psychoanalytic theory. Kovel underlines Freud's "heteronomous or double registration [of] basic psychoanalytic concepts: the objective discourse of force uneasily combined with the subjective discourse of meaning" (p. 23). Yet he does not see this as a reason for dismissing one concept in favor of the other. Instead, he suggests that such heteronomous functioning "is part of human truth and hence needs to be theoretically represented" (p. 26).

As Kovel clearly states, natural science concepts cannot be "lopped off" with benefit to psychoanalysis. What I would stress is that human beings belong to nature. However blurred, the interface between biology and psychology is crucial. Crucial not only for the theoretician but for the clinician as well. Szondi, for one, understood this. His psychiatric theory and practice derive from his belief in the genetic base of human psychology and psychopathology.

In my opinion, meaning-giving symbolic processes, such as language and value-oriented action, are *not* fundamentally heteronomous from biological "forces." Both Portmann (1965) and Langer (1967, 1972) have suggested that a proclivity toward form creation is inherent to organic nature. Evidence of this can be found in the orderly morphogenesis of all living things. Growth and development denote movement toward some form. The structuralization of the human psyche is a special instance of this organismic tendency.

I have already cited Cassirer's dictum that we are *by nature* symbol-making beings. As we saw in the last chapter, the very act of perceiving engages us in a selective and constructive process. It is our inborn capacity for symbol formation that enables us to condense the diffuse stimuli impinging upon us from within and without into delineated form, thereby producing order (Deri, 1974).

The impetus for this order-directedness can be found in the roots of our inheritance—in the genes themselves. A telling point is made by Schrödinger (1945), who derives the tremendous determining force of the genes from their structurally built-in disequilibrium. He describes the structure of genes as that of aperiodic crystals, which are not built on the principles of repetition and symmetry. Such an aperiodic structure would explain the great variety of patterned content which can be compressed into the genes. Moreover, Schrödinger assumes that the genes' power to send messages to the total organism, messages that direct highly complex and varied form development, stems from this asymmetry. In other words, we might say that the genes act as incomplete gestalts pushing the organism toward a more stable, better-equilibrated whole. More recent discoveries about the role of DNA and RNA do not present logical incompatibilities with Schrödinger's views. Indeed, this research ties genetic mechanisms to a theory of communication through "symbols." The nucleic acids use a four-letter "alphabet" to dispatch their instructions for form development to the various cells. The cells then read or translate this code to produce the proteins necessary for growth.

Biologically, then, the genes are par excellence the form-creative substance of the organism. But how does the knowledge fit into our conceptualization of the psyche? At one point Freud describes the id as "the oldest of [the] psychical provinces," containing "everything that is inherited, . . . that is laid down in the constitution—above all, therefore, the instincts which originate from the somatic organization" (1940, p. 145). In my opinion, this definition would include the powerful organizing forces of the genes as content of the id.

There is no need to postulate an antagonism between the seething caldron of instincts in the id and the controlling, formative forces of the ego. Consider Anna Freud's statement: "On their way to gratification the id-impulses must pass through the territory of the ego and here they are in an alien atmosphere" (1936, p. 7). Here the ego comes out as the "enemy" of the id, not its ally. Rather than trespassing through the ego, I would say that the id impulses are *transformed* into ego intentions. Natural tendencies propel the formation of an organized ego. Cassirer's dictum of man being a symbol-making animal is equivalent to asserting that man is an ego-making animal. Symbol-forming, order-making, and ego-constructing processes are constitutionally given human "drives." The psychic proclivity for pattern formation originates in the dynamic urges of the id; it is not simply superimposed by the "exigencies of outside reality."

Unfortunately, the idea of a biopsychological urge toward form creation was not part of Freud's metapsychology. To view psychic evidence as a unitary and hierarchically ordered series of transformations was not ego-syntonic to Freud's way of perceiving and conceptualizing. Instead, Freud's model of the mind was based on antagonistic tendencies vying for power, on conflict between separate psychic institutions. It is precisely this dualistic, segmented formulation that has proved most thwarting for a unified psychoanalytic theory of orderly psychic structuralization and form creation.[2]

[2] To give but one example of the distortions Freud's view has engendered, let me cite a passage from *Civilization and Its Discontents* (1930). Here Freud explains that order, "like cleanliness, applies solely to the works of man. . . . Order is a kind of compulsion to repeat which, when a regulation has been laid down once and for all, decides when, where and how a thing shall be done. . . . Human beings exhibit an inborn tendency to carelessness, irregularity and unreliability" (p. 93). Freud appears to view order as an anal reaction formation. Later, he refers to astronomical regularities as a possible "first point of departure" for order. Strange to mention "astronomical regularities" instead of the orderly symmetry of the human body—a model lying much closer to hand.

A Reexamination of Freud's Ideas

Because Freud's metapsychology ignores the principle of *natural* gestalt formation, his combining of concepts of force and meaning was always an uneasy marriage, and the gate was left wide open for "reformers" of psychoanalytic theory to simply shut out one side of the dualism. Yet I believe that, despite the limitations of his dualistic thinking, Freud has much to offer us in formulating a generic theory of symbolization. Freud's theory-making has the scientific elegance of introducing a minimum of concepts to explain observations of qualitatively different phenomena. Although one can disagree with some of the ways in which he linked these concepts together, the best way to sharpen one's own psychoanalytic thinking is to study Freud's writings—arguing points as needed. Nobody else has approached the firmness, scope, and parsimoniousness of Freud's conceptual scaffolding.

It should be clear that, in particular, I consider Freud's concept of the binding of energy crucial for a unified theory of psychic structuralization.[3] A significant corollary of this idea is the distinction between primary and secondary processes. In my opinion, these two suppositions are the most heuristic hypotheses of psychoanalytic metapsychology. The characteristics of the three different psychic systems—unconscious, preconscious, and conscious (the topographic model which actually Freud never really abandoned)—derive from these two suppositions. As we shall see, in all his theoretical papers, including his posthumously published *Outline* (1940), Freud

[3] Actually the distinction between bound (tonic) and unbound (mobile) psychic energy was first postulated by Breuer in his theoretical chapter in *Studies on Hysteria* (Breuer and Freud, 1893 –1895). Although Freud was aware that this key concept had been contributed by Breuer, his references to Breuer decreased over time. In the first Clark University lecture (1910), Freud explicitly named Breuer as the true founder of psychoanalysis, but by 1914 in the "History of the Psycho-Analytic Movement," this respectful attribution had vanished.

never ceased to grapple with the conceptual difficulties inherent in the notion of "binding" energy.

Still, it is before he set forth the "official" structural theory in *The Ego and the Id* (1923) that Freud came the closest to throwing light on the *processes* underlying energy transformation, the development of secondary-process functioning, and the change of psychic material from an unconscious to a preconscious, and thus potentially conscious, state (in other words, the dynamics of ego formation). These early concepts lend themselves much better to theorizing about unitary transformational processes than does the descriptive label "ego," which so easily lends itself to anthropomorphizing, concretizing use. Even Freud fell into the latter trap, with his images of the ego "fighting" to change the id (1940). In his pre-1923 works, however, Freud's approach to energy transformation is more unitary, more process- and function-oriented than struggle- and fight-oriented. It is to these writings that I shall now turn.

Freud's Earliest Views on Psychic Structuralization and Their Relevance to a Generic Theory of Symbolization

Since psychoanalytic treatment is essentially language treatment, it is almost redundant to state that the function of language was of prime interest to Freud from the very beginning. His first major psychophysiological work, *On Aphasia* (1891), deals with the central role of language in the functioning of the preconscious. This early work foreshadows Freud's later efforts to formulate a model illuminating the role of language in consciousness, in thinking, and in psychic structuralization. In other words, since language is the most articulated system of symbolization, I would describe Freud's initial interest as centering on the role of symbolization in consciousness and in the structuralization of the mind.[4]

Freud's early cathartic treatment of hysterical patients was based on the theory that verbal recall of "forgotten" visual memories dissipates the pathological effect of these "forgotten" (repressed) traumas. Defensive forgetting results in the damming up of harmful affects, while verbal recall "brings to an end the operative force of the idea which was not abreacted . . . by allowing its strangulated affect *to find a way out through speech*" (Breuer and Freud, 1893–1895, p. 17; my italics). The curative power of speech is not attributed to emotional catharsis alone, but also to the "associative correction" that comes with the introduction of the forgotten material into consciousness. Thus, Freud and Breuer seem to consider verbal recall the lever for transposing mental content from one region to another and thereby bringing about transformation in psychic functioning.

In his early theoretical writings—and later, too—this transforming function of words was central to Freud's interest. As we shall see, it intertwines with the concepts of binding energy, the preconscious, delayed action, the reality principle, reality testing, thinking, the secondary process, and the ego. And it is the generic process of symbol formation that ties together all these concepts. Together these ideas represent the specific *human*ness of human beings. *Binding instinctual energy is the juncture where human action takes off from biological behavior* and enters the specifically *human* universe. This is the universe of thought and meaning leading to action that serves purposes beyond simple survival.

But how does such specifically *human* behavior come

[4] To say this is not to deny my contention that Freud restricted the concept of symbolization to its pathological modality, to the "hiding" of "true" content found in repression. He himself did not refer to meaningful communication through language as symbolization.

about? What makes it possible to change the course of "selfish" id impulses so that human beings act for the benefit of others, search for truth, produce art? In the language of the biologist, how did the "selfish genes" build an organism with the mental equipment to turn "against the tyranny of the selfish replicators [the genes]" (Dawkins, 1976, p. 215)? Dawkins, an outstanding zoologist-geneticist, ends his book on evolution with this question, a question that is closely related to the problem that concerned Freud throughout his life. This is the riddle of "humanness" (the German word *Menschwerdung* is a better expression). In my opinion, this question remained Freud's focal interest throughout his life, with all the neurophysiological and philosophical implications this fundamental problem entails.

I believe that Freud knew that consciousness is more of an enigma than the unconscious. But, for whatever reasons, Freud eventually withdrew from clear-cut neurophysiological theorizing as well as from philosophy. Yet, in his correspondence with Fliess, Freud referred to his lifelong wish to become a philosopher: "I secretly nurse the hope of arriving . . . at my own original objective, philosophy. For that was my original ambition" (1887–1902, p. 141).

A good example of Freud's concern with a neurophysiological approach to the problem of consciousness is his *Project for a Scientific Psychology* (1895). That remarkable study aimed at explaining how the human mind works under normal conditions. Questions about speech, memory, consciousness, and binding energy are central to the *Project*, which focuses on general "laws" of human mental functioning, not on pathology. Moreover, the *Project* contains the germinal ideas of *all* of Freud's later theoretical essays (see Amacher, 1965).

Freud's awareness that the nature of the preconscious system and the process of binding energy are the crux of "humanness" is evident not only in his earliest works, but also in his great metapsychological essay "The Unconscious" (1915c) and in his conclusive work, the *Outline* (1940). Yet his exploration of the unconscious continues to be seen as the hallmark of his work. A paper on the relation between the preconscious and conscious systems is mentioned in "The Unconscious," but this paper, unfortunately, has never reached readers. (A similar fate almost befell the *Project*, which only saw the daylight of print in 1954, more than half a century after it had been sent to Fliess.)

Freud's Letter 32, which followed the dispatch of the *Project* by twelve days, is one of his most exalted pieces of writing. It serves as a paradigm for the elation the creator experiences when surveying with one quick glance the whole of his just-finished piece of creative work. Freud describes the sudden illumination he experienced in the course of a "strenuous night," when he "saw" "all the way to the very conditioning of consciousness," to "the factors determining consciousness as a perceptual function" (1887–1902, p. 129).

Clearly, it is the discovery concerning consciousness as a perceptual function that excited Freud here, that prompted his ecstatically joyous letter to Fliess. Yet the bulk of his later clinical observations did not focus on the functioning of the preconscious-conscious system. The concept of the preconscious remained, as it were, a stepchild of psychoanalytic theory, even though it is the locus par excellence for binding energy, for symbolizing form development, in other words, for mental creativity.[5]

Freud's failure to concentrate on the pathology of the preconscious parallels the limited treatment of symbolization in psychoanalytic theory. His emphatic insistence on unconscious *conflict* in pathogenesis—a point on which he parted

[5] As far as I know, only Kubie has emphasized the role of the preconscious in creativity and symbolization, and in the psychological freedom underlying the capacity for change (see Kubie, 1958, 1978).

ways with Janet and Breuer—may have led him to overlook the possible consequences of a primary defect in preconscious synthesizing and form-creating processes. An underendowment in the internal symbolizing capacity might predispose a person to psychic conflict, as well as the other way around.

Serious consideration of primary disturbances of the preconscious would have brought Freud's views closer to those of Janet and Breuer, as I discuss below. Could it be that Freud's withholding of his paper on the "preconscious-conscious" was connected with the break in his friendship with Breuer, just as the long-buried state of the *Project* probably had to do with his break with Fliess? We cannot know the answer; we only know the loss.

Integration of the Janet-Breuer constitutional theory with Freud's conflict theory would have led to deeper understanding of the functions of the preconscious, and consequently to some new diagnostic categories and altered therapeutic interventions. Some "interminable" analyses might have become "terminable" if emphasis had shifted from "making the unconscious conscious" to helping the patient redirect attention cathexis and improve the synthesizing-symbolizing function of the preconscious. Some patients now lumped into the vague category "borderline" seem to suffer from this kind of malfunctioning of the preconscious. They exhibit subtle aphasia-like thought disturbances and difficulties in verbalization. Due to the weakness of their internal symbolizing capacity, these patients' "preconscious ego" is in disarray, as if a synthesizing glue that held complex spatial and temporal gestalts together were missing. Treatment of these patients requires a combination of "uncovering" type interpretations with helping them to redistribute their attention cathexis. Focusing their attention on the malfunctioning of their thought formation, specifically on arrested stages of concept formation (fixation on and overcathexis of visual imagery, which easily lead to fragmented thought processes), as well as on the fragmentation of their intentional acts, has proved useful in my experience. Actually, redirecting the patient's attention cathexis is a way of making what has been *non*-conscious conscious. Increased awareness of preconscious malfunctioning can have good self-corrective effects.

Had Freud continued his line of thought started in his neuropsychological work, such as *On Aphasia* (1891) and the *Project* (1895), this puzzling group of patients might have benefited from more accurate diagnosis and a more specific treatment modality. Instead, when thrown into the category "borderline," the therapist's attention is directed by his or her own mental symbols appropriate for that group (such as malevolent and/or split introjects), rather than focusing on the formal malfunctioning of the patient's preconscious symbolizing-synthesizing capacity.

At this point we should turn to a closer examination of the theoretical issues involved in Freud's controversy with Janet and Breuer, since these two psychiatric practitioners and profound thinkers stood for the pathogenic significance of a primary defect in the patient's mental synthesizing capacity.

The Points of Disagreement with Janet and Breuer

Freud's ideological estrangement from Breuer hinged on two main differences in their views: (1) the role of sexuality in the etiology of neuroses, and (2) the role of constitutional predisposition toward dissociated mental states (Breuer's "hypnoid" states) versus the role of psychic conflict and the effect of "defenses" against it (Freud) in the genesis of hysterical symptoms. Breuer's thinking on the etiology of hysteria paralleled that of Janet, who spoke of a splitting of consciousness, which he saw as based on an "innate weakness of the capacity for psychical synthesis, on the narrowness of the field of consciousness" (cited by Freud, 1894, p. 46).

The Breuer-Janet hypothesis deserves our attention. Precisely because the push toward organismic form development originates in the genes (in the id), there is no reason to doubt that this capacity, like any other inherited tendency, can be constitutionally present in a variety of strengths. Janet's proposition (which accorded with Breuer's) was that hysterical patients are "*inherently* incapable of holding together the multiplicity of mental processes into a unity and hence arises the tendency for mental dissociation" (cited by Freud, 1910, p. 21; my italics). One could paraphrase this as: An autonomous ego deficit in the internal gestalting, or symbol-forming, capacity predisposes toward mental disorganization. (I have already noted that the capacity to digest stimulation by transforming it into meaningful symbolic forms is something like the mental equivalent of the physiologically given "stimulus barrier.")

For Freud, however, the conflict theory of hysteria was essential. He argued: "*The splitting of . . . consciousness is the result of an act of will*" (1894, p. 46). Here Freud was referring to the defense of repression, which the ego enlists when "faced with an experience, an idea or a feeling which aroused such a distressing affect that the subject decided to forget about it because he had no confidence in his power to resolve the contradiction between the incompatible idea and his ego by means of thought-activity" (p. 47). In the "Five Lectures" (1910), Freud again explicitly opposed Janet's (and Breuer's) idea of an "innate incapacity for synthesis on the part of the mental apparatus." Instead, he contended: "We explain it dynamically, from the conflict of opposing forces . . . [as the] outcome of an active struggling . . . of the two psychical groupings against each other" (p. 25).

Freud's Earliest Treatment of Binding Energy and Ego Development

Yet Freud's ideas are not incompatible with those of Breuer and Janet. In the *Project* (1895), Freud explored the *neurophysiological* basis of consciousness and of binding energy. That means, he explored the neurophysiological substratum of ego development and mental structuralization. In Part III, he postulated specific ego neurons that carry a constant amount of cathexis, i.e., that *bind* cathexes within themselves. By binding cathexes, these neurons intercept the free flow of discharge processes, thereby bringing about delay in manifest action—*the* necessary precondition for thought processes. Binding of energy and delay of action are necessary for sustained consciousness. As I shall explicate below, time is required for thinking *about* things—the hallmark of human symbolic thinking. The specifically human universe of symbols spreads out on *the dimension of time*. In other words, by providing time, cathexis-binding ego neurons make symbol formation, or secondary-process, planned activity possible.[6] Energy-binding ego neurons counteract the "constancy," or "pleasure," principle that aims at the fastest direct discharge. Freud wrote: "the ego itself is a mass of neurons . . . which hold fast to their cathexis (which, that is, are in bound condition)" (p. 425). Here Freud offered a constitutional theory of energy binding, and consequently of the genesis of the preconscious ego.

Some brains may have more ego neurons than others. Con-

[6] That delay of action is the *conditio sine qua non* for thought processes implies that the preconscious ego is a retardative structure. The primary retardation principle as the basis of human development, both physical and social, has been described by Bolk (1926). Weyl expands on Bolk's ideas in his paper "Retardation, Acceleration, and Psychoanalysis" (1959). Scientific and artistic creativity imply a combination of both principles: retardation and acceleration of mental processes, i.e., binding and unbinding of "energy" (see Chapter 9).

sequently, some individuals have a greater innate capacity to bind energy, to think, to synthesize diffuse urges into formed thoughts. Freud's early neurophysiological theory of ego functioning does not contradict Janet's and Breuer's theory of a constitutional predisposition toward dissociated mental states. It is also in agreement with my belief in a constitutional-neurological foundation for the capacity and necessity to symbolize. Had this early neurophysiological view been integrated into psychoanalytic theory, the enigma of ego development could have been resolved—at least to a considerable degree. The ego develops because the binding of energy is a natural, innate function of the human brain, as is internal (centrifugal) and perceptual (centripetal) symbol formation.

To my mind, a major limitation of Freud's theorizing is the lack of connection between the idea of binding energy and symbolizing form development. His is a dualistic cathectic theory, in which psychic change comes about by psychic energy attaching itself to various "presentations" of external objects. Psychic energy is one "thing" that cathects another thing, the presentation. Indeed, beginning with the *Project*, Freud treated energy (quantity) and formed meaning (quality) as essentially different realms of discourse. In his view, psychic energy, or quantity, which is derived from biological instincts, is something that flows, analogous to a current of electricity. As it flows, this formless state of energy can attach itself to entities of a totally different nature, such as percepts, memories, ideas, or fantasized imagery. Quantity is never *transformed* into quality. Instead, it "mechanically" cathects quality, or detaches itself from one quality and is displaced to another.

For Freud, the primary motivation of the organism is tension discharge. Thus, if unobstructed, instinctual energy attaches itself to (cathects) the object, or idea of an object, that best facilitates tension discharge. Freud calls these discharge-promoting ideas the "psychical" (ideational) representatives of the instinct. In his words, the instinct representative is "an idea or group of ideas which is cathected with a definite quota of psychical energy . . . coming from an instinct" (1915b, p. 152). The object of an instinct is the thing in regard to which or through which the instinct is able to satisfy its aim. The instinct "is not originally connected with [the object], but becomes assigned to it" (1915a, p. 122).

There *is* something mechanistic about this view of psychic energy as an independent current, settling itself on ideas that promote its discharge. Sufficient energy discharge is not enough for whole-some organismic functioning. "Release of tension" is neither a complex-enough nor specific-enough dynamic construct to account for the pattern-forming directedness of human activity. It is the confluence of *form-creative*, *expressive*, and *tension-regulating* activity that gives human life its specifically human quality. Symbolization is the guiding concept that ties together the above three functions.

Psychoanalytic psychology needs the concepts of both instinctual energy and an inherent tendency to pattern formation—an organismic creativity. Both properties originate in the id, although Freud did not specify form creation as an id function. Locating the origin of psychic form creation in the id, which contains all the inherited proclivities, integrates the tendency toward tension reduction with the psychobiological urge toward expressive form development. If the expressively form-creative, symbolizing function of the psychic organism is deficient, then the driving quality of instincts may indeed change the organism into something analogous to a badly functioning machine, which simply seeks release of tension without meaningful, ordered action. These are the impulse-ridden patients who feel powerless to modify their compulsive repetitive behavior. Addictionlike symptoms are often characteristic for them. They cannot symbolically transform their instinctual cravings.

But let me return to Freud's writing. What is of particular interest to us is Freud's early awareness of the pivotal role of perception and perceptibility in the preconscious-conscious system, i.e., in the ego. In the *Project* (1895) and *The Interpretation of Dreams* (1900), one finds the recurrent question: What attracts attention of consciousness to itself? Freud's answer highlights the role of speech, or rather, speech residues, memory traces of speech. Thus, again, we see that the role of language in forming human consciousness was central for psychoanalytic theory from its beginning.[7] Freud always believed that language provided the means for psychic content to become preconscious-conscious thought. (As a matter of fact, the significance for the preconscious of a proper matching between the "idea of the word" and the "idea of the thing" is mentioned as early as 1891 in *On Aphasia*, well before Freud's statement of this idea in 1915.)

Specifically, in the *Project* (1895, pp. 417–422), Freud claims that speech has the kind of quality characteristic of *perceptions* and *that* is what makes conscious thought possible. Perceptions give rise to "indications of quality," which attract the "cathexis of consciousness." In other words, through their "indication of quality," speech residues make thoughts consciously perceivable and thereby make it possible to recall thoughts. Thoughts, like perceptions, can be remembered: "thought, which is accompanied by the cathexis of indications . . . of speech, is the highest and most secure form of cognitive thought-process" (p. 431).[8]

[7] It is worthwhile emphasizing this in view of the recent focus on language as an important constituent of psychic structure (particularly in France, among Lacanians).

[8] Freud's nineteenth-century terminology here is hard to understand. Explicated in terms of gestalt perception, it means that speech residues, words, give perceivable form to thoughts. Only delineated thoughts with perceivable form-quality can be stored and recalled like any other percept, and thus can serve as firm, constant tools for thinking.

Admittedly, in these pages of the *Project* the relation between perceptions, indications of quality, and consciousness is confused. In my view, language and verbal memory have acquired gestalt characteristics ("indications of quality") and therefore can be picked up by consciousness, which is a perceptual function. That is, perceptions do not give rise to indications of quality but the other way around.

In *The Interpretation of Dreams* (1900), Freud actually describes consciousness as a sense organ, receiving excitations from both outside and inside. Freud's image of consciousness is spatial, a region that receives excitations "from the periphery of the whole apparatus." In contrast to the manifold of diversified perceptions originating from outside, "excitations of pleasure and unpleasure . . . prove to be almost the only psychical quality attaching to transpositions of energy in the inside of the apparatus" (p. 574). What Freud suggests here is the existence of internal, as well as external, perception: "the preconscious (*Pcs.*) system needed to have qualities of its own which would attract consciousness . . . [and] obtained them by linking the preconscious processes with the mnemic system of indications of speech, a system not without quality. By means of the qualities of that system, consciousness . . . also became a sense organ for a portion of our thought-processes. Now . . . there are *two* sensory surfaces, one directed towards perception and the other towards the preconscious thought-processes" (p. 574).

Yet the question remains: What is the quality provided by language that can attract consciousness and thus make thought possible? Freud's answer insists on cathectic and discharge processes. The new quality of preconscious internal excitations is derived from discharge processes that accompany speech, whether audible or internal. (This is similar to a "motor theory" of thinking.) In either case, Freud states that consciousness is now able to follow complex thought processes, independent of perception of external objects or of sensations of pleasure or pain. This independence from sensations of pleasure or pain makes unemotional, objective thinking possible. It explains how memory images of painful events become "tamed" (1895, pp. 437–440), how we can recall a painful event without experiencing the full intensity of pain originally accompanying the event.

My argument with Freud here rests on the dualism set up by this cathectic model, in which quantity and quality remain separate. According to my hypothesis, the purely pressuring energies are *transformed* into "tamed" affects, intentions, thoughts, images, by becoming contained *within a symbolic form.* (This is quite different from the idea that instinctual energy, as it flows, becomes attached to, "cathects," already-formed "presentations.") The function of instinctual energies is not solely to seek expression through "processes of discharge" (Freud, 1915c, p. 178). Instinctual energies themselves are "raw material" that undergoes a transformation, a formative unfolding, in the course of which "quantity" and "quality" *blend* in dynamically potent new structures. "Quantity" and "quality," as they merge in form, produce a *sui generis* new state; they are not just present as an aggregate. This new dynamic form is what can be picked up by internal perception exactly because it is a delineated, bounded gestalt, a symbolic form. This view of internal perception differs from Freud's dualistic one in which discharge processes of "quantity" are supposed to attract the attention cathexis of consciousness.

The distancing, objectifying aspect of verbal memory that Freud points to, and upon which secondary-process functioning hinges, seems to me to be tied up with the form-creative aspect of internal symbolization, rather than simply resulting from discharge processes. Internal symbolization creates forms that can be perceived. The blending of raw energy with form in internal symbols is the essence of *binding energy*. Perception implies distance between the perceiver and what is perceived. Excitations of pleasure and pain are formless and result directly in sensation. Sensations and feelings per se are immediate experiences of the sentient subject without the interpolation of distance between the subject and the feeling-sensation. "I hurt" is the experience, not "I perceive pain." Internal symbolization transforms this total subjectivity into distanced, more objective perception. Verbal therapy helps along this transformation.

Perceptible internal images and binding of energy are needed for the capacity to think *about* "things," to "think thoughts," as Bion would say. "Thinking about" implies distance between the thinking subject and the thought-about object. To "think about" is the earmark of symbolic mental activity. That is the reason why human beings can be analyzed but animals can only be trained. Without internal form development, there is no binding of energy, no preconscious, no distanced internal perception, no "thinking about," only "reacting to." Acting-out people, who cannot "think about" but immediately "react to," suffer from a deficit in their symbolizing capacity. (More on this later.)

On the Relation between the Unconscious and the Preconscious

It is in "The Unconscious" (1915c), the great theoretical essay of Freud's middle period, that he comes closest to a unitary conception of mental functioning. In this study Freud depicts a cooperative relation between the "institutions" of the mind that we do not find either in his earliest works or in his very last, the *Outline* (1940). Strachey calls "The Unconscious" the culmination of Freud's papers on metapsychology. I would agree. Moreover, I believe this essay (especially Sections VI and VII) has special significance for the theory of mental structuralization presented in this book. Here Freud does not talk about a compartmentalized "mental apparatus" but about "psychical systems" mutually influencing each other, as the following quotations illustrate:

> How are we to arrive at a knowledge of the unconscious? It is of course only as something conscious that we know it, after it has undergone *transformations* or *translations* into something conscious [p. 166; my italics].

> It is wrong . . . to suppose that communication between the two systems [*Ucs.* and *Pcs.*] is confined to the act of repression. . . . On the contrary, the *Ucs.* is alive and *capable of development* and maintains a number of other relations with the *Pcs.*, amongst them that of *co-operation*. . . . the *Ucs.* is continued into what are known as *derivatives*, . . . it is accessible to the impressions of life, . . . it constantly influences the *Pcs.*, . . . and is . . . subjected to influences from the *Pcs.* . . . [There is no] clear-cut distinction between the two psychical systems [p. 190; my italics].

Evidently, here the "psychical systems" are not treated as antagonists (the picture conveyed in the *Outline*, more than twenty years later). In this 1915 essay, Freud emphasizes that the unconscious is not simply an "abyss" into which repressed material from the preconscious is discarded; instead, the relation is a mutually transforming one. As we shall see, it is this assumption of a constructively transforming influence, originating in the "lowest" system (the unconscious), which affects the organization of the "higher" system (the preconscious), that is missing in Freud's late work, the *Outline* (1940). In that work, the task of transforming energy into a bound state is allocated to the ego alone. The energy-transmuting function comes from "above," as the ego reaches down in some undefinable way into the seething caldron of the id. This view seems to me a theoretical regression from Freud's 1915 view, in which the dynamically transforming influences are located in the id as well. Moreover, in contrast to the 1940 presentation, in 1915 the preconscious does not originate solely in external perception, but instinctual urges also participate in the creation of this "ordered" region.

What Freud portrays in "The Unconscious" is an unsegmented relation between the three psychic systems (an idea that disappears after his introduction of the "official" structural model in 1923). In this essay, Freud describes how the upward impetus of unconscious psychic content results in increasingly perceptible and organized structures. In the course of this ascent of unconscious content into consciousness, freely mobile instinctual energy becomes bound. How this binding might be effected is not spelled out. The most relevant passages are the following:

> [Among] the communications between the *Ucs.* and the other systems . . . [the following] is most prominent. At the roots of instinctual activity the systems communicate with one another most extensively. One portion of the processes which are there excited passes through the *Ucs.*, as through a preparatory stage, and reaches the highest psychical development in the *Cs.*; another portion is retained as *Ucs.* . . . The content of the system *Pcs.* (or *Cs.*) is derived partly from instinctual life (through the medium of the *Ucs.*), and partly from perception. . . . A complete divergence of their trends, a total severance of the two systems,

> is what above all characterizes a condition of illness. . . . The derivatives of the *Ucs*. . . . act as intermediaries between the two systems [1915c, p. 194].

Yet Freud's own emotional resistance to his own presentation of unsegmented mental functioning comes through even in "The Unconscious." After presenting the cooperative and continuous relation between the unconscious and the preconscious, he conjures up his usual imaginary adversary who will be completely disappointed at the lack of "clear-cut distinction between the two psychical systems" (p. 190). Following Freud's teachings about interpretation, one can assume that the "adversary" represents Freud's own resistance to a "psychic apparatus" in which systems not only "fight" but also cooperate in an uninterrupted, constructive way.

In the passage cited above, Freud is obviously referring to the "original," not the repressed, unconscious. What is particularly important is that he postulates the beginning of psychic form development in that region and indicates that processes of "instinctual activity" pass "through the *Ucs*. as through a preparatory stage." Unfortunately, Freud did not follow through on this insight. In most of his other writings, the unconscious is not cited as the locus of origin for form-creative processes. Form-creative acts, whether in dreams or art, are ascribed to the ego, which achieves form by fighting and counteracting the impulses of the unconscious. At one point, Freud says the artist "bribes" the audience by camouflaging his or her unconscious impulses under the "guise" of "pleasing form" (1908, p. 153). Statements to the same effect abound in his dream theory. In contrast, the above quotation lends support to my view of an innate human tendency to give form to diffuse inner and outer stimulation.

Let me underline a few more points. The "derivatives of the *Ucs*." that "act as intermediaries between the two systems" (the *Ucs.* and the *Pcs.*) are the symbolized, meaning-giving expressions of less-formed instinctual urges. They are "intermediaries" in the sense that all symbols are. The function of symbols is always to bridge over and connect separate regions. Note that Freud himself explicitly states: "A complete divergence of their trends [the trends of the *Ucs.* and the *Pcs.*], a total severance of the two systems, is what above all characterizes a condition of illness." In my opinion, this remark suggests that a preponderantly antagonistic relation between the two systems indicates pathology. This is the illness of power-seeking exemplified in the character of the obsessional neurotic (which I shall describe later).[9]

Yet, even in "The Unconscious," Freud vacillates in his insistence on cooperation between *Ucs.* and *Pcs.* Although the following quotation shows Freud's insight into the phenomenon of "multiple function" (Waelder, 1936), it also reveals his emotional resistance to a synergic constellation:

> Co-operation between a preconscious and an unconscious impulse, even when the latter is intensely repressed, may come about if there is a situation in which the unconscious impulse can act in the same sense as one of the dominant trends. The repression is removed in this instance, and the repressed activity is admitted as a reinforcement of the one intended by the ego. The unconscious becomes ego-syntonic in respect of

[9] An analogy to the power-seeking of Prometheus comes to mind. Prometheus tried to steal the secret of creative power from the gods. As punishment for such hubris, Prometheus had to suffer the pain of vultures gnawing on his insides. Freud's Promethean wish to "steal" the secrets of the unconscious and to fight the "creative father" is, I think, relevant to understanding the whole structure of psychoanalytic theory. Freud's often-mentioned depression may have been self-punishment for his own "hubris": the wish to "conquer" the power of the unconscious, a wish he knew was impossible to fulfill. His great work *Analysis Terminable and Interminable* (1937a) is a majestic testimony to a "Prometheus Bound."

> *this single conjunction* without any change taking place in its repression apart from this. In this co-operation the influence of the *Ucs.* is unmistakable: the reinforced tendencies reveal themselves as being nevertheless *different from the normal*; they make specially perfect functioning possible [1915c, pp. 194–195; my italics].

In other words, contributions from the unconscious do not necessarily disrupt organized ego activities (they are not necessarily "enemy aliens" trespassing in ego territory); they can also improve them. Indeed, Freud here describes a process quite similar to my depiction of internal symbol formation by way of isomorphic matching of unconscious impulses with preconscious symbolic forms. Except that Freud refers to this synergic matching as something exceptional, irregular, while I consider it the normal course of energy-binding psychic structuralization. Freud calls this reinforcing relation between the *Ucs.* and the *Pcs.* "different from normal," and strangely, exactly because it results in "perfect functioning."

What Freud describes here is "multiple function," one of the greatest concepts in psychoanalysis. To widen the area of life activities where multiple function constructively prevails could be used as a definition of the aim of psychoanalytic treatment. The more the person's activities constructively fulfill the "principle of multiple function," the more harmoniously integrated the person is and the more satisfaction he or she will derive from life. And, after all, that *is* the aim of treatment. A good capacity for "true," isomorphic symbolization is necessary for achieving this state.

In the last section of this essay, Freud deals with the process whereby unconscious content is changed into a preconscious state, a change that implies binding of energy. The essence of this change is described as "matching" (or linking) of the unconscious "thing-presentation" with its corresponding preconscious "word-presentation." The point of matching and joining up with is the crucial juncture where unconscious psychic material changes into the preconscious state. Once preconscious, the content has easy access to consciousness.

Thus, in the concluding passages of "The Unconscious," Freud, without using the term "symbolization," comes close to giving a generic theory of symbolization. True, Freud refers explicitly to a change in "cathexis" at the juncture where the thing-presentation links up with its corresponding word-presentation. But the essence of this change is evidently a change in *state*: Unbound energy becomes bound energy. Moreover, Freud's description of the matching of the unconscious thing-presentation with its corresponding preconscious word-presentation suggests the gestalt principle of "pair formation by isomorphic similarity" (Köhler, 1929), which underlies my generic theory of symbolization. Freud's "search for perceptual identity" implies the same principle. So does "internal symbolization," when unconscious content is "searching" for its matching preconscious form.

We cannot leave our discussion of this pivotal essay without citation of the passage that succinctly describes the transmuting function of words for otherwise unavailable (i.e., unconscious) psychic content. Here Freud describes what, in my terms, is the energy-binding and ordering function of internal symbolization:

> What we have . . . called the conscious presentation of the object can now be split up into the presentation of the *word* and the presentation of the *thing*; the latter consists in the cathexis, if not of the direct memory-images of the thing, at least of the remoter memory-traces derived from these. We now seem to know . . . what the difference is between a conscious

> and an unconscious presentation. . . . the conscious presentation comprises the presentation of the thing plus the presentation of the word belonging to it, while the unconscious presentation is the presentation of the thing alone. The system *Ucs.* contains the thing-cathexes of the objects, the first and true object-cathexes; the system *Pcs.* comes about by this thing-presentation being hypercathected through being linked with the word-presentations corresponding to it. It is these hypercathexes . . . that bring about a higher psychical organization and make it possible for the primary process to be succeeded by the secondary process which is dominant in the *Pcs.* . . . [What repression] denies to the presentation is *translation* [my italics] into words which shall remain attached to the object. A presentation which is not put into words, or a psychical act which is not hypercathected, remains thereafter in the *Ucs.* in a state of repression [pp. 201–202].[10]

I believe this long quotation from Freud offers the foundations for a generic theory of symbol formation. The "higher psychical organization" points to the order-making function of symbolization. What is problematic is Freud's continued emphasis on cathexis instead of form development. Making "hypercathexis" the primary cause of "higher psychical organization" and consequently of secondary-process functioning presents, to my mind, the proverbial fallacy of putting the cart before the horse. Hypercathexis depends on "attention cathexis," which implies perception. Yet perception can

[10] Freud reminds the reader that the above insights were already reached in *The Interpretation of Dreams* (1900). (In fact they were already put forward in 1895, in the *Project*, but we know Freud treated that work as "non-arrivé.") He recapitulates: "being linked with word-presentations is not yet the same thing as becoming conscious, but . . . makes it possible to become so; it is therefore characteristic of the system *Pcs.* and of that system alone" (1915c, pp. 202–203).

only function if there is a delineated form *to be perceived.* As we saw, Freud (1895) indicated that it is because speech residues possess "quality" (form) that they are able to attract the "attention of consciousness." What needs to be underlined is the *translation* of "thing-cathexes" into a form (words), from which perceptual "attention cathexis" follows. An unconscious "thing-presentation" is not a clear-cut mental picture of a "thing," but more an unshaped, primordial affective phenomenon. Even Freud states that the "presentation of the thing" consists more in its "cathexis" (i.e., affect) than in its being a "direct memory image."

In emphasizing the importance of *form* for thought, it is important to remember that not only words but also visual or auditory imagery *can* be raw material for thinking. Indeed, the latter *is* often the raw material in artistic and even scientific creation. These creative activities involve cognitive processes of their very own. The end-result of these cognitive processes is the "presentational symbol," an ordered and ordering structure that is not translatable into elements of discursive, symbolic language (Langer, 1942). While the full meaning of these presentations cannot be put into words, they are well articulated and not unconscious. And because they have articulated form, they too *can* be "hypercathected" with attention. Words are but one instance (maybe the most frequent one) of offering a formative template for expressing less formal emotional processes. On the one hand, we would say that what repression denies to a "presentation" is perceivable articulation, be this articulation in words or any other form. On the other, we would describe the preconscious as containing all kinds of articulated forms, which are available for the "attention cathexis" of consciousness.

Freud ends his great essay on "The Unconscious" by characterizing the peculiarity of schizophrenic thinking. Schizophrenics overcathect the word-presentation while withdrawing instinctual cathexis from the thing-presentation. This strange cathectic arrangement represents an attempt to regain the lost object, but the result is that these patients "find themselves obliged to be content with words instead of things" (p. 204). Freud also warns about the dangers of philosophizing "in abstractions," for in this way we too "may neglect the relations of words to unconscious thing-presentations" (p. 204).

Freud's remark shows profound insight into the schizophrenic's ambivalent struggle toward and away from "objects" (Guntrip, 1969). But we know, as we discussed earlier, that symbolization always fulfills this double function. It is one of the multiple "Janus-faces" of symbols. To reiterate: Symbols connect and separate. A symbol is formed when the *real*, concrete object is unavailable, or has to be given up, but connection with it is still desired. Symbolization facilitates separation from primary "objects" by keeping connected with them via symbol-bridges. The symbol is *la présence d'une absence*.

What Freud points to here is the need for some of the original "affective cathexis" to permeate language. Verbal communication becomes sterile if there is no connection to "unconscious thing-presentations," to the affective roots of language. Although verbalization binds energy, binding energy beyond an optimum degree facilitates the defense of isolation. This untoward effect of verbalization is by no means reserved for schizophrenics or philosophers. It is a widespread communication defect in everyday life. It can vitiate the psychoanalytic process, and by no means exclusively from the patient's side. An analyst may give correct, intelligent interpretations that correctly organize the patient's primary-process material, and yet his or her communication can be defective, and therefore therapeutically ineffective, if divorced from the affective roots of language. This kind of communication defect seems widespread among highly intellectual, obsessive characters (see Chapters 10 and 12). I would even argue that much of professional literature suffers from this defect.

Although the pervasive danger of verbal language leading to the defense of isolation, inside and outside of psychoanalysis, was left out of Freud's discussion, he did strictly demarcate the boundary between what is "pathological" and what is "normal" with regard to language. In other instances, however, he generalized from observations of pathology to "normal" psychic functioning and structuralization. In particular, I am referring to Freud's insistence on the antagonism between the ego and the id. We saw that in the *Project* (1895), as well as in "The Unconscious" (1915c), Freud tends to assume a synergic, cooperative relation between the unconscious and the preconscious systems much more than he does in his later writings, in which the ego vies with the id. This change took place with the formulation of his "structural model" (1923). In my view, the emphasis on the oppositional dualism between ego and id, between primary and secondary processes, had a negative effect on the further development of psychoanalytic theory; in particular, it restricted the development of a generic theory of symbolization. The limitations of this oppositional dualism are readily apparent in Freud's conclusive work, the *Outline* (1940), in which he moves away from the potentially unitary, harmonious model of psychic structure development presented in his "prestructural model."

Freud's Final View

The *Outline* (1940), Freud's posthumously published expository work, is the best source for studying his conclusive views on psychoanalysis. Strachey, in his Editor's Note, calls it: "A master's last account of the ideas of which he was the creator" (p. 143). Of particular interest for us is that in this, his final summing up, Freud was still grappling with the difficulty of defining the process of binding energy, as well as the relation between bound energy, the quality of being preconscious, and the ego. He felt, and I could not agree with him more, that these questions represent "the still shrouded secret of the nature of the psychical" (p. 163).

Also of interest is that even in this late work, Freud repeatedly combined his original topographic model with his post-1923 structural model. He speaks in the same breath of the unconscious or the id, the preconscious or the ego (see 1940, p. 164). His flexible combination of the two models shows that the structural model did not simply supersede the topographic one but rather represented an alternative mode of conceptualization. The structural hypothesis is not a "better" model than the topographic one. Rather, the character of the phenomena under observation decides the use of one conceptual framework or the other, or their combination—a method Freud followed to the end of his life. Certainly, it is regrettable that nowadays the structural model is considered the only acceptable framework, no matter what the topic under consideration.[11] Actually the topographic model, far

[11] Some psychoanalysts today voice outright condemnation if an author refuses to fit his or her data and ideas into the "official" structural model. To take but one example of this dogmatic bias: In his review of Arieti's *Creativity: The Magic Synthesis* (1976), Paul Kay sarcastically refers to Arieti's "cool" decision not to use " 'recent developments of the Freudian school' because he could not 'attune' his research to them!" (1977, p. 412). The exclamation point here would seem to imply that Arieti's decision is quite obviously ridiculous. Elsewhere, again with an exclamation point, Kay sneers at Arieti's adopting the "concepts of primary process and sublimation [as] more useful" than the structural theory (p. 411). This is quite simply a misrepresentation of Arieti's remarks. What Arieti (1976, p. 411) does find more pertinent are Freud's concepts of primary and secondary process—not "sublimation," as Kay would have it. I can only assume that Arieti's refusal to conform to the structural framework left this reviewer so annoyed that he misread the actual text.

from being *passé*, fits the discussion of symbolization and cognitive phenomena much better. No harm is done in combining the two, just as Freud did when he equated the preconscious with the ego.

According to Freud (1940), the content of the ego is preconscious and this quality implies a bound state of energy. The great question is: Just how does energy change from a freely mobile (unbound) state to a bound one? Freud's conclusive description is that "a hypercathexis [of psychic material] brings about a kind of synthesis of different processes—a synthesis in the course of which free energy is transformed into bound energy" (1940, p. 164). And he goes on to stipulate:

> At any rate, we hold firmly to the view that the distinction between the unconscious and the preconscious state lies in dynamic relations of this kind, which would explain how it is that, whether spontaneously or with our assistance, the one can be changed into the other. . . . We have found that processes in the unconscious or in the id obey different laws from those in the preconscious ego. We name these laws . . . the *primary process*, in contrast to the *secondary process* which governs the course of events in the preconscious, in the ego [p. 164].

Freud says that "the ego was developed out of the id by the continual influence of the external world" (p. 163). This categorical statement harbors the question: Can external influences produce order in psychic processes if these processes by themselves do not have the proclivity for producing ordered gestalts? (See the earlier quotation from Freud [1930] about the externally imposed origin of order [fn. 2].) My answer, in agreement with Cassirer's and Langer's theory, has been given already: The ordered ego develops because symbol-forming, order- and ego-constructing processes are organismically inherent human "drives" (tendencies). Human beings are symbol-making, i.e., ego-making animals. External influences shape the specific manifestations of this human, constitutional and dynamic predisposition.

Freud was committed to his dualistic, cathectic theory, but, I think, one can detect in the above statements an awareness that the creation of preconscious psychic content necessitates a new principle of transformation—"a kind of synthesis." True, Freud clung to his idea of "hypercathexis," a purely energic occurrence that is supposed to synthesize qualitatively different processes. Yet, by introducing the term "synthesis," Freud suggested the need for a unifying process. What remains a question is how a purely energic (quantitative) occurrence brings about a qualitative transformation.[12] Before examining this issue further, however, let me quote another relevant passage from the *Outline*:

> Id and unconscious are as intimately linked as ego and preconscious . . . the ego was developed out of the id by the continual influence of the external world. In the course of this slow development certain of the contents of the id were *transformed* into the preconscious state and so taken into the ego; others of its contents remained in the id unchanged, as its scarcely accessible nucleus. . . .
>
> Having now decided upon the *topographical* dissection of the psychical apparatus into an ego and an id, with which the difference in quality between pre-

[12] Some theorists of evolution, J. B. Haldane among them, suggest the possibility that intense sources of energy, such as ultraviolet radiation and electrical discharges, are responsible for the prebiological synthesis of organic compounds (see Dickerson, 1978). Whatever the problems in drawing an analogy to psychic processes, at least here we have an example of how a great amount of supplementary energy can bring about a synthesis that results in new forms.

> conscious and unconscious runs parallel . . . a further question faces us. What . . . is the true nature of the state which is revealed in the id by the quality of being unconscious and in the ego by that of being preconscious and in what does the difference between them consist?
>
> But of that we know nothing [1940, p. 163; my italics].

Again, we see Freud's groping for a principle of successive organization, without, however, answering his own question. If we think of internal symbolization in terms of increasingly delineated gestalts, with each successive level increasingly structuring the meaning of the previous one, we may come closer to understanding the difference between unconscious and preconscious psychic content. An attempt to clarify this question in terms of perception psychology will be offered after some more of Freud's views have been presented.

> Starting from conscious perception [the ego] has subjected to its influence ever larger regions and deeper strata of the id. . . . Its psychological function consists in raising the passage [of events] [Strachey's insert] in the id to a higher dynamic level (perhaps by transforming freely mobile energy into bound energy, such as corresponds to the preconscious state); its [the ego's] constructive function consists in interpolating, between the demand made by an instinct and the action that satisfies it, the activity of thought [1940, p. 199].

Yet again we find Freud grappling with the problem of binding energy. (It is amazing how glibly some analysts use the expression, as if we *really* understood what "binding" meant!) It is somewhat obscure what "raising the passage [of events] in the id to a higher dynamic level" means, but obviously it has to do with "binding" energy. I would add that, equally obviously, it has to do with the generic process of symbolization, since interpolation of thought between instinctual demands and action results from "raising the passage of events." It must also relate to perception since the main characteristic of a preconscious state is its accessibility to consciousness, and perception is a correlate of consciousness. This connection between symbolization, perception, the *Pcs.*, and consciousness is evident in Freud's remark: "The inside of the ego, which comprises above all the thought-processes, has the quality of being preconscious. This is characteristic of the ego and belongs to it alone." Moreover, he says:

> . . . internal processes in the ego may also acquire the quality of consciousness. This is the work of the function of speech, which brings material in the ego into a firm connection with mnemic residues of visual, but more particularly auditory, perceptions. Thenceforward the perceptual periphery of the cortical layer [of the ego] can be excited . . . from inside as well, internal events . . . can become conscious, and a special device is called for in order to distinguish between the two possibilities—a device known as reality-testing. The equation 'perception = reality (external world)' no longer holds [1940, p. 162].[13]

[13] Freud's continual telescoping of his topographic within his structural model is also evident in this passage. His related spatial metaphors treat the ego as a "container" with specific content "inside." He even describes a "periphery," a "cortical layer," of the ego. All this adds up to a view of the ego as a "preconscious mental region," at least when Freud is discussing psychic qualities and thought processes. The strict adherents to the structural theory insist that the ego has to be viewed as a group of intercorrelated functions and *not* as a bounded region with an "inside" and a "periphery." Yet, as I have already argued, for theorizing about symbolization, language, and creativity, the topographic view of the ego (such as Freud gives here) is more fitting.

But we still have not dealt adequately with the problem of binding energy. I believe that a specific thought-hurdle arises in Freud's attempt to derive the process of binding energy because he counterposes the functions of the ego and the id. By positing antithetical "psychic institutions," Freud ends up depicting the *segmented* functioning of a conflicted mind, rather than a synergic, "unitary" process of gestalt formation. In other words, what he presents is a model of dis-ease. The source of disturbance would seem to lie in an over-intense need for power—power *over* all forces experienced as stemming from unknown sources, such as the unconscious "instinctual" forces originating in the "nucleus" of the id. Never are these "instinctual" id forces mentioned by Freud as the natural point of origin for psychic organization and creativity, as forces that create the ego and later can work in synergic harmony with it.

In Freud's last formulations, id and ego are described as antagonists in a fight. The ego is the strict, disciplining agent, trying to defend itself against the "enemy," the id (1940, p. 200). The ego defends itself by "gaining control over the demands of the instincts" (p. 146). "The severest demand on the ego is probably the keeping down of the instinctual claims of the id, to accomplish which it is obliged to maintain large expenditures of energy on anticathexes" (p. 172). Freud's antagonism to the forces originating in the id comes out in his choice of words: "whenever we have been able to detect any of its [the id's] derivatives in the ego we have pointed out their *illegitimate* origin and have instigated the ego to reject them" (p. 179; my italics). Strange to call id origin "illegitimate." And what does Freud mean by instigating "the ego to reject them"? He can only mean rejecting them from action, for the aim of psychoanalysis is to *include* in the ego, and thus in our awareness, *all* id derivatives uncovered by means of verbalization. On the face of it, this statement would seem to contradict what Freud elsewhere claims to be the goal of interpretation. Only his subjective antagonism to the powers of the id could have led Freud to seemingly invalidate his own discovery. The ego, on the other hand, is depicted as valiantly "fighting" against its "internal enemy" (p. 200), meaning the demands that originate in the id.

I believe it is this postulated antagonism between the ego and the id, with its portrayal of the id as the "enemy" to be "conquered" by the ego, that has landed the problem of "binding energy" in such limbo. A logical conundrum arises from Freud's formulations. To begin with, the id is depicted as the nucleus of disorganized urges clamoring for direct "satisfaction." The ego develops only later, "out of the id," under the "influence of the external world." But then, this id *derivative* (the ego) somehow acquires so much power that it can subject "to its influence ever larger regions and deeper strata of the id." Where does this "binding" power of the ego come from? Certainly not from "conscious perception," which brings the ego into existence. Nor can it stem from the id—at least not according to Freud's conclusive statements in the *Outline*—for here the id is the "enemy" against which the ego fights in self-defense. There is simply no way to account for the transformation of mobile id energy into a "bound" state if the derivative "middle layer" of the "psychic apparatus," i.e., the ego alone, is supposed to effect these transmuting incursions from *above*, by *reaching down* into the seething caldron of the id.

Modern ego psychologists have tried to get around this logical conundrum by postulating "primary ego energies" or "neutralized ego energy." But these are just new terms; they do not tackle the problem of how energy becomes bound. In effect, they sidestep the issue, replacing the phrase "bound energy" with "neutralized energy." To my mind, this is a great conceptual loss. I strongly believe that it should be the other way around; that a more thorough understanding of what "binding" means would eliminate the need for a concept of "neutralization." One can postulate any number of qualitatively different energies and then play mental chess with them. Logically and scientifically, however, it is more attractive to postulate "something basic" that undergoes development, and thus becomes differentiated in its perceptible manifestations. (Admittedly, logical attractiveness does not necessarily coincide with the true state of affairs.) Lacking any compelling evidence for the existence of id-independent ego energies, it does seem scientifically more appropriate to stay with the concept of transformation, through "binding" impulses, all of which originate in the id.

"Neutralized" might be all right as a descriptive adjective, denoting behavior that is calm and thoughtful, as opposed to more tempestuous and impatient. But "cathected with neutralized energy" adds nothing to our understanding, except to restate that something was done calmly. Yet, due to the "magic" (black magic?) of words, expressions like this are often uttered in speech and writing, with a certain ponderousness, as if some illuminating, dynamic explanation had been conveyed. How well Mephisto understood the spurious use of words! Talking to the eager student, he advised:

> Im ganzen—haltet Euch an Worte!
> Dann geht Ihr durch die sichre Pforte
> Zum Tempel der Gewissheit ein.
>
> Denn eben wo Begriffe fehlen,
> Da stellt ein Wort zur rechten Zeit sich ein.
>
> [Yes, stick to words at any rate,
> There never was a surer gate
> Into the temple, Certainty.

For just where no ideas are,
The proper word is never far.]

—Goethe, *Faust*, Part I
[Walter Kaufmann's translation]

Freud never followed Mephisto's "advice," as his lifelong attempt to grapple with the concept of "binding energy" shows. In his efforts to explore the *meaning* of that concept, he tried to understand the *process* whereby unbound energy is changed into a bound state. Freud saw two sets of phenomena that differ in function from each other: (1) unconscious, id, unbound energy, primary process; and (2) preconscious, conscious, ego, bound energy, secondary process. True, he did not really succeed in describing the process whereby the second group derives from the first, but neither did he look for new words to "cover up" the problem. His goal was not the "temple Certainty."

Toward a New Theory of Symbolization

As I have already indicated, binding energy and the preconscious are the two Freudian concepts most relevant to a theory of symbolization. The essence of this theory lies in the connecting and order-making function of symbols. This order-making comes about as symbol formation produces a more perceptible, more sharply delineated gestalt than the gestalt qualities of whatever has been symbolized. Freud's emphasis on the perceptible quality of "speech residues" relates to this idea. Had he reached out to the work of perception psychologists and of the pioneers of Gestalt psychology, all of whom were active during his lifetime, Freud might have conceived a less "machinelike," less segmented model of the mind. Instead of portraying the mind as an "apparatus" (a painfully unfitting word still used today), he might have drawn a more organic picture, in which "organismic" form development would have accounted for mental structuralization. But, as we have seen (p. 82n), Freud (1930) bypassed the idea that order-making is a natural process, rather than a superimposed, anal-compulsive one.

On Schilder's Contribution

In contrast to Freud, his contemporary (and admirer) in Vienna, Paul Schilder, aimed at integrating the findings of psychoanalysis, neurology, brain pathology, Brentano's and Ach's "intentionality," and experimental Gestalt psychology. Consequently, he conceived a much more unitary model of the mind than did Freud. Yet Schilder's concepts did not "make it" into psychoanalytic theorizing. Why certain concepts become fashionable, while others fade into the background and remain unused, has often little or nothing to do with the quality and appropriateness of the concepts themselves. It has more to do with personalities, transferential group dynamics, and even geographic factors. It is a great pity that Schilder's way of looking at the functioning of the mind has been "repressed" by psychoanalytic theorists. Many of his views are congruent with my ideas on internal or centrifugal symbolization, with the "model" of the mind based on the gradual (serial) gestalting function of symbol formation.

Schilder's (1920) "sphere" includes Freud's unconscious region and primary-process functioning, but extends into the preconscious and partakes in secondary-process functioning as well. It is the "storage place" for drives and for experiences of life. Schilder compares this "unarticulated background" of all experiencing to the effect of the germ plasm on the fully developed organism (an image of organic form development in contrast to an "apparatus"). Since he does not postulate separate, discontinuous "psychic institutions," questions about "the mechanics of thought" or the separate origin of "the ego" do not even arise within his conceptual framework. His "sphere" serves both the drives *and* reality. (Waelder's [1936] later idea of "multiple function" describes the mode of functioning for the *total* psyche.) Primary and secondary processes, affect and cognition, intermingle in the sphere. Thought, symbol, and image development all originate in this matrix, from which they emerge into consciousness through "continuous reformulations." Drive "orientations" are "reformulated" into increasingly clear, reality-adapted "gestalten," without losing the "halo" of their previous, more obscure forms. This never quite dissipated "halo" gives "color and richness to mental life."

The analogy to germ plasm indicates Schilder's concern with *the* basic problem: the unitary *creation* of organic form, of which creation of ordered mental gestalts is just one instance. At one point Schilder (1920) even states that "every thought repeats the natural history of creation."

The Relation of Energy to Form

Let us turn now more specifically to the problem of energy, which recently has been so readily excised from psychoanalytic metapsychology. We must remember that ultimate theoretical concepts tend to be hazy, in theoretical physics as well as in metapsychology. Our knowledge (psychologists' as well as physicists') of the relation between "form" and the nature or "behavior" of energy is insufficient for formulating a detailed theory of what really takes place when "energy" becomes "bound." Not to mention the fact that energy itself is one of those "ultimate" concepts physicists use without being capable of truly defining. Therefore, what I propose is more in the nature of a sketch.

Particle physicists assume that the formal organization of "energy particles" accounts for their different "behavior." In other words, the characteristics of energy cannot be separated from the form in which the particles are present. I find this hypothesis useful for thinking about the transformation of "psychic energy" as it flows into (not "cathects") various symbolic forms, i.e., gestalts. These forms, which act as "containers," originate in images of external perception. This is analogous to the role of day residues and presleep dream suggestions in the formation of the dream (Nachmansohn, 1925). Unconscious impulses do not hide behind, but express themselves by merging into these structures. These preconscious memory images lend form to the id drives, and it is this molding into form that constitutes "binding of energy."

Here I would disagree with Freud's assumption of the practically total amorphousness of id forces. Id forces do already have *some* form. Even Freud differentiates between libidinal and aggressive "instincts." However, in Freud's theory, form and structure are superimposed by the ego on the amorphous id impulses. Other systematizers of depth psychology attribute marked form-creative tendencies to the deepest layer of the original (not the repressed) unconscious. Jung's analytic psychology and Szondi's genetically based instinct theory, which underlies his system of *Schicksalsanalysis* (destiny-analysis), treat the origin of psychic form and structure development in a totally different way from Freud. According to their theories, the formative creative processes exert their power from the depths of the psyche upwards.

On Jung's Contribution

The creative function of the unconscious is most important for Jung, as can be seen in four essays by the most outstanding Jungian theorist, Erich Neumann, which appeared under the title *Art and the Creative Unconscious* (1954). Neumann points to the analogy between the creativity of the unconscious and the creative principle in nature which produces atoms, crystals, organic life, and the world of stars and planets. The substratum of the psychophysical world is creative; it is forever bringing forth forms. The collective unconscious is the source of all psychic creation—of all symbolic forms, of consciousness, and of art. The contents of the collective unconscious are the archetypes. Art creativity derives from the formative power of the archetypes; by themselves these are "intrinsically formless psychic structures" (p. 82), but they become visible in art. The archetypes, then, are inherited form-giving principles in the deepest layer of the unconscious. In dreams, fantasies, hallucinations, and art, the archetypes become visible in the form of images.

One and the same archetype can gain manifest form in an infinite variety of images. The forms of archetypal images are molded by the epoch, the place, and the psychology of the individual who brings them forth. Neumann reminds us of the varied styles of the mother archetype, depending on whether the mother image was formed in Egypt, Mexico, or Europe, or in ancient, medieval, or modern times. He talks about the "paradoxical multiplicity" of the archetypes' "eternal presence," about the "infinite variety of forms of expression," since each form is realized by "man in time"—"its [the image's] archetypal eternity enters into a unique synthesis with a specific historical situation" (p. 82).

The archetypes of the collective unconscious are the creative driving power, although by themselves they are imageless and nameless. They represent an inner order of the unconscious, on which "the development of man and his consciousness" depends (pp. 89–90). "As magnets order a field of iron filings, so do the archetypes order our psychic life" (p. 124). This archetypal world is "transpersonal" (in contrast to the individually repressed unconscious). But the "transpersonal can express itself only through the medium of man, and takes form in him through creative processes" (p. 87). Artists have to obey both the powers of their inner archetypal world and the traditions of their epoch, the "cultural canon" of their time and place, which represents the consciousness of the collective. The unconscious archetypal contents are projected onto the existing phenomena of the particular epoch's cultural canon. These new forms, then, become part of the "dogmatic heritage of the group" (p. 87). These expressions of the archetypal world, in the form of art, music, poetry, and religious rites, become possessions of the collective. The function of art and religious ritual is to symbolically represent the archetypal. These are the "numinous" points where the collective unconscious extends into lived reality.

"Numinous" or "numinosum" are Jung's terms to denote the fascinating quality of the nonpersonal "eternal" archetypes. Immediate contact with powerful archetypal imagery can elicit numinous experience in the viewer. This experience has the quality of the sacred, tremendous, terrifying, and fascinating. We all know such experiences, whether in response to Beethoven's last quartets, Verdi's *Requiem*, Mozart's *Don Giovanni*, Bosch's or Signorelli's paintings, primitive art, or whatever moves us in that special "numinous" way. It happens when the specific archetypal ground that, unbeknownst to the artist, strove for visible manifestation elicits a resonance in the analogous segment of the viewer's collective unconscious—a kind of "matching." The experience, then, is overwhelming exactly because it involves the "transpersonal," transcendent realm of the unconscious.

Let me add another quote from Neumann (1954): "the creative power of the unconscious seizes upon the individual with the autonomous force of an instinctual drive" and can lead to ecstatic frenzy or psychosis. But "the artist takes full responsibility and a formative, interpreting consciousness plays an essential part" (p. 98).

Obviously, my view on the locus of origin of form creativity is very much in line with that of Jung and Neumann. There is agreement with regard to the unsegmented (under conditions of health) "model" of psychic structure formation, in which the content of the deepest layer of the unconscious is assumed to possess its own impetus "upward" and to manifest itself in perceptible form.

It is Jung's concept of archetypes, the inherited content of the collective unconscious, with its supposedly mystical connotations, that sets many psychoanalysts against Jungian psychology. This is not the place to discuss this topic in depth. Here we should only remind ourselves that Freud's own views were not that totally different from Jung's with regard to inherited psychic tendencies. He defined the id as containing everything that is inherited; in other words, the id, in contrast to the repressed unconscious, is viewed as a transpersonal region. It contains the "instincts," with their inherited strength and tenaciousness (Freud, 1937a). And let us not forget that in Chapter VI of *The Interpretation of Dreams* (1900), Freud reserves the term "symbol" for manifest dream images with supposedly inherited and specific unconscious meaning. Moreover, in *Group Psychology and the Analysis of the Ego* (1921), he talks about "the ego's nucleus, which comprises the 'archaic heritage' of the human mind" (p. 75), as well as of the hypnotist who "awakens in the subject a portion of his archaic heritage . . . which had experienced an individual re-animation in his relation to his father" (p. 127). (Here the son's actual oedipal relation to his father is assumed to be the revival of an inherited constellation.) Later, he says: "The uncanny and coercive characteristics of group formations . . . may . . . with justice be traced back to . . . their origin from the primal horde" (1921, p. 127); and "hypnosis is solidly founded upon a predisposition which has survived in the unconscious from the early history of the human family" (p. 128). Or, still later: "Both . . . hypnosis and group formation are an inherited deposit from the phylogenesis of the human libido" (p. 143). These quotations have a definite Jungian flavor, but Freud himself neglected their implications in discussing psychic structure formation. It is interesting, though, that it is in connection with the "uncanny" phenomenon of the subject's "fascination" with the hypnotist that an accumulation of "Jungian" explanations appears. The "numinous" fascination adhering to archetypal manifestations comes to mind.

There are also less obvious parallels between Jung's (or Neumann's) and Freud's thinking. And I feel a particular affinity between my own and Neumann's theory of symbol formation. The nameless and intrinsically formless Jungian archetypes, which can be known only through the images given to them by humans, can be seen as analogous to Freud's (1915c) "thing-cathexes," which are nameless and formless (quality-less) and therefore unknowable until they meet with their matching word-presentation. At this juncture, they acquire "quality" (form) and can be named; hence they are ready for entering consciousness. Freud's original "thing-presentations" or "thing-cathexes" are the "archetypes" of the individual, unrepressed unconscious. They are the prototypes which, from the depth of the unconscious, influence later conscious choices. It is due to Freud's dualistic, cathectic conceptualization that, unlike Jung, he does not call this process the form- and consciousness-creating function of the unconscious. Yet the infantile "archetypes" do form the individual's conscious destiny.

Neumann's emphasis on the archetype's unique synthesis with a specific historical situation, and the intrinsically formless archetype's projection onto the existing phenomena of the particular epoch's "cultural canon," parallels my emphasis on the form-creative function of the preconscious. The preconscious is the mental depository of the memory-images of external perceptions, and thus the mental representative of our historical time and place. The "cultural canon" of our time is represented in the preconscious by way of centripetal symbolization. Neumann disregards the symbolizing function of perception and memory-image formation, nor does he use the concept of preconscious. When he talks of the forms of the external world, he means their internal representations. But he does see art and dream symbols as the formative synthesis between the form-giving power of the archetypes and their isomorphically fitting expressive forms, to be found among the existing plethora of shaped things offered by the cultural canon. I see this as analogous to the instinctual drive's blending into (or with) its fitting preconscious "container," the fitting symbolic form in the preconscious, which originated in external perception. This is internal or centrifugal symbolization, which derives from the instinctual drive's inherent impetus toward form creation. It is a creative symbolizing act continuously active in the human psyche. Without synergic cooperation between the unconscious and the preconscious, the forces of the unconscious can overthrow the preconscious ego and produce frenzy or psychosis. In these pathological states the person's integrated individuality and communicative creativity get lost, while the transindividual (transpersonal) id instincts take over with compulsive intensity. The person has lost his or her human freedom. It is not only the artist whose "formative consciousness" (preconscious) prevents these pathological irruptions of the unconscious. In this respect, Neumann's Jungian view of the specificity of archetypes, as opposed to instinctual drives in general, leads to conclusions different from mine.

On Szondi's Contribution

Szondi's genetically based instinct theory is grounded in biology and thus avoids the theological connotations of Jung's archetypes. Szondi's basic problem concerns the original instinctual forces that shape human destiny, hence the name *Schicksalsanalysis.* He extricates the concept of destiny from its fatalistic connotations. The destiny-spinning *Moirae* are our genes, handed down to each individual by an indeterminate number of ancestors. This biological substratum forms the inherited layer of the unconscious. To differentiate it from the Jungian "collective" and the Freudian "repressed" unconscious, Szondi calls it the "familial unconscious." The contents of the familial unconscious are the eight genetically laid-down "instinctual drives." They correspond to the eight forms of mental disturbances Szondi considers genetic in their origin. Genetically laid-down tendencies imply their autonomous striving toward expression in perceptible form. The power of these tendencies, or "factors," of the familial unconscious manifests itself by directing the individual's significant destiny-shaping choices. Genetic endowment influences the choice of sickness, including the form of death, the choice of mate, friends, and occupation or vocation. It is through these channels that the genes "attempt" to fulfill or complete their prototypical form (note the biological analogy to the "constellating" function of Jung's archetypes).

The eight factors are represented in Szondi's (1947) experimental choice-test by photographs of patients belonging to the eight categories of mental disorder. As noted in Chapter

5, the subject chooses "likes" and "dislikes" from each of six presented groups, containing eight different types of patients. The eight types correspond to the eight factors. These eight factors are conceptualized as the genetic "radicals" (archetypes?) of the familial unconscious, common to all humanity, though in individually different proportions. The manifestation of the eight factors is multipotential (analogous to the multiform manifestation of archetypes), which accounts for Szondi's conception of "directable destiny." Each factorial tendency can express itself in a variety of forms, from serious pathology to character traits to fitting forms of socially constructive activities. Szondi's postulated eight factors function as *a priori* forms of the total range of human experience, normal as well as pathological, of everyday life activities as much as of artistic creation. In other words, Szondi's system offers an eight-dimensional, biologically based formative template that contributes formal aspects to human character, thinking, and behavior. (This is in contrast to Jung's archetypes, whose formative effect is supposed to manifest itself only in the numinosity of art and religious symbols.)

The familial unconscious is not an amorphous caldron of "instincts" upon which structure is superimposed by the ego. Instead, Szondi postulates the familial unconscious as an eight-dimensional drive system in which the specific quality of each drive *ab ovo* (in the literal sense) implies rudimentary structure. The eight factors are the ordering principle of the unconscious. Szondi believes that even though the genetic tendencies set the outer limits to the possible forms of individual destiny, within these outer limits there is a wide range of possible channelizations and patterns of combination of the constitutionally given instinctual tendencies. The aim of therapy is to facilitate the constructive forms of such patterns and channelizations.

In contrast to Freud, sexuality is not viewed as the exclusive instinctual source of energy for sublimation. Rather, the eight factors represent qualitatively different instinctual energies, each with their own specific formative power, but all of equal primary order. Each can lead to specific forms of pathology or specific forms of socialization and sublimation.

Szondi coined the concept of "operotropism," which means that dangerous instinctual strivings can be channeled into specifically fitting occupations. After evaluating the "existence-possibilities" from the test profiles, Szondi actively guides the patient to genetically fitting "work-channels." In this way the genetically laid-down formative tendencies are respected, while at the same time they are harnessed into isomorphically congruent but higher levels of manifestation.

Like psychoanalysis, *Schicksalsanalysis* aims at making the unconscious conscious. Except, unearthing forgotten memories does not help the "choice-sick" (*Wahlkrahke*) patients for whom *Schicksalsanalysis* is the appropriate treatment. Uncovering the forgotten does not help them because their etiology has a pre-personal history. Szondi confronts them with their hereditary background. He aims at making them aware of the formative powers forcefully acting from the deepest biopsychological layers of their unconscious. These are patients who are driven to make the "wrong" choices at crucial points of their biographies. Understanding how the deepest biological-genetic urges influence these destiny-ruining choices decreases the repetitive tyranny of the genes, which always aim at the reestablishment of previous forms of life. The formative power of the genes is the biological root of the repetition compulsion. The biological repetition compulsion drives the individual toward choices that lead to the reestablishment of forms of life from the repertoire of the person's familial past. Particularly dangerous are past forms of pathology which, in the subject (patient), are "repressed" from open manifestation due to the overpowering effect of the dominant genes. The biologically "repressed," latent-recessive gene anlagen, like all repressed content, strive for appearance on the surface in whatever roundabout way possible. Szondi's genetic-statistical research on family trees has shown that influencing the destiny-shaping choices in the direction of the original familial pathology (for example, the choice of a mate or friends whose sickness exhibits in a more manifest form what is latent in the "chooser") is the "roundabout" way for these biologically repressed tendencies to exert their formative power. To reduce this potentially harmful, genetically driven, repetitive acting out, and to lend flexibility and "directability" through conscious knowledge of the genes' obstinate and literally conservative driving force, is the aim of Szondi's *Schicksalsanalysis*. By confronting patients with their hidden "ancestral strivings," their ability for free choice will increase. This "free choice," however, will have to respect and build on the formative tendencies of the familial unconscious.

Schicksalsanalysis is the treatment modality for patients whose previous psychoanalyses ended in failure. Instead of writing them off as hopeless character disorders with negative therapeutic reactions, Szondi formulated for this group a genetically based etiological theory and principles of treatment based on the form-giving tendencies, negative as well as positive, of the familial unconscious. The aim is to decrease the compulsively driven, harmful choices and to increase the range of human freedom. But, in accordance with Spinoza's philosophy, human freedom means the acceptance of the limits set by necessity. The aim of *Schicksalsanalysis* can be summed up by a quotation from Goethe's *Faust*:

> Was du ererbt von deinen Vätern hast
> Erwirb es, um es zu besitzen.

> [What from your fathers you received as heir, acquire if you would possess it.]
>
> [Walter Kaufmann's translation]

Jung's and Szondi's theories regarding the form creativity and structure of the unconscious (the id) were presented because of their affinity to my own theory of internal, or centrifugal, symbolization. In Szondi's case, it is more than a coincidental "affinity" since my whole thinking about human psychology and destiny was molded by the years I spent in his clinic. These were the years he worked out his theory of *Schicksalsanalysis* and his experimental choice-test. I had the privilege to work with him on these.

Binding as a Process of "Blending Into"

Let us now turn back to the problem of symbol formation—specifically, to the genetically laid-down instinctual tendencies and autonomous striving toward expression in *perceptible* form. How should we imagine what happens in the course of this upward "striving"? We have to rely on metaphoric language and imagery to formulate a hypothesis that gives the sense of how internal symbol formation might come about.

The matching of isomorphically fitting—though not identical—forms is crucial to this hypothesis. In their upward trend, the instinctual impulses or demands search for their appropriately matching, preconscious, perceptual memory image. One could say that the symbolic forms in the preconscious are "scanned" to find the appropriate expression for the less formed id impulse. Once this matching image is found, it will serve as a formed container for the less formed, more unbound energy that constitutes the instinctual need (or impulse, or demand).

Freud's example of the hungry baby's search for the breast (or bottle) can be used, with some modifications. It will somewhat clarify what I mean by harnessing or binding energy in form. The young infant, when hungry, exerts unbound "energy" through restless movements, crying, and other signs of distress. These are the infant's rather formless expressions of the drive: "I want, I need." After memory images of satisfying experiences at the breast or with the bottle cluster in the preconscious, the situation changes. The distressing hunger-need, as it reaches the preconscious, finds its fitting memory-image "container" in the form of the breast or the bottle. At this point the unbound energy of the hunger-need blends into the form of this image. By merging with a delineated form, the need loses its unmodulated impetus toward direct energy discharge. It is as if the unimpeded current of the drive energy were slowed down and restrained by merging with the image of the bottle or the breast. As a limited analogy, one might think of the intensity of a current of water rushing straight downhill, and how this intensity is restrained when the water has to spread through a complex pattern of channelization.

In the case of drive intensity merging with its fitting memory image, the outcome is not only a slowing down of the drive-current but a change of meaning of the whole constellation. The drive becomes differentiated into a wish or intention ("I want the bottle"), while the image or perception of the bottle acquires its own energy, almost like a magnet, pulling the infant toward a goal. This is how what Kurt Lewin describes as the valence-character of objects comes about. The form and the "drive" at this point are not separate but fused. It is not a question of a current of energy "settling" on some object; rather, the two merge to form a new structure.

I think of this binding process not as "cathecting" but as "*blending into.*" By blending into a more delineated form, the originally more diffuse instinctual urge acquires a more specific directedness, a more precise aim. The nature of the energy that constitutes the urge is also modified.

It is this binding that, to quote Freud, "makes more delicately adjusted performances possible" (1900, p. 574)—"more delicately adjusted" because they are steered more by perceptual-cognitive processes than by immediate sensations of pleasure or pain. The "blended schemata" are more gestalted than the unconscious urges, and therefore more perceptible, more "thinkable."

These blended schemata both constitute and "inhabit" the preconscious. They are the preconscious symbolic structures that make secondary-process functioning possible. What is important is that through their "double parentage," their derivation from both (external) memory images and (internal) instinctual urges, they connect the outside and the inside. They function as bridges between the two, imbuing each with the other. As I have said, symbols have a Janus-face, looking in opposite directions simultaneously. The symbolic structures in the preconscious look "back" at the turbulent, highly intense occurrences in the id (unconscious), one of their two sources. Within the preconscious structures themselves, this turbulent intensity has been "bound" or "contained." Yet, it colors the opposite vista of these Janus-faced structures—the outside environment. The object world is enlivened with subjective emotional significance because as objects are "looked at" and recognized, they are matched with their appropriate preconscious symbolic forms. The felt intensity or flatness of the world depends on the process of mutual assimilation (blending) between the instinctual (emotional) urges and the primary perceptual memory traces. If the latter preponderantly exert the function of assimilating to their own form the instinctual urges, then clear perception of the outside objects ensues—without, however, the experience of deep emotional significance. In this case, "a spade is a spade" and that is all.

On the other hand, if the instinctual urges exert more of the assimilating function, then the resulting preconscious schema will bestow more of the instinctual intensity on the perceptual world. The preconscious schema performs double, and opposing, functions. It binds and tames primitive emotional intensity originating in the id, while it enlivens the perceptual world with subjective emotional significance. These enlivening emotions can be intense and deeply personally meaningful, but they do not have the driving quality of "unbound" urges. They do, however, endow the person's lifespace with "valences"; that means the person experiences a meaningful, directed, intentional tension between him- or herself and his or her milieu. Life has goals and meaning. This is the opposite of the anhedonic, apathetic experience of emptiness and meaninglessness. Well-formed preconscious symbol-bridges are the antidote to the feeling of unmotivated, apathetic emptiness.

The "working-through" phase in analytic work consists of repeated reverbalization of the "same" events in the patient's history—except, repeated recall and reverbalization of the "same" event always implies some change. The process implies serial resymbolization, which results in binding emotional intensity to an increasing degree. In this way the intensity of painful memories decreases. On the other hand, the newly formed preconscious symbol-structures connect the person more fully to his or her object world. These therapeutic effects of "working through" take place thanks to the double function of preconscious symbolic forms. By serial resymbolizing, the disturbingly intense emotions calm down, while a more meaningfully motivated stance to the object world increases. These beneficial effects of working through can be derived from the energy-modifying effects of intrapsychic form development.

Form development by way of symbolization is the core event in mental structuralization—specifically, in the formation of the preconscious, on which reflective thinking and purposefully motivated actions are predicated. The importance of form development and gestalt perception in mental structuralization and the creation of the "thinkable" preconscious was, I believe, a major omission in Freud's theorizing. True, sensations of pleasure and pain are at first the only guideposts in steering behavior. They are the first, vaguely formed content of internal perception. As long as this is the case, there is no preconscious or bound energy. This initial unstructured state, however, soon gives way to increasingly structured "layers."[14] This development is a *natural* one, tied to the propensity for form development in the organic universe (see Portmann, 1956, 1960).

My point is that energy becomes bound *in* form. As instinctual energy ascends from the id toward consciousness and eventually becomes manifest in external form, it assumes increasingly more articulated form-quality and more articulated meaning. This is the route of centrifugal symbolization, which orders our internal and external universe (our "psychic apparatus" and external object world). It is through this hierarchic, serial transformation or *re*formulation of psychic content that the directly driving, unbound id energies become bound into goal-directed, modulated intentions. Energy bound in form makes "delicately adjusted performances" possible. In contrast to this view is Freud's statement that "in

[14] Spatial metaphors can be useful in theorizing about physically invisible events, whether in particle physics or psychology. They are a way of giving "shape" to ideas.

order to make more delicately adjusted performances . . . the preconscious system needed to have qualities of its own" (1900, p. 754). (We know that by "quality" Freud means perceptible form, as opposed to the formless intensity of "quantity.") In my view, the preconscious is formed *due* to the form-producing symbolizing propensity of the human mind. Without "qualities," i.e., formed, perceptible structures, there is no preconscious.

On the Use of the Topographic Model

From my remarks on the intertwining of energy and form, it should be clear that I find the topographic model useful in describing mental structuralization. Such a model allows us to envision a continuum that begins with the formless (although not totally formless) unconscious (the id) and continues through increasingly formed "layers" of the preconscious until it reaches the visible "daylight" of the conscious. In this view, what is unconscious is unconscious because it does not have any perceivable gestalt qualities, while consciousness equals the perception of such qualities. Indeed, I believe that by using perceptibility as a guideline, we can clear up *some* of the often-criticized ambiguities in the topographic model.

The term "out of awareness," for instance, should be used in many places where the term "unconscious" is now used. Some allegedly "unconscious" memories "uncovered" during analysis fall, I believe, into the category of moving neglected *preconscious* content into the center of awareness. Preconscious content is descriptively *not* conscious until attention cathexis brings it into focus. A patient may simply avoid focusing on a certain memory, without taking the drastic step of repressing it into the system "unconscious." These memories which, once focused on, emerge in full detail, without any difficulty, were never truly forgotten; they were just kept incommunicado. These are memories the patient "chose" (and here we meet the problem of "will") to exclude from communication with the analyst, as well as from his or her own perception of self. For whatever reasons, these memories did not fit the patient's self-styled biography. There can be considerable emotional investment in keeping the self-written "story" of one's life in a particular shape by repeatedly recounting it in the same way, to others and to oneself.

"Not to recall," then, is not the same as true repression, though admittedly they might be situated at different points on a continuum representing increasingly strong forces to push content out of awareness. These forces can range from decathexis to anticathexis. Some resistance forces must be assumed to operate within the manifold of the preconscious, forces that can keep certain memories "tucked away" from frequent recall. In the course of analysis these memories can enter the patient's communication, not because true repression has been removed, but because the patient's whole emotional stance to his or her self-created biography has changed. Trust in the analyst is an important factor in facilitating this change. The patient can now risk verbalization of memories that do not fit his or her integrated life story. These "forgotten" memories are closer to "secrets" hidden in a safe place than to truly repressed material. True, sometimes one can hide a thing so well, in such an out-of-the-way place, that after a while one forgets where the hiding place is.

These questions belong in the problem area of the dynamic relation between the preconscious and the conscious, or of the dynamic organization within the segments of the preconscious. The clinical reverberations of the various ways of conceptualizing these phenomena are great. The therapeutic methods for lifting material from the true unconscious imply reconstruction. Unconscious memories do not simply suddenly appear in perfect verbalization, accompanied by visualization in exact detail. This type of sudden "repression removal" with sudden total recall is the Hollywood version of psychoanalysis. In real analysis reconstruction of unconscious memories is hard work, in which the analyst's "educated guesswork" strongly participates. It is very different from a patient's fluent account of an event not mentioned for years, just because "I did not happen to think about it." "My father used to take me to museums" or "play with me in the park" can be told after years of having described the father as a stern, uncaring person. Or, the most ideally described mother is suddenly recalled in her "hysterical yelling fits." Psychoanalytic treatment did something very therapeutic by facilitating the alteration of the patient's willingness to change his or her "officially" guarded life history.

The therapeutic interventions used to bring about this alteration are quite different from those aimed at true repression removal. The creation of an atmosphere of trust is crucial for enabling patients to really talk about everything they know—everything they know but prefer not to think and talk about. After having told such previously "not-thought-about" but not-unconscious material, patients usually say: "But I knew this all the time. This was never unconscious." They are right, and the analyst should confirm their rightness, even if the analyst adds that to know something and to talk about the same thing to another person have psychologically very different meanings. Unfortunately, analysts often refer to such recall as if "it were retrieved from the unconscious"; yet giving patients credit for what they know they always knew is therapeutically important. Trust has to go both ways within the psychoanalytic situation. From reported case histories one can gather that analysts interpret (maybe not to patients but to themselves and to their colleagues) remarks similar to the one above as resistance to giving the analyst credit for removing true repression. Such a belief on the analyst's part, even if not verbalized, contaminates the atmosphere with undertones of tension stemming from mutual narcissistic competitiveness—an atmosphere not conducive for productive analytic work.

Freud himself seems to have been of two minds on the question of whether everything withheld was due to resistance guarding repression,[15] or whether it was closer to unwillingness to tell the truth. In his case histories and vignettes, he often seems to treat patients' "resistance" not as an unconscious defense, but as a willful withholding of unpleasant truth. Although the judgmental tone with which he admonished Dora (Freud, 1905) does not facilitate the free, trusting communication necessary for analytic work, this kind of intervention indicates that in his clinical work Freud treated phenomena he conceptualized as "unconscious" as if they were "preconscious secrets." Still, to uncover the unconscious was, for Freud, the earmark of psychoanalytic work, not the reorganization of the preconscious. I would argue that his strict division between the unconscious and the preconscious lay behind his reason for defining psychoanalytic work exclusively in terms of "making the unconscious conscious." What I am proposing is a more fluid situation, as suggested by Schilder's concept of the "sphere."

My approach to the dimensions unconscious–preconscious–conscious is in terms of the increasing perceptibility given by increasingly delineating symbol formation. In this conceptualization, the topographic model does allow us to account for the structuralization of the mind. The "official" structural model was introduced precisely because of the

[15] Indeed, Freud must have been aware of the possibility that mental content can be withheld in the preconscious without bona fide repression. In his essay "The Unconscious" (1915c), he refers to a paper that deals with the censor between the preconscious and the conscious. This is the paper that has never reached readers.

multiple use of the term "unconscious" to designate non-conscious functions within the preconscious (the ego), the dynamically repressed unconscious, and the original (never repressed) unconscious. Certainly, this state of affairs was untenable, but it could have been corrected by a truly structuralizing redefinition of the topographic model. A theory of symbol formation applied to intrapsychic form development attempts to fulfill this task. My viewpoint limits the meaning of what is truly unconscious and enlarges the realm and therapeutic significance of the preconscious.

Where Freud's view differs from mine, then, is in his more fragmented or divided view of the human mind, of what he calls the "mental apparatus." The word "apparatus" itself reflects a mechanistic separation into parts. With Freud's introduction of the structural model, as we have seen, this divisiveness came to predominate, with the ego pictured as battling forces from the id. Although the topographic model "divides" the psyche into different "layers," there is always the possibility of a natural movement (flow) "upward," toward more delineated and more perceptible symbolic forms of expression. This conceptualization gives more of a sense of continuity than does a model of distinct "agencies."

Why the topographic model "fits" a theory of symbolization best becomes clear if we view symbolization, whether perceptual (centripetal) or internal (centrifugal) as a process of *mapping* the overpowering multitude of external and internal stimuli onto a delineated preconscious "map." It is a symbolizing, schematizing projection of "raw material" from the id and from the external world onto the preconscious. This "symbolized map" is by necessity a narrowing down, a compression of the initial manifold of raw material in the id and in the external world. Symbolization delineates or unfolds one form of the multiple potentialities inherent in the diffuse raw material.[16] Just as the hub of a wheel holds together the radiating spokes, so does the symbol hold together the multiple meanings of the symbolized in the central hub, i.e., the manifest symbol. Even though one of the potential meanings is more manifestly elaborated, all the others too reverberate in the symbol. This gives symbols their richness in "connotations" (in contrast to the one-dimensional meaning of signs). Let us remember that *symballein* in Greek means: to throw together, to unite separate parts.

That our by-itself-unknowable unconscious inside and manifold outside reality are "mapped" in preconscious symbolic forms gives a special significance to the preconscious. Because the preconscious symbol-structures unite instinctual urges with perceptual memory images, one can view the preconscious as the locus where goal-directed intentionality supersedes the more "driven-from-below" causal principle of human functioning. The preconscious mental structures lend something like "free will" or "free choice" to human beings. Our preconscious "map" structures our world in terms of goals and valences.

The Process of Matching

In speaking of symbolization as a kind of mapping, we need to take a closer look at the process of *matching*. To my mind, it is significant that in his essay on "The Unconscious" (1915c), which relies on the topographic model, Freud deviates from

[16] My views of internal symbolization are somewhat related but not identical to the ideas of Matte-Blanco (1975). He presents an almost totally undynamic, mathematical (and theological?) model deriving the "asymmetrical" world of consciousness from the "symmetrical" "underlying reality" (p. 6) of the "more comprehensive mode of being" (p. 57), which he identifies with the id. While his application of mathematical concepts to the different modes of psychic functioning opens up new avenues for thought and understanding, his neglect of instinctual forces is, in my mind, a major shortcoming.

his usual emphasis on deriving changes from purely cathectic processes and focuses instead on the *matching* between the unconscious "thing-presentation" and the preconscious "word-presentation." This is the juncture where Freud's explanatory concepts overlap with gestalt principles of organization.

The rules governing "unit formation" or "group formation" concerned Gestalt psychologists from the beginning. As was mentioned in Chapter 2, Wertheimer (1923) found that in visual fields the contents of particular areas are perceived as "belonging together." This was the beginning of Gestalt psychology. Besides similarity, proximity, and good continuation, the symmetrical position of similar entities proved to be an important factor in unit or group formation. A gestalt unit, consisting of two identical or similar subparts, is a pair. The tendency toward "closure" acts as an autochthonous force of attraction between the separate but potentially "fitting" subparts of a good gestalt. Gestalt processes (Köhler calls it "requiredness") give rise to field forces that regulate events in the field in the direction of reducing field tension by bringing about equilibrated, "good" gestalt structures. Pair formation results in symmetrical, well-equilibrated structures; it is one manifestation of the dynamic self-regulation of field forces. In Köhler's (1938) words: "If a context is not balanced its forces constitute a pressure in the direction of balance" (p. 346). And he says: "Whether any force operates between two objects [he means "entities"] depends on the characteristics of *both*; it is the nature of *both* which determines whether such a force will tend to . . . repulsion or to . . . attraction" (p. 361).

Isomorphic processes tend to form functional wholes within the organism (in the phenomenal sense: within the person). Köhler's main case in point is the isomorphic matching between perceptual organizational phenomena in the phenomenal world and their underlying brain processes. The lawful coordination between these two sets of processes can be considered as a serial set of functional pair formation. Analogously, Freud's hypothesis about the matching between the unconscious thing-presentation and its fitting word-presentation can be considered a serial set of functional pair formation based on the forces of "attraction" between isomorphically congruent subparts of a new gestalt.

Isomorphic matching, or pair formation, is pivotal to my theory of psychic organization by way of symbol formation. In symbolization, a more amorphous content finds abbreviated expression in an isomorphically matching but more articulated structure. The latter is what I have called the "true" symbol for the former (the symbolized). If the matching is isomorphic, then the sense of the symbolized will be meaningfully articulated in the more readily perceivable form of the symbol. In this case, symbolization leads to good, meaningful communication.

My assumption is that psychic structuralization, as well as the creation of perceptual order in the outside world, takes place through a series of such matchings. In the course of these serial events, new gestalts are formed and energy conditions are altered. The field tension existing prior to the serial, new unit formations is equilibrated with the formation of new gestalts. Equilibration through gestalt formation accounts for the order-making function of symbols. The drives from the id find more stabilized expression by "fusing into" more delineated, fitting memory structures in the preconscious. I do not, however, see this as a one-step transformation (i.e., as *one* event where the unconscious "thing-presentation" meets its fitting "word-presentation"), for I view the preconscious as a continuum of "layers" of increasing delineation, stretching between the amorphous unconscious and the clearly perceivable conscious. Schematically, one can visualize the transposition of psychic content from layer to layer as a series of transformations based on isomorphically fitting forms matching, uniting with each other. The matching of the inner "schema" with the external object by way of visual perception is the last step in these serial matchings.

Actually, this is the step Freud refers to as the "search for perceptual identity." The role of "perceptual identity" in structuring external reality has been discussed in Chapter 4, in terms of the guiding function of symbols. Freud's conception is that the cathected memory image (a symbol) of the satisfying object is compared to the form of outside objects and the correct match between the two indicates that the searched-for object has been found.

Gombrich's (1960) analysis of pictorial representation can be compared to Freud's "perceptual identity." Gombrich is concerned with image-making, with the "secret" of how artists produce the illusion of reality by putting patches of color on a two-dimensional canvas. He points out that artists interpret the world in terms of their own "mental schemata" (actually, this is true for everybody). These mental schemata, and consequently art itself, are influenced by convention (remember Neumann's [1954] emphasis on the particular epoch's traditions on the appearance of the art symbol). Artists rely on a "vocabulary of forms" (I would specify this "vocabulary" as the storehouse of symbolic forms in the preconscious). The existence of different styles depends on changes in the conventions that underlie the vocabulary of forms. In other words, depending on the conventions or traditions of a particular era, people actually *see* differently. Different styles result from different ways of seeing.

Children "make" pictorial objects on the basis of their knowledge of things. They rely on a minimum of preformed visual schemata. In the intertwining creative process of "making and matching," children's productivity leans heavily toward "making." In contrast, if we look at the creative process of eighteenth- and nineteenth-century "realistic" landscape painters, for instance, it leans toward "matching." As Gombrich explains, "All representations are grounded in schemata which the artist learns to use" (1960, p. 313). With these schemata, the artist *makes* something, which can then be *matched* with what he or she sees right then (the search for perceptual identity). Without making, there can be no matching. Artists have to "invent comparisons which work" (p. 301). Their visual experience is influenced by guesses, expectations, hypotheses.

Gombrich reminds us that the "innocent eye is a myth" and that the inductive method in science is a mirage (p. 298). He quotes Karl Popper (1959) on the nature of observation. Every observation is the result of a question from nature which implies a tentative hypothesis. This hypothesis may then need modification to make it fit (match) the new observation. The same is true in art. The creative act does not start with pure observation, followed by recording. Artists, too, start with a "hypothesis," which is their schema. Just as in science, this schema may need correction to make it a good match with visual observation. But a starting point, a standard of comparison, is needed to begin the creative process of "making and matching and remaking." Artists cannot start from scratch. Their "experiments" consist of the "tentative projection of works of art into nature, experiments as to how far nature can in fact be seen in such terms" (Gombrich, 1960, p. 322). Will their projections match their perceptions? Is there perceptual identity between the preexisting symbol and the new percept? The artist's "secret" for producing the illusion of nature on canvas is a serial "making and matching."

The great innovators in art—for instance, Constable and Turner—modified shapes (creating a new style) "to match the here and now of their appearance" (Gombrich, 1960, p. 295). In the innovator, "matching wins out over making." And the artist's creative new "matchings" can teach the public to see in new ways; the artist can teach a new "visual language." Artists' special gift, says Gombrich, is their capacity to see the ambiguities inherent in the visual world and to attain different "readings" of the same given configuration. Their innovative creativity lies in their capacity and readiness for alternative interpretations. They can create new classifications and dissolve old ones. Fluidity of categories characterizes artists' inner and outer worlds. Creativity is the discovery of the ambiguities of vision, and art "becomes the innovator's instrument for probing reality" (p. 324). This does not mean that the inner schemata born of tradition are put aside completely. Innovation for its own sake does not create a new communicative language; it produces "gibberish" (see the discussion of psychotic art in Chapter 7).

Gombrich's remarks connect with the relation of the "symbolized map" in the preconscious to the infinite manifold of "raw material" in the id and in the external world. The symbol is always by necessity a narrowing down of the initial manifold. The richness of a symbol consists in its allusions to all the potential meanings which were not manifestly included in the symbol. And the richness of symbolizing perception is to sense the potential manifold of meanings implied in the formed gestalts surrounding us. This is the artist's way of looking at the world that Gombrich describes.

More specifically, Gombrich talks about literally perceiving visual configurations in terms of Rubin's (1915) ambiguous gestalts (see Chapter 4), and this has relevance for therapy. Psychoanalysis "teaches" patients to see the ambiguities in their memory configurations. It aims to make their memory, perception, and thought categories more fluid. In other words, psychoanalysis, if successful, makes patients' perceptions more creative, allowing them to symbolize the "raw material" of their biographies in new, less painful, ways. Just as the innovative artist presents the public with a new way of seeing, so does the good analyst present to the patient a new, flexible set of mental schemata for probing and enriching reality.

There is great variability among patients in their capacity to change their perceptions. Some cannot "learn" to see their intrapsychic or external world as "ambiguous figures." Their psychic energy (libido, aggression) remains imprisoned in the forms of their original preconscious "containers," the mental symbol-schemata with which they probe reality. These patients' probing does not lead to innovative new forms—they are victims of fixation. Their perceptual rigidity is the opposite of Gombrich's description of the artist's fluid perceptual categories.

There is also a wide interindividual variability in the degree to which the capacity to shape diffuse raw material into isomorphic symbols is present. The internal symbolizing (gestalting) capacity of creative artists is particularly strong (see Chapter 9). A person with constitutionally low internal gestalting capacity, on the other hand, has a lowered capacity for binding energy, i.e., for forming a well-organized preconscious and conscious ego. The ego's "synthesizing function" (Nunberg, 1931) is deficient. Here is an integration of Freud's idea of conflict with Breuer's and Janet's hypothesis of an "innate weakness in the capacity for psychical synthesis." A person with a deficient gestalting capacity will be more prone to experience conflict. A handicap in "binding energy" leads to increased pressure from unbound energy, and thus to the tendency toward "hysterical" attacks. Without the connecting function of symbolization, the mental field tends to split in disruptive tension; whereas isomorphic symbolization holds the "mind" together. Psychoanalytic therapy heals splits and reduces tensions by helping patients to adequate verbal symbolization of their psychic content.

Specifically, as I shall detail in the next chapter, repression splits the wholeness of the mind and "narrows the field of consciousness." At the same time, paradoxically, repressing forces are "gestalt forces" attempting to hold the ego's organized structure together. They repudiate material that might disrupt the ego's unified organization. What we have here is an instance of premature closure of a gestalt because the ego's creatively synthesizing capacity is deficient.

The "creatively synthesizing capacity" refers to the capacity for forming complex gestalts which have subparts of opposing content, yet are integrated into an encompassing whole. The equilibrium of such a gestalt is balanced in the whole but is not as rigidly fixed as in a simple, unambiguous gestalt. The complex wholes resemble more "ambiguous figures," which lend themselves for different perceptions and therefore represent possibilities for change in the psychic structure. Individuals with low ambiguity tolerance have to resort to repression in order to hold up an unambiguous ego structure. Material beyond the ego's symbol-forming capacity has to be repressed, which is a gestalting function of a simpler order.[17]

[17] Although Bion's (1956, 1957, 1965, 1967) ideas came to my attention after writing this, it is worth noting that his approach, more than any other analyst's I know of, is based on principles of gestalt organization, even though he makes no reference to Gestalt psychology. Order versus disorder is basic to his conceptualization. Moreover, his notion of a "container" is similar to what I call "the preconscious storehouse of symbolic forms," or Freud's "inside of the ego which . . . has the quality of being preconscious" (1940, p. 162). Recall that Freud, who obviously telescoped his topographic with his structural model here, treats the ego as a container with a preconscious inside and an undefined outside.

Bion's "container" contains the well-formed structures of "alpha elements." The "alpha function" transforms the "by itself unknowable 'O' " into "thinkable thoughts." The unavailability of the "real" thing originates the alpha function. "Ultimate reality" can be known only through its "transformations." Bion's alpha function seems to correspond to what I call "isomorphic symbolization," internal or perceptual. Total internal or external reality is unknowable; we have to deal with their symbolized preconscious or conscious registrations. Symbolization is always predicated on the unavailability of the desired real thing.

Bion's "beta elements" represent "unmetabolized things-in-themselves," not "thinkable thoughts." They are disturbing elements, which cannot be stored in

Thinking About: The Hallmark of Humanness

It is the constitutionally given gestalting-symbolizing capacity that distinguishes the human mind and allows for "thinking about." To "think about" means conscious perception of a formed mental image as it appears on the "internal screen" of the conscious mind. This internal screen functions as a mirror, reflecting the transmuted forms of symbolized events originating in a different region, whether in the unconscious or in the external world. Because of their delineated form these symbol-gestalts can be consciously perceived. Conscious internal perception of these forms sets in motion a second mirroring process, producing "second-degree" symbolic transformations. These, in their turn, can be internally perceived and reflected from yet another "mirroring screen," with "third-degree" symbolic transformation . . . and so on.

Perception and thinking about thus constitute an infinite series of symbolic transformations. Human consciousness and its corollary, reflective thinking, can be likened to an infinite

---

the container and need to be "evacuated." The "not-transformed" beta elements cannot be used for thinking or remembering. The function of the "contact barrier" is to selectively control entry of new elements into the "alpha-elements container." The contact barrier is the basis for the normal relation to reality. However, the contact barrier can be destroyed, in which case the alpha elements change into beta elements and form "bizarre objects."

Bion, in spite of his strange language, has orderly thoughts about the function of internal gestalt formation (what I call internal symbolization). Order in the preconscious "ego-container" depends on a good transforming, symbolizing capacity. The beta elements correspond to the psychic material beyond the ego's symbolizing capacity. Since they disturb the ordered conditions in the preconscious, they need to be "evacuated." Bion here refers to projective identification, while I emphasize repression as the order-upkeeping defense. His "bizarre objects" are related to desymbolization, which will be discussed in the next chapter. I obviously find Bion's organizational views congenial to my gestalt-oriented view of symbol formation and mental structuralization. He derives mental malfunctioning from the unfittingness of "unmetabolized" (unsymbolized) elements in the ordered "thinking apparatus" (the preconscious storehouse of perceivable symbols). Bion does not point to the unacceptable *content* of disruptive ideas, but to their unacceptable, chaotic *form*.

hall of mirrors, although it must be added that each successive reflection entails some change. This is due to the ever-active symbolically transforming function of the human mind. Thinking about something we have previously thought about always involves some change; it always involves a further degree of symbolization. The truth is that we cannot think twice about *exactly* the same thing. Nor can we recall the "same" memory in exactly the same way repeatedly.

Highly intelligent narcissistic patients are often painfully aware of the unavoidable changes caused by speech. They cannot speak with easy spontaneity because they experience the process as speaking *about* their thoughts instead of speaking their thoughts. They are continually aware of their internal "mirrors" and notice the changes in the serial reflections. These patients look at the reflection of their thoughts in much the same way that Narcissus looked at the reflection of his body. They are in *love* with their thoughts and cannot tolerate the necessary transformations implied in symbolization. At times they become enraged because they are convinced that the analyst does not *see* them as they *really* are but only "through the glass darkly." Any comment from the analyst is thrown back as proof that he or she functioned as a distorting mirror. Of course such obsessively heightened self-consciousness and lack of trust in the other has a long history from earliest childhood. In analysis this attitude is enlisted in the service of resistance. Still, the phenomenon these patients desperately and aggressively focus on does in fact exist, although it need not interfere with communication. Moreover, if we add to these transformations due to the "serial mirroring" the idea that symbol formation, in words as well as in other media, is by necessity a selecting and condensing "creative act," we can better empathize with the pain some people experience in the "creative act" of expressing feelings and thoughts in words.

Wilhelm Stekel, in his "The Polyphony of Thought" (1924), beautifully expresses the psychic "struggle" involved in expressing thoughts in language.[18] He says: "Man has a hidden world of thoughts which cannot be expressed in language. . . . This discrepancy, . . . between what we want to say and what we can say, is due mainly to the fact that we never have single thoughts but always many, an entire polyphony, of which speech expresses but one melody. The other voices and the counterpoint remain hidden" (p. 313). And he adds: "The thought-process shows a remarkable condensation. Verbalization is preceded by a struggle" (p. 314). In other words, Stekel saw that condensation is not limited to primary-process thinking but that secondary-process thinking and language by necessity imply condensation. According to my view, all forms of symbolization imply condensation, but only in true symbolization is the product of condensation isomorphic with the raw material that is symbolized.

These theoretical assertions regarding the symbolic transformation of underlying raw material bear directly on the psychoanalytic method of treatment. It should be kept in awareness that whatever the analysand or the analyst says is but one articulated gestalt lifted out from the manifold of underlying content in the speaker's mind (conscious and not conscious). Each uttered word or sentence is the hub of a wheel of potential, but silent, meanings. For true communication, the analyst, as well as the analysand, has to hear the reverberations of the "polyphony" within the linear "melody" of spoken sentences. Awareness of this multivalent, multi-

[18] Rapaport (1951) includes Stekel's paper in his volume as an example of the incorrect representation of the psychoanalytic theory of thinking. He reminds the reader that Stekel was not in possession of such concepts of "modern psychoanalytic ego-psychology" as "conflict-free ego-sphere" and "inborn ego-apparatuses." To me, it seems that Stekel, in his understanding of the discrepancy between word-symbols and the underlying raw material they symbolize, was ahead of his time.

potential relation between symbol and symbolized guards against naive insistence on one truth or against simplistic one-to-one interpretations of "latent meaning" hiding behind manifest expressions (see my discussion in Chapter 7).

We should also note that although "working through" in the analytic process allegedly consists of repeated recall and reverbalization of the "same" events in the patient's history, recall of the "same" event always implies some change. We saw that "thinking about" and "thinking about thinking about" never refer to exactly the same mental "object." Serial internal perception equals serial resymbolization, which implies "binding" of concomitant emotional intensity to an ever-increasing degree. This is one of the important consequences of working through. The painful intensity of past frustrations and feelings decreases by virtue of the "energy-binding" function of repeated reformulations. On the other hand, the newly formed preconscious symbolic schemata, imbued with feeling, connect the person more meaningfully to the object world and, to quote Freud (1900) again, make "more delicately adjusted performances possible." All this happens thanks to the double function, the Janus-face, of preconscious symbolic forms.

Conclusion

The "inside" registration of the outside world through perception (centripetal symbolization) and the expression of the "inside world" through serial transmutation of instinctual urges into perceptible forms (centrifugal symbolization) together represent the *cycle of the creative process* that is part and parcel of the functioning of each human being. Full-fledged artistic or scientific creativity is but a special instance of this cycle of creative symbolization. Creative geniuses are rare. They are endowed with extremely high capacity for creative perception and creative expression, in other words, with a rare capacity for creation of symbolic forms. I assume that in the case of creative geniuses this capacity is based on genetic endowment, even though this capacity could not flourish without the effort of serious learning. We can, however, view scientific and artistic creativity as existing on a continuum, with the rare geniuses on one end, the talented creators in the middle, and the many individuals whose creative perceptions and activities fuse into their daily lives on the other end. There are creative individuals whose creativity is not associated with any one specific work of "creation." Yet they lend beauty to the world by their perceptions and life patterns.

There are also individuals whose "cycle of creative symbolization" is impaired, in whom we find the opposite of order-producing symbol formation. The next chapter deals with the symbolization impairments of this group: with desymbolization and missymbolization. Both these processes result in impaired communication, impaired dialogue between "outside" and "inside"—that means, impaired relation to reality.

CHAPTER 7

Desymbolization and Missymbolization

Up to now symbol formation has been discussed as a specifically human process that transforms chaotic inner and outer stimulation into orderly, perceptible gestalts. The psychic regions of Freud's topographic model have been described in terms of their increasingly delineated and perceptible psychic content. Symbolization is a communication process, in which perception conveys information to the perceiver, who can be called the "addressee." This perceiver may be another person or a particular perceptual region within the symbolizer. (The latter results in communication with oneself.)

True symbols isomorphically represent what is symbolized, thus providing a good cognitive map. For this to happen, the symbolizer's mental field, or "psychic apparatus," must be well articulated, with qualitatively different areas separated from each other, yet allowing communication between them. By bridging over permeable boundaries, isomorphic symbols connect what is disparate. At the same time, by establishing delineated structures, they bring order to unbounded chaos. To perform this organizing function, the true symbol reveals the essential and disregards the unessential or confusing detail in the symbolized. As I stated earlier, symbols both *connect and separate*; they also *hide and reveal.*

Neurotic symptoms are not true symbols. They are cryptosymbols, to use Piaget's (1945) expression, for they hide meaning more than they reveal it. That Freud, Jones, and later analysts limited their discussion of symbolization to this pathological modality has already been pointed out. Yet, somewhat paradoxically, it is through the communicative, *symbolizing* function of the symptom that the analyst gains insight into the patient's hidden psychic reality. Despite his narrow focus on the disguising function of the cryptosymbol, Freud's discovery was the method of deciphering the symbolic language concealed in the patient's symptoms. The poorly communicating symbolic language of symptoms, however, is the outcome of impaired symbolization due to the effect of defense mechanisms. The next section deals with pathology of symbolization due to the impeding effect of repression.

Repression and Impairment of Symbolization

Repression and other defense mechanisms disrupt the process of meaningful inner form development through symbolization. In the last chapter, I described how psychic content migrates "upward" from one layer to the next, more delineated one. In the course of this "upward migration" of psychic material, transformations of form and state of energy are brought about by a series of *matchings* and blendings of isomorphically fitting forms. Repression obstructs the proper matching of isomorphically fitting forms. The inappropriate merging of an unconscious content with a preconscious structure results in a symptom rather than a true symbol. This symptom then acts as a "foreign body," disturbing the whole-some functioning of the total organism. A symptom is the product of missymbolization.

To understand the dysfunctional symbolization of the symptom, we must look at defects in the symbolizer's internal boundary formation. Both neurosis and psychosis imply boundary malformations. If boundaries exist where they should not, or if they too rigidly separate neighboring mental "regions," then the impetus of psychic content toward more perceptible expression will be impeded and defective symbolic communication will ensue. A rigid "repression barrier" is *not* a desirable permeable boundary within a well-articulated mental field. It is a particularly rigid boundary, i.e., a "barrier" fortified by countercathexes, producing split segmentation within the psychic organization. Transposition of mental content across the repression barrier results in missymbolization, in the maladaptive "bad" gestalt of a neurotic symptom. The true meaning of symptoms is not understandable to the neurotic person who produced them. Symptoms constitute a misguiding preconscious-conscious "map" for psychic orientation. These pathological cryptosymbols indeed need a specially trained interpreter who can unravel their meaning.

Obstruction by the repression barrier can lead to two different types of impairment: (1) *desymbolization* and (2) *missymbolization*. Recall that in "The Unconscious," Freud explains that what repression "denies to the presentation is *translation* into words which shall remain attached to the object. A presentation which is not put into words, . . . which is not hypercathected, remains . . . in the *Ucs.*" (1915c, pp. 201–202; first italics mine). Denying a presentation *translation* into words means denying a vaguely structured urge expression within a more articulated, and thus more perceptible, form. The unconscious content, if not "translated" into preconscious form (i.e., not symbolized), will continue to obey the "syntax" of primary process, with its impetus toward direct, tension-relieving discharge of unbound energy. Put slightly differently: If unformed instinctual urges are denied access to the appropriate formative template of preconscious symbolic structures (words are such formative structures), then thoughtless striving toward immediate tension release and avoidance of pain will steer behavior.

What is crucial in the symbolization process is the energy-binding effect of preconscious symbolic forms. Freud (1940) describes this as the ego's "constructive function" which, he says, "consists in interpolating, between the demand made by an instinct and the action that satisfies it, the activity of thought" (p. 199). Actually, "interpolating" is not the best term, for, in my view, instinctual urges are not simply put to one side, with thought inserted in between. Rather, they are *blended* into their isomorphically matching preconscious forms. It is this blending that *transmutes* the primitive urges into meaningful and thoughtful human action. Primary repression obstructs this symbolizing transformation by "closing the door" between primary urges and their corresponding preconscious, expressive forms.

Subsequent repression, "after-repression," aims at expelling content *from* the preconscious, back into the unconscious. These "after-repressed" contents are those that prove to be beyond the ego's capacity to synthesize permanently within the organized "territory" of the preconscious. With repression, the preconscious form tends to disintegrate and the psychic content once again falls under the sway of the primary process. It is *desymbolized.* The primary-process pressure toward immediate tension discharge now prevails, precluding thinking *about* as a step preliminary to action. Repression causes desymbolization by changing preconscious material into primary-process demands clamoring for expression with instinctual intensity. Freud says: "An excessive strength of instinct can damage the ego . . . it can destroy its characteristic dynamic organization and change the ego back into a portion of the id" (1940, p. 199). Let me expand on this statement, since it is crucial for the process of desymbolization.

This is exactly what happens dynamically due to repression—that a portion of the ego is changed back into a portion of the id. And this reacquired portion of the id poses particular danger to the ego precisely because it has already been preconsciously symbolized. In other words, it is psychic content with enough "push" to have worked its way "up" into the "organized territory" of the preconscious ego, only to be "pushed back" after having been perceived and deemed unfit to remain there. One can assume that the particular content was contradictory to that of the existing preconscious ego and the synthesizing-symbolizing capacity of the ego was too limited to form a permanent, complex symbol-gestalt containing contradictory subparts. With more symbol-creativity, repression could have been avoided. Yet, with limited capacity for complex symbolization, repression cannot be avoided. The unbound instinctual energy of the unconscious id then tends to assimilate to its own state the energy and form-quality of the psychic material driven "down" into it by repression—hence the pressure and primary-process mobility of the repressed content.

The particular upward-driving power of desymbolized material derives partly from its particularly strong impetus (shown by the fact that it has achieved symbolization once). Plus, one can assume that special gestalt forces are active, driving toward achieving the previous preconscious form, which might not have totally disintegrated into the fluid forces of the id. The result of this whole dynamic process is what Freud called the proclivity toward "the return of the repressed." This return is likely to take the form of missymbolization, i.e., of cryptosymbolization in the form of a symptom. Symptom formation is caused by the failure of repression to be totally effective, although it is effective enough to prevent the correct resymbolization of the upward-pushing, previously repressed content. The outcome of this internal conflict situation, in which opposing forces act upon the emergence of one and the same mental content, is the cryptosymbol, or symptom. In their formal characteristics, these cryptosymbols fit into the organized preconscious because they have perceivable, delineated structure. However, they fall short in conveying meaningful information since repression impedes the proper blending between the upward-striving instinctual-emotional urge and its isomorphically matching preconscious form. This mismatch between impulse and preconscious form accounts for the diagnostic sign of a symptom, namely, the inappropriately intense emotions invested in a seemingly neutral object. Phobias and compulsive acts result from missymbolization due to the misleading effect of repression.

The repressing forces could actually be considered "gestalt-upkeeping forces" that "aim" at holding the ego's organized structure together when confronted with "undigestible," i.e., unsymbolizable, instinctual strivings. The presence of not-symbolically-structured id content would endanger the organized, unified character of the preconscious-conscious ego—hence the need for repudiation by means of repression. (This is analogous to Bion's conception of the function of the "alpha barrier" and the disturbing role of the "not-transformed" beta elements.)

Thus, repression by means of cryptosymbolization (symptom formation) does safeguard a certain formal organization of the ego and symptoms do bind energy. All this, however, at the price of furnishing faulty information to the perceiving, cognizing aspect of consciousness. Cryptosymbols are perceivable internal representations that the symbolizer can "pick up" and think about, except he or she will think about the "wrong" thing. Cryptosymbols furnish a misleading cognitive map, pointing to wrong connections between events because the matching between the "deeper" urges and their preconscious manifestations was not isomorphically fitting.

If the repressed content does not reappear in the preconscious in the guise of a cryptosymbol, then more disorganized symptomatology ensues. In such instances, the destructured, "desymbolized," repressed material influences behavior from the unconscious. Unconscious urges held back by primary repression from entering the preconscious, and desymbolized material "banished" from the ordered preconscious into the more chaotically "organized" unconscious, share this in common: They both act as intense driving forces with an urgency toward action that precludes symbolic "trial action," i.e., "thinking about" before acting. Compulsively driven, repetitive, unmodulated "acting out" is frequently the consequence of this "unsymbolized-desymbolized" psychic constellation.

The destructuring of preconscious form involved in repression brings about a critical loss of internal perceptibility. After repression, the desymbolized preconscious material loses its delineated gestalt quality. Without delineated form, there is no-thing to perceive. Perception is perception *of* something, implying distinction between perceiver and perceived, a certain distance between the perceiver and what is perceived. One does not really "see" chaos. Lacking a preconscious structure, a shape, mental content is not so much perceived as simply "experienced." Thus, desymbolization, by destroying delineation, also destroys the distance necessary for reflection and thinking about—the hallmark of human symbolic thought processes. Shapeless driving forces are experienced as sensations and feelings. They have an immediate, pervading presence so that the sentient subject becomes a subject who, in a sense, *is* feeling. In order to distinguish and evaluate one's feelings, one needs distance to objectify them, one needs to be able to step back and observe oneself, to re-present (symbolize) what is happening. Desymbolization works in the reverse direction. The consequence may well be unmodulated acting out under psychic conditions of practically total subjectivity.

Acting Out as a Deficiency in Symbolization

Acting out indicates an impoverished storehouse of preconscious symbols. Rather than thinking about the situation, the person acts impulsively, in an attempt to reach the desired goal fast. There is a lack of good communication with self and with others. In extreme cases, massive acting out deprives the person of much of what makes a human being specifically human. He or she is driven by the pressure of unmodulated, unsymbolized impulses.

In less severe cases, acting out may appear only in a particular area of the person's life, and here we can see clearly the desymbolizing effect of repression. In these cases, acting out tends to be circumscribed as the target area of repression. If, through analytic intervention, we succeed in lifting the repression, then the desymbolized becomes accessible to resymbolization. Verbal interpretation *translates* the pressing but unconscious impulse into a delineated form (words). As the impulse acquires shape, as it becomes perceptible, it can be contemplated and thought about. The working-through process with acting-out patients hinges on the energy-binding and distancing function of symbolization through language.

The acting-out person can be said to live in a distance-less world. Symbolic representations bring about articulation of the internal world, making for distance between self- and object representations. For acting-out persons this distance is lacking. The boundary between self and object is not clear. They act as if the self and the object world were contiguous. They expect to be able to "touch" anything they desire.

What happens if the desired object is out of reach, unavailable? The acting-out person's reaction tends to be disproportionately intense. His or her frustration tolerance is close to nil. Without proper symbol formation, delayed action becomes inconceivable. One has no means of moving gradually *toward*, across space, in time.

It might be conjectured that the acting-out person's deficient symbolization is a corollary of pathologically intense instincts. Such extreme intensity can destroy or prevent energy binding and consequent articulation of the psychic sphere. Again, Freud (1940) asserts: "An excessive strength of instinct . . . can destroy [the ego's] characteristic dynamic organization and change the ego back into a portion of the id" (p. 199). In the câse of the acting-out person, one might assume that the urgency of id demands contributes to the direct, immediate involvement of the motor system. One might also assume a primary ego defect with regard to symbol formation. In either case, the constitutional deficiency results in the accumulation of unbound, unformed instinctual strivings. Direct action becomes the only means of tension release. "I want what I want when I want it" is the motto of these impetuous people. They simply cannot accept the unavailability (however temporary) of somebody or something desired, for they are unable to use symbol-bridges to connect to what is not directly reachable. Theirs is a concrete, present universe where *the absent* does not subjectively exist. The sense of striving toward some future goal is missing. Without symbols, the dimensions of time and space only separate; there is no connecting. Mental operations within the abstract dimensions of time and space are predicated on the existence of full-fledged symbols.

Signs versus Symbols in Acting Out

"The human brain is constantly carrying on a process of symbolic transformation of the experiential data that come to it" (Langer, 1942, p. 47). In the acting-out personality, the brain-mind does not function as a reliable symbolizing transformer. These people's transformers seem to produce *signs* instead of symbols. Symbols *represent* something *absent*. Signs *indicate* something *present*. A temper tantrum indicates the presence of rage; it is not a symbolic (distanced) representation of rage. Similarly, smoke is a sign, indicating the presence of fire, just as steam indicates that the water is boiling.

Generally the expression of an affective state starts out as a sign, but in the course of time this expression undergoes a change in function, so that the sign evolves into a symbolic means of communication. It was in fact Freud (1895) who originally described such a change in function, in pointing to the shift in the infant's crying from a pure discharge phenomenon (a sign of hunger or other discomfort), to communication addressed to the mother. Acting-out individuals, however, show little change in function from sign to symbol. Indeed, they live in a universe of signs.

Signs, acknowledging no absence, operate within concrete contiguities and immediate action. The acting-out person lives in a concrete action-space without the "buffer zone" of thoughts to mediate between desire and action. The direct invasion of pressuring impulses into the system of motor discharge represents the predominance of primary process. Symbols, in contrast, allow for delay of action (i.e., secondary-process functioning). Symbols evoke the *conception* of a thing that is absent. To conceive a thing is different from reacting to it directly and overtly. We might draw an analogy between signs and a conditioned reflex. The dog does not think *about* food when the bell rings but overtly salivates as if the food were present. In a similar fashion, signs *announce* their object and trigger a rigidly preformed, immediate response. The reaction is direct and overt, without the pause of conceptualization.

For acting-out persons, even slight environmental stimuli may act as signs, evoking an almost stereotyped response. A particular facial expression, movement, or word can provoke a seemingly uncalled-for outburst. "I cannot stop before the whole thing is out" was how one patient described her uncontrollable seizurelike reactions to certain visual stimuli. In childhood, certain of her mother's facial expressions had acted as "releasing stimuli," prompting ritualized fits of anger. Later, as an adult, the sight of someone who looked aloof or arrogant (at least to her) or who seemed elegantly dressed could serve as a "release," leading to a set, patterned response. If, for instance, she saw a woman who was (in a specific way) "well-dressed," she had to immediately shop for loads of unnecessary clothes at all the bargain places. She would then invariably regret the waste of money and bemoan the lack of closet space for her newly bought clothes. Of all this she was fully aware while the shopping fit was "on." In a similar way, a glimpse of her own nose in profile in a mirror might fill several analytic sessions with stereotyped cursing of her "impossible looks." (The patient was in fact extremely good-looking and always elegantly dressed.) After these hours would come the equally stereotyped self-reproaches for having "wasted" analytic time in such a "stupid" way. "When the demons are set going," she explained, she simply could not stop them.

In retrospect, such repetitive, compulsively acted-out scenes evoke a feeling of humiliation—at least in the more mature patients whose acting out is restricted to certain unresolved conflict areas. In these cases, where desymbolization results from intense but focalized repression, sign-governed functioning is not pervasive. Since, most of the time, these patients are able to exert secondary-process control, the appearance of their "demons" is especially disconcerting. When they look back at their behavior, they are aware of the disproportionate intensity of their reactions. They feel, in some sense, dehumanized.

In fact, this form of focalized acting out does resemble the function of "sign releasers" in animal behavior (Tinbergen, 1951). As discussed in Chapter 5, sign releasers elicit *total* instinctive action patterns in animals. But these environmental releasers and their corresponding behavior patterns are well fitted, guaranteeing that the animal does the right thing at the right time. In contrast, humans are not "made" to be either as instinct-bound or as stimulus-bound as animals are. The basic "blueprint" for human beings implies their functioning as "animal symbolicum." Instead of preadapted instinct patterns, we have symbolic thought processes to guide our choices. And this basic blueprint of the species must be respected, or else the person (or the member of any other species) will be shipwrecked. Thoughtlessly acting-out persons do become shipwrecked because they lack good orienting, symbolic "dialogue" with their environment and also with themselves. Because their mental "transformer" seems to produce signs instead of symbols, they are both "human manqué" and "animal manqué."

A person's symbolizing potential can be enhanced by appropriate psychoanalytic therapy. Although massively acting-out patients do not take easily to psychoanalytic treatment, I believe this is the method that holds the most promise for developing the patient's capacity for correct symbolic communication. Many of the new modalities of treatment (various forms of "gestalt" therapy, "primal scream" therapy, and others) seem to be based on a hybrid mixture of inauthentic symbolization and (actually equally inauthentic) acting out. Psychoanalysis, on the other hand, combines discursive language treatment with a therapeutically useful form of acting out, which is the transference neurosis.

Secondary-process, discursive language represents the order of the world (see Wittgenstein, 1958). The analyst's verbal interpretations help to order the patient's "inner world" by naming, and thereby shaping and binding, chaotic drives and impulses. Words lend organization to the initially diffuse content of the unconscious. Word-symbols throw the "light" of consciousness on the darkness of the unconscious. Only in light can we perceive. In darkness we are blind. The massively acting-out person acts "blindly." Repression causes "blind spots" which cause lacunae in the perceptual field. Psychoanalytic interpretations aim at clarifying the patient's exteroceptive and proprioceptive "vision." Analytic treatment aims at clearing the "blind spots" caused by repression and opening up the patient's total perceptual field through the correct symbolization of the previously unsymbolized. What is important to remember here is that, in addition to light, one needs a certain distance to see clearly. Close up everything becomes a blur. There must be some separation between perceiver and perceived. Symbols, in contradistinction to signs, provide this distance.

The Role of Distance in Symbolization

Symbolizer, symbolized, symbol, and addressee—these are the four anchoring points of the symbolizing process. In order for true symbolization to occur, there must be some separation, some distance, between these points. This distinction implies differentiation between self and object, as well as between internal mental products and external reality. The notion of communication already assumes a distance between the speaker (symbolizer) and the addressee, or "other." The experienced existence of an addressee is needed for the motivation to initiate and perform symbolic communication. To quote Sartre: "language . . . presupposes an original relation to another subject. . . . Language is therefore not distinct from the recognition of the Other's existence" (1943, pp. 485–486). Without adequate separation, there is no "other" and consequently no symbolization. At the same time, however, symbolization is a means toward separation. It is a circular process with no definable point of causal origin.

In children we can perhaps see most clearly how symbolization comes into play with the experience of distance from a desired person and the wish to bridge that distance. A young child will use a transitional object to cope with mother's absence or unavailability (Winnicott, 1953b). The teddy bear or soft, cuddly blanket serves a protosymbolic function. Later, the full-fledged symbolic systems of language and thought connect across a distance. Children first have to experience a space separating them from the mother before they can turn that space into a "connecting space" by symbolic play or language. (Just how the mother can foster or thwart the child's capacity for symbolization will be discussed in Chapter 8.)

My point is that autistic traits (i.e., noncommunication) relate to a lack of separation—a lack of acknowledging the separate existence of the "other"—necessary for symbolic communication. In this regard, Luria and Yudovich (1959) describe an interesting case of nonverbalizing twins. The twins seemed to live in a closed universe of symbiotic union. After they were forcibly separated, however, language development began and proceeded at a rapid rate. One might say that with physical separation, each twin experienced distance from the "other." To cross this distance, they mobilized their (until then unused) innate capacity for symbolic communication. The case history of these twins illustrates the effect of both environmental circumstances and the innate symbolic language generativity of the human mind (brain) (Lenneberg, 1967). At the other extreme, we need to consider that an innate weakness in the symbolizing capacity may itself prevent wholesome separation.

With the massively acting-out individual, we encounter a somewhat different picture. Yet massive acting out also indicates lack of respect for separation from objects and consequently impairment in symbolic communication. Massively acting-out people do not tolerate or acknowledge the limitations imposed by separating distance. Yet the fact that they *do* talk in a grammatically correct fashion points to constitutional anlagen different from those of autistically nonverbal children. The acting-out person has a predisposition to direct motor discharge, a propensity which also leads to impaired symbolization and might be the differentiating factor between the symptomatology of acting out and autistic mutism. Both imply lack of separation, impaired symbolization, and lack of true connectedness to an "other." The latter characteristic might be deceivingly camouflaged in acting-out individuals by surface charm and talkativeness. Yet closer observation reveals their almost total self-centeredness, lack of empathy, and the pseudo-character of their "object relations." Other people are *used* for selfish needs, as if they were mere serving puppets. There is no reciprocal dialogue between inside and outside, no symbolic mediation between the two. The acting-out person sees only his or her needs, not the different (separate) needs of the other.

Psychotic Art as a Form of Acting Out

We have discussed the need for cathexis of the "addressee," the person to whom symbolic expression is directed. (This cathexis may be directed toward the internal representation of the addressee.) Without awareness of the otherness of the other, there is no real communication. This situation is clearly reflected in art work by psychotics. Hospitalized schizophrenics can be driven to draw or paint as if under some "creative spell" (Kris and Pappenheim, 1946), but the strangely stereotyped forms they create reveal their "general contact disturbance."[1] These frenetic bursts of "creativity" appear to derive more from a compulsively repetitive need for energy discharge than a felt creative need to express inner content within the perceivable outside world. One might compare these drawing fits to the compulsively acted-out, stereotyped scenes of acting-out individuals.

The psychotic's mental field (or psychic organization) lacks articulation. The psychotic does not possess a well-organized preconscious with delineated symbol structures, which can facilitate expression of, while also "taming," unbound instinctual urges. The homeostatic need to alleviate inner pressure is present in the psychotic, but not the differentiated inner equipment for binding raw impulses into good gestalts. Unsymbolized or desymbolized urges push toward direct expression. Under these energic conditions no truly communicative symbol can be created.

How we "explain" the psychotic's "emergency" state depends on our conceptual framework. If we choose an object relations perspective, then we might emphasize a distance-

[1] Schizophrenics produce more art than other types of hospitalized psychotics (see Reitman, 1951). Fascinating examples of schizophrenic art can be found in Kris (1952), Kris and Pappenheim (1946), Reitman (1951), and of course Prinzhorn (1922), who initiated the psychiatric study of psychotic art.

less, symbiotic closeness to the mother as the "cause" of the psychotic's noncommunicative, autistic pseudo-symbolization. In terms of Freud's libido theory, we might talk about impoverished object libido. Or, taking Freud's (1920) dual instinct theory, we might speak of a defusion of Eros and Thanatos (in which case destructive tendencies always seem to dominate). It is possible that pathologically intense aggressive impulses (evidenced in schizophrenic rage) demolish or prevent the development of organized mental structures. What all these formulations point to is an accumulation of unbound instinctual strivings and the impairment of symbol formation. Yet, even with an impaired symbolizing capacity, there is always an organismic need to keep the inner tension level within a tolerable homeostatic equilibrium (Bertalanffy, 1952). Energy strives toward discharge in whatever way possible.

The repetition compulsion is the primitive form of tension regulation that operates "beyond the pleasure principle" (Freud, 1920). Activities patterned on the repetition compulsion may be used to fight against the disruptive internal excitations caused by the pressure of unsymbolized or desymbolized psychic content. The compulsively repetitive features of psychotic art seem to serve this function (Reitman, 1951; Prinzhorn, 1922; Kris and Pappenheim, 1946).

Reitman (1951) differentiates the work of artists from that of psychotics—even those psychotics who show signs of artistic talent—on the basis of the final product's "ordered pattern," or lack thereof. Disturbing disorder and jarring fragmentation permeate all psychotic art. (These features were evident in my own collection of drawings by institutionalized psychotics, collected long ago, during my internship in a state institution near Budapest.)

The artist's final product is by no means a point-by-point copy of what is seen. Even so-called naturalistic painters, such as Corot or Constable, restructure the externally given stimulus pattern. This also holds for portrait painters. Visual perceptions are filtered through the artist's apperceptive and symbolizing schemata before they are recorded on canvas for perception by others. This filtering process imbues the art work with subjective symbolic significance. It also accounts for the recognizable style of an artist. While the deeply subjective elements in this reconstructive process may come from the artist's unconscious, the formal organizing principles stem from the preconscious-conscious system. The artist *wants* to communicate with an audience (addressee) and *wants* to be "understood." Implicit here is a kind of "automatic" (preconscious) assumption that the basic laws of gestalt perception hold equally for the creating artist and the appreciative audience. These gestalt laws involve the figure-background differentiation in visual perception or the effect of a framework, in this case the effect of the picture frame or simply the edge of the picture. Psychotics' art lacks these basic organizational principles, hence the difficulty for the viewer to simply visually "understand" it.

Art is not evaluated on the basis of subject matter but on the basis of the quality of the art work's structured pattern. The quality of this structured pattern, which includes the "fittingness" between form and the meaning the artist intended to symbolize, evokes the feeling of aesthetic pleasure—or lack of it—in the viewer. There are painters, for example, the cubists and surrealists, whose pictures radically restructure the features of our everyday "object world." In Picasso's paintings, for example, bodies and faces are intentionally fragmented in complete contradiction to anatomical possibility. In Chagall's case, objects appear in the most unlikely juxtaposition, such as a human being within a cow's head. Yet, however unexpected, these works do not evoke the jarring feeling of being faced with disturbingly incomprehensible disorder or chaos. We experience that the artist has *re*ordered the universe. The "language" of modern art does have a syntax. The combination of lines and color is far from arbitrary. The modern artist's symbol formation implies deliberately chosen, selectively organized form.

In contrast to the compulsively "driven" psychotic, the true artist exerts control over the shape and rhythmic distribution of line and color. There is a kind of inner vision of structural relationships that acts as a generative guiding principle. I do not mean that the artist has a precise mental blueprint that dictates every move. In the course of creation, a "*dialogue*" takes place between the artist and the work. Each brushstroke creates a new situation on the canvas, which poses new demands for the next stroke. The original "inner vision" and the gradually evolving relation between the canvas and the frame (the edge) shape the unity of the finished work. There is a continual *matching* (probably on a preconscious level) between the external and the internal that takes its shape through the "dialogue" between the artist and the visible work. The outside feeds into the inside, which again looks out—maybe changed due to the effect of what has been seen on the canvas. The final work possesses a self-consistent system of relations, which is the essential "subject matter" of all art forms. Topical subject matter is not essential, it is not even needed, as the term "nonobjective art" indicates.

Yet art is more than *just* a system of relations. Even though topical subject matter is nonessential, the artist is motivated by the need to give symbolic expression to a "content" deeply meaningful to him or her. This "deep content" may be expressed in a variety of symbolic forms, by means of representational subject matter as well as through a totally nonobjective but self-consistent pattern of relationships. The basic, motivating "deep content" may be unconscious, preconscious, or conscious (or a combination of all three) to the artist. The artist's talent (genius is very rare) for visual symbolization manifests itself through finding the symbolic form that "fits" or "matches" the "deep content" that needs to be symbolized. The unity we feel and "see" in a real art work is the result of this "good fit" or "good match." Even though the process of matching might to a large extent take place below the level of consciousness, *some* preexisting mental core image or conception is needed for executing a meaningfully ordered pattern of art, a unified and communicative composition, which is the *sine qua non* for art in any medium.

Implicit in the ongoing dialogue between the art work and its creator is a distance across which the dialogue can take place. In the course of artistic creation, fusion between creator and creation alternates with the artist's stepping back—literally as well as metaphorically—in order to experience a distanced view of the work. These "pauses" of distanced looking feed into the judgments that make the work communicate to others.

Even before the distanced view of the work in progress is the artist's internal viewing of his or her generative initial conception. This internal viewing, too, is predicated on the existence of distance between the artist's inner vision (a function of the observing ego) and the generative conception. Maybe "viewing" is not the best term since the initial internal conception is not yet a visible pattern of relations. Before translation into really perceivable form, the initial notion is a mental content of vague outline, although definitely experienced as something in need of more clarified expression. It may be clarified by means of musical structure, visual composition, or cognitive conceptual elaboration. Whatever form this symbolizing translation or elaboration takes, distance is needed for the creator's internal perception to in-spect his or her emerging mental contents.

Artists' or creative scientists' talent for creative introspection is particularly acute; they can discern and hold onto internal events that would fall below the threshold of the internal perception of most people. Artists' keen internal perception is part of what we call "inspiration." This is a subjective occurrence but a necessary step toward further objectifying elaboration, which is the creatively symbolizing work itself. Inspection, introspection, inspiration, symbolizing elaboration, all partake in the creative process and all need the existence of distance between the perceiver (symbolizer) and what is perceived (symbolized). This separation is fundamental to all forms of symbolization. It is the cornerstone of symbolic thinking, which is always thinking *about*.

Artistic creativity thus is a *sui generis* cognitive process, involving "thinking about"—first "about" emerging internal content, to which the externally perceivable work is added later. In the case of the artist, thinking about the inner guiding vision (or "image," although it might also be an auditive, musical motif) does not mean verbal conceptualization. It is rather a form of perception that implies relational inspection, planning and ordering, which leads to the creation of a "*presentational symbol*" (Langer, 1942). A well-articulated art work is always a presentational symbol. Discursive conceptual thinking is not the only form of cognition, just as a discursive verbal symbol is not the only communicative, true symbol. Presentational art symbols are at least as communicative and well articulated as discursive verbal symbols. A presentational symbol is a complexly interwoven unity of thoughts, feelings, and imagery. Its meaning is not built up, in a linear fashion, from separate, definable elements, but has to be grasped in a simultaneous perception of the whole. Although, later, subgestalts as parts can be successively focused on, it is in their togetherness, and not simply their addition, that they carry meaning.

Ostensibly, this definition of a presentational symbol refers to the way the spectator comprehends the art work. But on a more basic level, it also indicates the way the artist grasps the meaning of his or her initial internal conception that serves as the core from which the finished art work unfolds.

Without formative perception, the urge for creation would be experienced mainly as energic pressure seeking discharge. If this push for discharge were realized in graphic activity, it might result in something similar to the psychotic's "creative spell." It is the somewhat distanced "cognitive" stance at the beginning of (as well as throughout) creative work that distinguishes the symbolized communication of the artist from the symptomatic acting out of the psychotic. Psychotic art, in its lack of coherence, bears the earmark of compulsively driven action, the need to get something "out," without time or distance necessary for cognitive patterning. The psychotic lacks the necessary differentiation between self and object for true creation. Without distancing between the artist and the work, there is the danger that the "language" will be a totally private (autistic) one, inaccessible to the outside spectator.

Actually, there is some contemporary art that leaves me, as the spectator, with the feeling that it does not communicate anything meaningful. Whether the fault lies in the limitations of my responsiveness or in the art work's lack of authenticity is hard to judge. True, the innovative artist is always introducing, and thereby teaching, the spectator a new visual language, a new way of seeing (Gombrich, 1960). And sometimes there is a time lag between the introduction of a new style and the development of viewers' capacity to perceive with aesthetic pleasure the new visual order presented to them.

Be it as it may with this "modern" art that is not communicative or enjoyable to me, I shall present my subjective reactions because they bear on the nature of psychotic art. The works I am talking about impress me as inauthentic in the sense that their form (or rather, lack of it) gives the feeling that the creator's purposeful wish was to "shock" with the unexpected instead of being the result of true introspection and symbolic translation of deep psychic content. Some of these fragmented works impress me as if their creator were deliberately out to produce schizophrenic-like features in his or her work. Yet these creations could not be taken for bona fide psychotic art. I think it is exactly the effect of intentionality resulting in a "mannered" quality (the French term *voulu* or the German *gewollt* describe what I mean) that differentiates these inauthentic works from the psychotic's authentic peculiarities.

At this point I would like to take issue with what I see as a misguided glorification of the psychotic, evidenced in R. D. Laing's writings on schizophrenia and dramatized in Peter Shaffer's play *Equus*. Freud's teachings (however watered down or misrepresented) have created a widespread fascination with the "subconscious mind," in dream states and in mental illness. In some quarters this interest has led to a high valuation of psychotic states, as if psychosis were a *via regia* to profound, untainted wisdom. By the same token, well-proportioned order is often equated with "surface defense."[2]

I believe that the misguided glorification of mental illness has something to do with the noncommunicativeness of what, to me, seems not-good modern art. The art I have in mind deliberately exhibits "acting-out" characteristics in tribute, I believe, to depth, spontaneity, and the supposedly inherent artistic order contained in "chance." I feel some affinity be-

[2] A misconception to which, unfortunately, Freud (1908) himself contributed. Even Ehrenzweig, a profound thinker on the psychology of art, falls into the trap of raising "Dionysian" principles above "Apollonian" notions of order (1953, 1967). His one-sided reverence for Thanatos is especially disconcerting. The problem lies in his dichotomizing view, which sets one set of principles against another. Dionysian Thanatos, according to Ehrenzweig, is the true creative force, while Apollonian Eros represents the surface "gestalt" principles.

tween these works and the deliberate "spontaneity" and (supposedly) "not-thought-about" acting out of some new modalities of therapy. The end-products of "willed" acting out still reflect the existence of an organized mind that planned this deliberate "spontaneity," even if that mind aims at overcoming its own organization. (This speaks for the physiological underpinning of truly psychotic disorganization.)

The content and form of schizophrenics' paintings directly reflect their creators' mental peculiarities. In a schizophrenic's drawing, figures may appear at random—as if strung together—without any meaningful connection to each other in either a narrative or compositional sense. As the disease progresses, composition and cohesion increasingly deteriorate. The pictures take on an increasingly bizarre character. Disconnected human figures, pure ornamentation, and written words often intermingle, without any structural coherence. Repetitive stereotypes of gestures and forms are frequent in psychotic art. The forms are often open, unfinished gestalts, as is the whole picture. These unfinished gestalts contribute to the poorly differentiated, or totally undifferentiated, figure-background relation. What one would expect to be "foreground" fuses into its surrounding space. One might speculate that such merging is linked to symbiotic lack of differentiation, which does not exclude the possibility of an organic underpinning to the pathology of *all* relations in the subjective world of the schizophrenic.

Schizophrenics are sometimes described as living in a dream state, and their art might be said to exude a dreamlike atmosphere. "Dreamlike" in the sense of the viewer's inability to grasp the whole—a feeling analogous to the loss of form one senses while dreaming or on waking from a dream. This sense of something there but being unable to discern or grasp it comes, I think, from the weird condensations of figures, in dreams as well as in psychotic art. If psychotic art is skillfully executed, this only adds to the viewer's uneasy feeling that he or she has missed the point and a more careful examination would reveal the meaning. But it does not. The experience is similar to an attempt at conversation with a hospitalized schizophrenic whose syntax is good enough to suggest to the listener that if he or she pays attention the patient's speech will be understandable in everyday terms. While parts of the patient's speech may seem to communicate, the connections are missing and the whole becomes "word salad." (This does not mean that with the conceptual tools of psychoanalytic interpretation some "message" cannot, at least sometimes, be unraveled from the schizophrenic's "word salad" or bizarre drawings.)

A total lack of respect for (or awareness of?) the separateness of "things" is reflected in the strange condensations found in schizophrenics' art products. This confusing of object boundaries, together with the lack of figure-ground articulation noted above, might be interpreted as a manifestation of these patients' unseparated, unindividuated, symbiotic "self." Similarly, schizophrenics' tendency to fill every bit of space with meaningless, repetitive elaborations could be seen as *horror vacui*, in the sense of "horror" of the lack of immediate contact, of existence as a separated organism surrounded by space. The same interpretation might hold for the frequently occurring duplicated, strangely connected symmetrical figures (which might also be an expression of symbiotic "twinning"). Schizophrenics' drawings often look like "doodles" with no beginning and no end—no points of separation. Moreover, what is inside or behind a human figure is frequently depicted on the same plane as a surface feature. These "transparencies" in their drawings (also evident in their Rorschach responses) indicate the experience of lack of substantiality, a lack of recognition of the three-dimensional solidity of objects, and especially of the human body.

In sum, schizophrenics' drawings suggest a lack of defined boundaries within their psychic "topology" as well as in their experienced world. Demarcation between the self and nonself is blurred or nonexistent. Under such circumstances, thought disorder follows by necessity, since thinking implies awareness of relations. Perceptual disorder entails thinking disorder and vice versa. In either case, erosion (or lack) of boundaries means erosion of the distances between the anchoring points necessary for true symbolization. Without distance between the symbolizer and the addressee, the distance between the symbol and the symbolized also vanishes, since there is no need for communication. The structured field, necessary for communication by symbolic means, such as language or art, is missing. Without proper symbolization, the psychotic person lives in disordered dimensions of space and time. The conceptually ordered dimensions of space and time are predicated on the capacity for symbolization.

A question that invariably arises is how much the psychotic's severe relational confusion results from constitutional defects and how much depends on the quality of the early mother-child relationship. The two seem intertwined. Nor do we know how much the early mother-child relationship is influenced by the infant's constitutional givens. Yet, in any case, it can be assumed that the confused features of schizophrenics' drawings do reflect the symbiotic, undifferentiated mental structure of their "makers."

Whether a disturbed, symbiotic mother-child relationship is the cause or consequence of a disturbed symbol-forming capacity (and the probability is that the relation is circular), focusing on this aspect has proved useful in planning corrective treatment (Mahler, 1968; Ekstein and Wallerstein, 1954). On the other hand, it is good to keep in mind the probability of organic contributors to symbiotic (and therefore symbolization) pathology. Too much emphasis on the mother's "mistakes" may lead to a one-sided treatment approach that may stabilize some unfruitful paranoid attitude in the patient. (The latter is a particular danger in the treatment of nonpsychotic "symbiotic characters.")

Reitman (1951) is one who has chosen a neurophysiological approach to the study of psychotic art. Citing studies of the effects of brain lesions and mescaline on visual perception and body image, he attempts to unravel the peculiarities of schizophrenics' concept formation, as reflected in their art. He assumes a noxious agent affecting the temporo-parietal area of the cortex which destroys categorical thinking, eroding the body concept and consequently any delineated feeling of self. Without boundaries, the "self" is not distinct from its spatial and temporal surroundings.

Reitman observes that in schizophrenics, patients with certain brain lesions, and subjects under the influence of mescaline, similar perceptual and thought disturbances appear. In all these groups, ordered conceptual thinking tends to be replaced by *visual images*. Thinking in concrete visual images instead of true symbols is also characteristic of young children and is related to eidetic imagery (Jaensch, 1930). Reitman points out that in EEG studies of eidetic imagery and mescaline intoxication, the records showed changes in the alpha rhythm of the visual cortex with the onset of eidetic imagery, as well as with the appearance of visual hallucinations in mescaline-takers. The onset of visual hallucinations also coincided with alterations in space-time perception. In Reitman's opinion, these data support the "markedly physiological character" of visual thinking. He particularly emphasizes the similarity of the effects of mescaline to the impaired conceptual and increased pictorial thinking of schizophrenics. (The disintegration of concepts into concrete imagery might underlie the special urge for picture-making in schizophrenics.)

For Reitman, the weakening of conceptual thinking in the

schizophrenic stems from the body-image disturbance, the loosening of the experience of the individual's own body schemata as well as those of the bodies of others. Noncategorical thinking, then, would be a consequence of the loss of body boundaries, i.e., the merging of body and environment. And schizophrenics' paintings would be the outcome of their noncategorical thought processes. Reitman assumes that schizophrenics' urge for painting resembles a self-healing process, re-creating a world that is in harmony with their altered experience of space-time relations. The weird fusions of parts, the lack of figure-ground articulation, the transparencies, all are derived from the patient's noncategorical thinking. It is insufficient, he concludes, to interpret schizophrenic art solely or mainly in psychological terms; the physiological disturbance must be considered.

Reitman's neurologically oriented interpretation of schizophrenics' art work reminds us of the possibility of an alternative to an object relations perspective. Admittedly, most psychoanalysts today would be more inclined to approach the peculiarities of schizophrenic art in terms of symbiotic fixation and early mother-child interaction than to assume a noxious agent affecting the temporo-parietal cerebral cortex.

Nevertheless, in the framework of a book proposing a generic theory of symbolization it is important to emphasize the various ways one can look at the same phenomena. We need to remember that our attempt to impute meaning and order phenomena is dependent on the template formed by the mental symbols stored in our preconscious. Even the nature of what we consider a "fact" or "datum" is not unequivocally *given* from the outside but selectively constructed ("created") by the ever-symbolizing perception of the researcher. We see and think through the filter of our preexisting mental symbols. As Susanne Langer expresses it: "it is not the essential act of thought that is symbolization, but an act *essential to thought* and prior to it" (1942, p. 45).

My point here is that any particular scientific outlook represents only one possible way of organizing the raw material under consideration. Physicists seem to be more aware of this need for flexibility in conceptualizing phenomena than psychoanalysts. The Newtonian versus the quantum mechanics view, the wave versus the particle theory of light, these are accepted modes of different conceptualizations. In the psychoanalytic literature, however, one often gets the impression that one theoretical outlook is *the* correct one. I have already commented on how the structural model has replaced the topographic model. Similarly, the conceptual framework of object relations theory has practically superseded Freud's libido theory. Emphasis on object relations theory—significant and useful as it is—has also tended to push into the background the importance of genetic, constitutional, and neurological factors in psychic structuralization, or misstructuralization. It is not that differing points of view are absent, but one seldom hears acknowledgment that the organizing symbols behind one's outlook are, to some extent, subjectively chosen. We select our conceptual framework not only on the basis of intellectual judgment but also because it is congenial to our way of thinking and because the type of clinical work that follows from it suits our personality. Being aware of this unavoidable subjectivity does influence the tone and style of therapeutic communications. It introduces a necessary and therapeutically welcome tentativeness to all interpretations.

I hope this epistemological digression has clarified the need for *both* neurophysiological and object relations approaches to psychotic art. Reitman's suggestion of a neurological basis for picture thinking, as opposed to categorical thinking, might lead us to look for a neurological predisposition in severe cases of acting out where secondary-process thinking gets relegated to the background. I have called psychotic art a form of acting out. Let us now examine more specifically the relationship between picture thinking and such stereotyped impulsive behavior.

Acting Out and Picture Thinking

In my own practice I have noticed that acting-out patients tend to think in *pictures* and to have an extremely vivid visual sense.[3] Greenacre (1971), too, repeatedly points out the relationship between a heightened cathexis of the visual functions and acting out. This combination of acting out and picture thinking is well illustrated by the case of an unusually talented patient.

"My mother was always in bed, reading mystery stories and eating cottage cheese with crackers." This was Jim's repetitive description of his mother. This was *the* picture, and the image enraged him. Other phases of his life were recounted in similar frozen frames. Highly intelligent, Jim was successful not only as an artist, but also in a number of other professions. Indeed, he alternated between professions as well as between lifestyles and personal attachments. Changes in his life pattern were abrupt. His restless exhibitionistic tendencies seemed beyond control and caused much trouble.

This man hated and distrusted words. He experimented with various acting-out types of therapy while still in analysis. Hypnosis appealed to him, with its spectacular age-regression imagery (I believe he just produced the imagery without ever being in a hypnotic trance). After a while, however, he concluded it was not helpful. Given his distrust of words, analysis was problematic. What he called "free association" consisted of an avalanche of spectacular imagery, without any further

[3] As a student in Hungary, I assisted a court psychiatrist who found eidetic imagery to be frequent in juvenile delinquents.

work. The fact that in the very long run we did achieve something was helped along by a mutual good feeling between us and the fact that we did understand each other.

Jim needed a way of life that allowed many changes and unrestricted personal freedom. His talents helped him to be successful in spite of this need to follow new turns whenever his spirit—which was mainly represented by his eyes—moved him. Life for him was a succession of visually exciting phenomena which pulled him in new directions with almost magnetic force. Yet in the midst of all this seeming turmoil, his art remained central to his life. His unusual talents helped to make him successful.[4]

What I am calling "picture thinking" refers to a kind of concretistic thinking that relies more on *signs*, calling for immediate *reaction to*, than symbols, which evoke *thinking about*. Picture thinking, exactly because it is concretistic, is also connected to magic omnipotence of thought. The mental vision of a concrete picture carries with it the total conviction of perceived reality—Jim's picture of his mother left no room for doubt that this was "it," this was how his mother was. The picture was a sign indicating "mother." "Thinking about" something in a more flexible, many-sided way needs the distance implied in symbolic thinking. Acting-out people who live by picture-signs cannot do this. Picture thinking is less conceptually ordered than language thinking. To think in pictures is to represent things in a static relationship, as if caught in the snapshot of the moment. Within such a set image, it is difficult to symbolize the process of change in time. All that is seen is that single view. As we saw in the case of Jim, acting-out patients keep their past in their heads in the form of frozen, framed pictures.

[4] The biographies of such well-known artists as Gauguin, van Gogh, and Franz Marc suggest that they too showed an acting-out pattern of life, with sudden changes due to overpowering visual experiences. Less talented patients of this type have a much harder time in finding an acceptable life for themselves.

Working with these patients, one encounters particular difficulties because they are not willing, or perhaps they are not able, to decathect their mental picturebooks. They readily display their pictures as proof for the legitimacy of their claims—claims on parents, on the analyst, on the world, to concretely and possibly immediately rectify their childhood injuries. Guided by their picture-signals, they make snap judgments with absolute certainty and act accordingly. They do not take time to ponder and think *about*.

Patients of this type may manifest harmful transferences that are difficult to use for healing, and sometimes impossible to work through. Because they detect clues (signs) in everything they see, paranoid features color their world, and these distorted perceptions can become particularly intense, verging on the psychotic, in relation to the analyst. They may, for instance, perceive ominous signs in the analyst's face, in the placement of the couch or chair, in the arrangement of objects on the analyst's desk, in anything visible. And they "know" what everything means. There is no "maybe," no hypothetical thought. In a universe of signs, the meaning is automatically given. These patients' lack of the category of the potential or possible calls to mind Goldstein's (1939) description of brain-injured patients, who had lost what he called the "abstract" attitude to their environment.

The paranoid acting-out patient, living under the dictates of visual signs or signals, does not have the mental flexibility to keep up the "double frame" needed for symbolic perception in general and for a workable transference in particular. To be workable, the transference must be experienced in the key of "as if." Although reactions to the analyst are felt as real, "true," in the back of his or her mind the patient dimly realizes that what appears to be present reality is in fact only a reflection of the past.

The Pictures of Three Women

The following vignette condenses the cases of three women patients of the acting-out type. In some ways these three women were extremely similar to one another. All were in their thirties, single, highly intelligent, and functioning well in their chosen professions. Yet they were unsuccessful in what they, supposedly, wanted most—to settle down in a good marriage and secure family life. The three were all picture-thinkers, depending on visual signs instead of symbols, particularly in their relationships to men, but also in other aspects of their lives. One could call them infantile characters, without severe manifestations of acting out, except that their inappropriate judgments and "spontaneity" got them into painful situations. They were definitely not psychotic, although at times they exhibited paranoid reactions because they felt badly treated by others, by life in general. People, mainly men and office superiors, often "let them down" by not living up to their unrealistic expectations or by not treating them as "special," as deserving "special" treatment and indulgence.

These women were analyzable, although I refrained from genetic interpretations for a long time. The reason for my holding back was that this was exactly what these patients clamored for, what they had received in their previous (ineffective) treatments. They would have liked me to talk about their good and bad (split) introjects, about their early traumas, thus keeping their daily misfunctioning outside analytic observation. Like so many patients, they were willing to be in analysis as long as that process did not impel them to actually change. In contrast to their expectations and demands, I concentrated for quite a while, maybe the first third of their treatment, on exploring their way of mental functioning in all those situations they continually complained about—the daily "injustices" in which they were treated "unfairly."

My intention was to demonstrate to them the harmful consequences of their picture thinking. I wanted to show them the connection between thinking in picture-signs and inappropriate acting-out behavior which repetitively leads to frustration. They "hated" me for this approach. I was repeatedly reminded that an analyst is not supposed to deal with the present but should explore the past. They readily opened their "frozen" picturebooks of childhood injuries, replete with neat labels given by previous psychoanalytic interpretations.

Despite their annoyance with me, our work proceeded and they did develop usable transferences. They had enough mental flexibility to keep up the double-framed "as if" attitude necessary for a workable transference. Although they frequently expressed anger and hatred toward me, they were able to use the transference situation in its therapeutically symbolic aspect. They did not show the severely paranoid patient's total identification of the transference with "real reality." They never lost sight of the fact that while they might experience me as a nuisance, I was basically on their side and was working on their behalf. This flexibility could exist because their mental apparatus was not flooded with unmodulated aggression. In other words, there was "basic trust," which always indicates that the forces of Eros are in lead over those of Thanatos. True, these women frequently acted out in a childish, self-defeating way, but even this acting out was fueled by immature libidinal forces rather than by sadistic impulses. I think it was this constellation of the two basic "instincts" that enabled them to benefit from treatment, to produce real psychic change.

Let me clarify now these patients' sign-directed (instead of symbol-directed) functioning. A major complaint was that men would simply disappear after the first or second date. The first date routinely ended in bed, which made them wonder whether "jumping into bed too fast" was the mistake.

They were looking for a “rule” specifying the proper time lapse between the first meeting and sexual intercourse. The analyst was supposed to know this rule. The idea of a natural timing, stemming from the development of a relationship, did not occur to them. Instead of observing their own and the man’s feelings, they immediately painted detailed mental pictures depicting their future life together. They had no mental category with which to experience fantasizing as qualitatively different from realistic assessment. The first phone call conjured up a complete vision of the future with everything “set”—the wedding, the house they would live in, in one case even the flower pattern of the dishes and the wooden kitchen utensils. Before the first date, this woman saw herself in her future home as an “old-fashioned country housewife,” baking bread without the aid of modern gadgets. Whatever the expectations, the corresponding mental picture was etched sharply and colorfully. A strong wish immediately became a vivid picture and, in this way, clamored for “perceptual identity,” for its match in outside reality. If outside reality did not oblige, then the woman felt terribly hurt, insulted, angry and depressed. If a man failed to call back after the first date, she reacted as if a lover of long standing or a husband had betrayed her.

The frequent repetition of the same pattern did not modify either the expectations or behavior of these women. They did not learn from experience. Their self-made pictures indicated unambiguously how things “are”—they showed with certainty how the future had to be. In addition, there were the selected scenes of childhood disappointment, also inscribed in vivid visual form, which functioned as supporting evidence that the world owed them special indulgent treatment to rectify the past. Careless negligence on their part was expected to be overlooked. Such behavior often caused minor annoyance to others and major trouble to themselves.

These women lived in a universe of signs, where perceptions, wish fulfillment, imagery, and the visual disclosure of a certain future coincided. The phone call was a *sign* that indicated the man's total fascination, his readiness to wipe out all other women in his life, and his willingness to commit himself to life together. In this context of certainties, going to bed on the first date was not a casual sex act. It was the "understood" beginning to a long, already manifest life story. Sign reading does not allow for space to look across and reflect, or to reverse the situation and see it from the other's vantage point. We know from Piaget that reversible mental operations are the hallmark of adult thinking. Without reversibility, there is no category for the possible or conditional, only for what "is."

It is no wonder, then, that in a universe of such certainties, if the man did not call up after the first date, the woman felt that he had broken his contract and cheated her of what was not simply hinted at but *actually there*. Signs always indicate what is supposedly *there*. A corollary of such faulty sign thinking is intense mood fluctuation, which all my patients showed. Euphoria suddenly reverses into angry depression—a bipolarity analogous to that seen in manic-depressives.[5]

An important similarity in these women was their use of "play-acting," their cultivation of a childish "ingenue" spontaneity. They saw their behavior as cutely feminine, the opposite of compulsive and petty. And they expected others, including their analyst, to appreciate their cute "brattiness." One may wonder to what degree such hysteroid play-acting is "chosen" and controllable and how much it is compulsively driven by constitutional-instinctual factors. I don't know the

[5] For all we know, heightened visual thinking may be part of manic-depressive pathology. Indeed, I have heard from a Hungarian physician that a visual hypersensitivity theory for manic-depressive disorder has been proposed in the USSR (Gabor Korosy, personal communication).

answer but assume the working hypothesis "as if" it were controllable. This is a double-pronged working hypothesis which fits these patients' "double-pronged" character. Indeed, these patients seemed to mix and confuse reality and play-acting with the ease of Pirandello characters. At times they even play-acted their play-acting, mocking themselves in a childish sing-song voice or caricaturing their imitation of a "naughty brat." Yet such confused "play" may serve as a vehicle for significant emotional communications. This manneristically "playful" style reminded me of the court jester who dons the fool's cap in order to say what he really means but can't say without the "play."

These patients' transference behavior reflected this quality of play within the play. Their reactions were intense, noisy, with a histrionic tinge. Often their transference responses were based on visual "perceptions" saturated with unreal meaning. They saw in my face or in my movements that I was overjoyed or annoyed at their arrival. All of them felt that in one way or another they were "special" for me, either my favorite or the patient I particularly dreaded. They took similar extreme positions in their attitudes toward me, supposedly in response to what they had perceived. "I hate you; you want me to suffer" alternated with "I love you; you are my good mother—but of course that's all transference." The last shows how, in their verbalizations, they preempted all the twists of transference and reality before I could say a word. The mocking here underlines that they of course know about the "transference play."

In contrast to the situation with paranoid borderline or paranoid obsessive-compulsive patients, the task with these play-acting patients was to help them see the reality side to their transference feelings. Sometimes I pointed out that they used their play as a defense, sometimes I just talked past their play-acting, as if it didn't exist, and addressed my remarks to what I took as serious in their "mock" communications. At such times they stopped the "cuteness" and became sad or angry. They felt quite uncomfortable if I ignored their "fool's cap" and talked to them as adults. What is important is that secondary-process language communication was able to reach them, and increasingly so with time. I tried to focus their attention on their own mannered functioning, connecting their inappropriate behavior to many of the mishaps they so frequently complained about.

The untoward consequences of their picture thinking were dealt with in a similar vein. The aim was to make their infantile picture-fantasy thinking ego-dystonic, to relegate it to the category of symptom, instead of cherished attribute. Distancing these patients' self-perception from their "spontaneous" acting-out behavior was the first step in transforming their sign-directed functioning into symbol-directed, thought-about action. Reflective self-observation ran contrary to their ego ideal. The danger was that they would become "gray" adults instead of colorful children. To counter this idealized "child" image, I demonstrated how each time they got into trouble with superiors, with men, with time or with money, these frustrations resulted from their "spontaneous," unthought-about actions. I had to show repeatedly how their picture-signs made for frustration. For example, they were always late for everything. According to their mental picturebook, they could get from one place to another in no time, since taxis or buses were visualized as waiting for them and dashing through traffic-less streets to their destination. It was somebody's fault (not their own) if this expectation was not borne out, as it never was. Money was spent on pretty things they saw and *had* to have, from dresses to luxury apartments—with total disregard for whether or not they could afford it. Loans and charge-card debts accumulated until they got themselves into serious financial trouble. An interesting common feature was their unwillingness to keep track of checks; consequently, important checks bounced, the telephone was disconnected, the electricity turned off. All this was somehow the "world's" fault. An unbalanced checkbook gave them the feeling of "infinite possibilities," since the limits were simply not visible. Another common feature was the conviction that they were being "victimized" by the petty rules and habits governing life. They should have been "exceptions."

In analysis, distancing and thinking about were introduced by my verbalizations, which stopped the patients' flow of words and forced them to listen. They produced a rush of what they considered to be "free associations," leaping from picture to picture without thinking about any of them. Working with these patients, I could almost literally feel the energy expenditure needed to *bind* their cathexes, at least for a while, to one topic, one instance in their lives. It was hard work to slow down their runaway verbal-visual productions.

These patients' "script" for analysis did not include effortful, slow work. Analysis was supposed to be a stage for unimpeded verbal acting out and play-acting, for denial of responsibility. Any painful turn of events was to be explained as a consequence of the parents' or siblings' misdeeds in the patient's early childhood. Moreover, the analyst was supposed to be delighted with the patient's spontaneity in talking and picture-making. These women started their acting the minute they entered my apartment. With their very first step on the stage, they commented on whatever struck their eyes. Leaving the waiting room was a noisy process, accompanied by laughs, groans, sighs, or mutterings. They came the laborious settling on the couch, fussing with the pillow, trying to shift position so as to face the analyst, adjusting the angle of the window blinds, occasionally asking for water, aspirin, even a thread and needle to fix some rent in their clothing.

My not reacting to this commotion was taken as much for an insult as my commenting on what I believed to be behind these histrionics (childish craving for attention). I was supposed to revel in their spontaneity.

My verbal interventions were simple. The concretistic thinking of the picture-thinker has to be met on almost, although not quite, the same concrete level. Only by little steps can one lift discussion of their stories to a more general, abstract realm. That is the way to establish distance between patients as "actors" (acting subjects) and their actions. As I noted above, I began with functional explications of their action patterns rather than genetic interpretations, because the latter would have been picked up as concrete "proof" and added to their mental picturebooks as "liabilities" from the past to be used as "credits" for future claims. Even the most correct "historical" interpretations would have been assimilated into these patients' mental picturebooks as showing yet again their eternal victimization. I could see this from the way they used good interpretations from their previous analyses.

Some theoretical remarks are in order here. Using Piaget's concepts, we can state that a mental schema of signs assimilates incoming material precipitously ("voraciously"), with almost no accommodation to the incoming content. The kind of slower, distanced taking in present with a symbolic schema is nonexistent with signs. A sign schema acts like a huge mouth devouring anything new it comes in contact with. This preponderance of assimilation over accommodation makes picture-thinkers' mental functioning rigidly subjective, or egocentric, which is very much the way young children think (Piaget, 1936, 1945). Piaget calls this the "adualistic" stage (borrowing the concept from Lévy-Bruhl) because the "other" does not exist with independent substantiality for the child at this developmental level (the same holds for the chronologically adult picture-thinker). The "other" is not really an "other," only "there," expected to fit into the child's (or picture-thinker's) already-existing mental picture-sign schema. Reversible thought operations are not possible under these self-centered conditions. The mental schemata work only one way—taking in wholesale, without forming a new, more complex mental schema by way of equilibrating the two dialectic functions (assimilating the new to the old while also appropriately accommodating the old to the new). Well-equilibrated new schemata result in good adaptation to the outside, with simultaneous consideration for the internal conditions. The subjective inside and the objective outside are then well balanced. Thought processes, judgments, are anchored in both poles of this well-equilibrated structure: in the subjective inside as well as in the objective outside. All true symbols span the distance between these two poles. Mental schemata made up of balanced symbol-structures do not immediately "eat up" what comes along, but "take their time" to perform time-consuming mental acts, such as surveying, comparing, judging. It is through these mental acts that we are able to find the proper "filing place" for the new within the old, so that together they form a new schema, a new mental symbol-gestalt. Time and perceptual distance are needed for this complex new form creation.

My childlike, picture-thinking patients did not have well-equilibrated mental schemata. The image of a "devouring mouth" seems an appropriate metaphor, for it is more than a simple description of the way the new stimuli are assimilated into a preexisting mental schema. "Devouring mouth" conjures up the intense oral craving of the young child. My acting-out patients were fixated at the impatient, devouring, oral stage. Oral incorporation is immediate, with no "buffer zone" between taking in through perception and action. Objective qualities of the "outside" are ignored, and mental processes are directed by purely subjective feelings and wishes. Inevitably, ensuing actions collide with outside reality, which exists in its own right whether or not the "actor" denies its separate existence. Such an actor "acts" out, totally guided by his or her own desires, which gain immediate access to transformation into pictures. These pictures, then, function as signs and drive for direct action.

My patients' thoughtless, repetitive actions often left them shipwrecked on the resistant substance of reality. Picture-signs only allow for what is there, within grasp. They cannot represent what is *absent*, contingent ("if . . . then"), possible but not certain, wished for but unlikely or impossible. Signs do not carry multiple connotations; only symbols do. The relation of the symbol to the symbolized is always one-to-many, for although it articulates one aspect of the multitude of potential meanings contained in the raw material, the non-articulated meanings still reverberate within it.[6] In other words, each symbol condenses a number of meanings. Every word, if truly used as a symbol, carries such condensation of meanings, called connotations. In true communication, word-symbols are not perceived rigidly but within an aura of connotations, varying with context and tone of voice. Because they do not hear the connotations, communication is especially problematic with sign-directed patients.

Given the intelligence of my acting-out patients, it was easy to mistake for meaningful communication what in actuality was not that. The analyst talks in symbols, but the patient may take in these words as signs without subtle connotations. For the patient, then, these word-signs indicate one concrete thing with certainty. Verbal and nonverbal communications

[6] Therapeutic implications of this proposition have been explicated by Angyal (1965), who describes the therapeutic process in terms of carving out a new symbol-structure from the multidimensional phenomena present in the patient's unconscious. A new form of symbolization equals new conscious meaning.

are registered by the patient as definite orders: "Do" or "Don't do." With my women patients, for example, the way I dressed indicated that they should dress "in the same dull way." My marital status was crucial. If I did not have a husband, it *meant* they should not have one either. Interpretations were taken in either as signs of love for and pride in the patient, or as insults. "You will be proud of me" was the usual introduction to a report of something good that had happened. My vacations "meant" I personally disliked them. All these reactions indicate their denial of our separateness and the concreteness of their thinking.

It was because of these patients' tendency toward "one-dimensional" intake of interpretations that I decided first to concentrate on explicating the way their minds worked rather than offer more "genetic" historical interpretations. Let me give an example that deals with their first-mentioned cathected topic: how to find a husband. My explications followed more or less the following lines. The gradations that develop with time in a relationship did not exist for them. I have already described how a *whole* picture-story would light up in their minds the instant a man called them. Their mental crystal ball showed the future with absolute certainty. The future was *there*, in the present. There is nothing to evaluate or think about if everything is unambiguously given, just as there is nothing to evaluate or think about when perceiving a traffic sign. The traffic sign tells one exactly what to do right then and there. To ponder over the meaning of a traffic sign gets one in trouble. One has to act immediately in one definite way. One cannot wait for the development of a "meaningful relationship" between the sign and the driver before obeying the order of the sign. In contrast, in reading a novel, one doesn't usually decide after the first page whether one likes it or not. Our appreciation of a good novel depends on a relationship to the author's style and the characters, on our involvement in the universe of the book. Time is needed for this involvement to develop.

Starting a new relationship in one's life is more like getting involved in a new novel than like seeing a traffic sign. Yet these women reacted to a man's phone call as though it were a traffic sign and not the first page in a story, which might have innumerable unpredictable ends.[7] Even though, interestingly enough, these women had no patience with novels either, my concrete similes did have an effect. The imagery I offered was visual enough to make an impression. Slowly, the idea of change over time, the concept of an abstract dimension of time along which life processes take shape, acquired form in their minds. They realized that there is a past, a present, and a future and that these three tenses exert different functions. They learned that past experience can be used in *planning* for the future; the past does not have to invade the present, and consequently the future, in a repetitive way. What Lewin (1935, 1936) describes as organization of behavior events along the dimension of time was my aim with these patients. Their speeded-up reactions-actions had to be slowed down by interposing the processes of observation and reflection. With these mental operations, they could change their sign-releasers into the bricks of thinking, i.e., into mental symbols.

Talking to my patients in secondary-process language about their "primary-process" behavior was instrumental in establishing reflective perception and reflective thinking. Listening is a form of identification with the speaker and if practiced repeatedly, under propitious transference conditions, it can change the mental structure of the listener. By listening to me, they could develop the distance and slowed-down tempo necessary for secondary-process thinking and symbolization.

[7] With acting-out patients knowledgeable about psychology, I have used the comparison to the sign-stimulus response of animals (see Chapter 5).

Out of a previously unobserved mass of confused behavior, certain features were lifted out and delineated as "things" to look at and think about. The Janus-face of true symbolization became evident in these patients: While symbolic thinking distanced them from an immediate experience of their past, it also served as a bridge, connecting across this distance. Gradually they came to reflect on how their frustrations came about and what their own share in this was. They reported fewer mishaps in their daily life, although they still had to pay the price (metaphorically and literally) for thoughtless actions in the past. The style of their speech and movement changed, too. The speech was slower, more articulated in intonation and punctuated by short pauses; it lost its child-like sing-song quality. Entering the office ceased to be a noisy invasion. They came straight in and lay down ready to work. In dealing with others, they felt less victimized as their expectations of "special" treatment decreased. They were better able to follow rules and keep some objective distance between themselves and others.

At this point our work on their way of recalling childhood memories should be described. Their memory for details was excellent, approaching eidetic imagery. But the catalogue of recalled images was rigidly repetitive—everything proved their victimized childhood. Once in a while, and increasingly more often with time, this litany was disrupted by an "unfitting" chance remark; a memory image slipped in that did not fit the usual picture. For instance, a mother who was usually described as resembling a psychotic "bag lady," totally unconcerned about her home and children, suddenly was referred to as a good cook. Or a father, "frozen" in the image of a self-involved, detached and absent man, was suddenly remembered taking his daughter to the park or movies. For a while I did not comment on these discrepancies, in order not to seem bent on "catching" them in contradictions and also to let the "unfitting" imagery accumulate.

Later, I contrasted these chance remarks with the stereotyped listing of devastating memories that depicted a totally terrible childhood. Again, the point was to demonstrate just how their picture thinking worked, how they were so used to pushing one button and lighting up pictures that made them feel victimized and sorry for themselves. I did not question the truthfulness of these memories but only pointed out their preselected nature. Theirs was a carefully chosen picturebook, guaranteed to evoke in them the same reaction every time. Memories that did not fit this purpose were simply left out of the catalogue. The discrepant images did not emerge from the repressed unconscious; they had simply not been "lit up" because ambiguity could not be tolerated. Sign language does not tolerate ambiguities. Real life, on the other hand, consists mostly of ambiguous, multilayered meanings. My patients' "new" memories did not arise from analytic reconstruction. They were not lifted from the unconscious. They were all there, at the patients' disposal, except that they chose not to put them into their repertoire of memory-pictures.

Thanks to their "basic trust" in the analytic process and in me, and after much work on the harmfulness of their repetitive acting out triggered by rigid picture thinking, they allowed new details to enter their memory picturebooks. The formerly excluded pieces had to be integrated into the old picture. This reorganization necessitated awareness of contradictory features within the same gestalt. In the course of this reorganization, their previous, unambiguous "sign-releasers" turned into more complex memory-symbols that evoked more complex reactions. We worked on the more complex reorganization of their preconscious. The preconscious changed from a colorful picturebook into a storehouse of true symbols, isomorphic with the much more ambiguous nature of their childhood conditions than what they wanted to believe previously.

That these women in actuality always knew the truth, but preferred to disregard it, fits denial much more than repression. To organize their thinking with complex symbols seemed "pedantic" (a favorite disparaging word). But they were never surprised at the emergence of their "new" memories; they knew that they knew them all the time. This kind of reaction convinced me that therapy had to concentrate on reorganizing their preconscious. This met with resistance because in their eyes, their mental pictures were wonderfully intense and colorful, and they believed that their acting out represented spontaneous honesty and something artistic. The fear was that thinking about something would make them drab, compulsively "neat," boring. Showing them the connection between their thoughtless acts and their failures in life did help. But particularly helpful was my drawing their attention to the compulsively repetitive character of their "spontaneous" actions, as well as to the amount of time and "boring" effort needed to straighten out the consequences of their heedless behavior. The "boringness" of their mindless behavior impressed them. They began to realize that the time gained by better organization could be spent on developing certain talents. Previously they had shied away from long-range projects, and learning technical skills seemed too effortful and dull. Speedy spontaneity was equated with being artistic.

A distinction needs to be made here. Artists, composers, and scientists do experience an accelerated spurt of activity at the height of the creative process. At these times creative thinking has the fluidity and speed usually attributed to primary-process functioning. What happens, however, is not "regression in service of the ego" (Kris, 1952), but a kind of accelerated "progression." Moreover, this speeded-up functioning is but one phase in the creative process (which involves a lot of hard work and thinking about). Nor is it usually a *modus operandi* in the artist's everyday life (though some visually creative artists' lives do show acting-out features). In contrast, with our acting-out picture-thinkers, high-speed functioning is a compulsively driven manifestation, indicative of the deficiency in symbol formation. It leads to repetitive frustration, not an art product. (The "creative spells" of psychotics show this compulsively driven quality.)

As my patients changed their mental picture-signs into mental symbols, their compulsively restless activities were replaced by thought-about goal-oriented actions. They had more time to follow up on their talents and more patience to allow for the development of better relationships. Mental symbols are the proper tools for realistic dialogue between the person and her (or his) environment, for building a traversable pathway between wish and gratification.

But why did these women become fixated at the childish level of picture thinking? Was their fixation the consequence of various early deprivations, or were they constitutionally visualizers? It should be obvious by now that I believe that the choice of neurosis or character disorder has constitutional roots. Reitman's (1951) belief in a physiological underpinning for visual thinking and Goldstein's (1939) neurological perspective on "concrete" versus "abstract" thinkers were cited in this regard. (My selection of these authors is of course already a function of my own mental symbols.)

In my presentation, I have purposely not specified the traumatic events in these patients' childhoods. The same traumatic situations can be reacted to in a multitude of ways. Given her background, it would have been understandable if one of these women had become an acting-out delinquent, but she did not. Another might have been expected to be a withdrawn "inner symbolizer," a type I shall describe in Part III. The third woman could have become a compulsively orderly person if reaction formation or counteridentification had been adopted as a defense. Yet all three "chose" to be infantile picture-thinkers. Visual fantasizing was their main activity from early childhood on. This fantasizing was their "real" life, furnishing them with everything they wished for. Their fantasies were accompanied by active, though not particularly creative, play. What is interesting is that, although these women came from very different family backgrounds, their behavior patterns seemed extremely similar, both in childhood and later when I met them. I take this to suggest that constitutional factors were decisive in their "choice" of character disturbance.

These women's willingness and capacity to change followed, I believe, from their basically nonsadistic nature. They did not enjoy causing others (or themselves) pain, not even in fantasy. As I noted before, however unrealistic, urgent, and egocentric their behavior was, it was basically fueled by childish libidinal strivings. The aim was unification rather than destruction. Considerable reactive anger followed their repetitive frustrations, but this anger never drove them toward revenge, or even revenge fantasies. Their anger led to childish, verbal temper tantrums, which were forgotten about when the next unrealistic hope appeared on the horizon. One could say that these women did have some sort of "love affair with the world" (Greenacre, 1957), however unrealistic. Primitive as the forces of Eros were, they were still usable for therapy. Their pleasure-seeking could, for instance, be channeled into the wish to make a better life for themselves. They were able to invest analysis and the analyst with basic trust and active hope. They had no hidden agenda to turn analysis into a failure and thus prove the degree of damage they had suffered in childhood. Nor did they harbor the profound feelings of guilt that so often lead to negative therapeutic reactions (Freud, 1920).

Metapsychological Considerations on Symbolization Deficiency

My picture-thinking patients exhibited *nonsymbolization*, rather than desymbolization due to repression. As we have seen, in these patients the preconscious "container" held colorful pictures of concrete events, which functioned as *signs* driving toward immediate action. Their wishes and desires entered the preconscious freely, where they obtained immediate pictorial expression. Their wishes were pictorially *presented*, not symbolically *re*-presented. At best one might call their pictures protosymbols, somewhat similar to the infant's supposed use of primary-process, hallucinatory wish fulfillment. The lack of symbol-structures in their preconscious was not due to repression and ensuing desymbolization. Their "mental transformer" was too speeded up for symbol formation.

Acting out, if driven by unsadistic picture-signs, has a very different character from acting out driven by unsymbolized instinctual urges that were kept from the representational region of the preconscious due to the function of the repression barrier. The former is more likely to exhibit unrealistic "storybook" features (much as in the above examples), while the latter is more likely to exhibit a certain fierceness characteristic of sadistic impulses. Sadistic impulses are more guilt-provoking, consequently more defended against by the repression barrier, than are childish erotic desires. Unamalgamated forces of Thanatos are the most dangerous motivating forces. (This is not to deny that proper amalgamation of Eros and Thanatos is needed for active creativity). These forces drive toward fierce action without symbolic representation in the preconscious. Unmitigated sadistic impulses are not gestalt-forming but gestalt-destructive impulses. In contrast, the plethora of "pretty pictures" in my patients' preconscious utilized forces of Eros (no matter in what unrealistic form those forces operated) for their formation. Had these women been able to distinguish between fantasy and reality, their pretty pictures could have been used to entertain themselves by looking at their "wishful fantasies," the way people enjoy movies without mixing up what they see on the screen with reality. Except, these patients did mix up movies with reality also.

Repetitiveness as a Primary Indicator of Symbolization Deficiency

A deficiency in symbolization always results in *stereotyped repetitiveness*. We have encountered this phenomenon in psychotic art and in picture-thinking, acting-out patients. The missymbolization found in symptom neurotics also engenders maladapted repetitive behavior, even if the general level of functioning appears to be more goal-oriented than that of the acting-out person. For instance, obsessive characters, with their extreme organization and frequent "super-intellectual" bent, also suffer from stereotyped rigidity. They lack the freedom to introduce new forms of pleasurable activity into their life patterns. They are particularly inhibited in activities that require the freedom of playful imagination.

Even though all forms of serious neurosis result in stereotyped rigidity of actions by curtailing freedom of choice, let us stay for a while with the obsessional characters because they appear to be the diametric opposite of the pleasure-oriented acting-out patients already discussed. Obsessives' behavior is not frenzied, not speeded up. Indeed, there appears to be slowness, hesitation. They *seem* to have the "buffer zone" of "thinking about." Yet obsessives' "thinking about" lacks direction; it is circular and repetitive, often not leading to any action. This circular thinking—or talking (in the analytic session)—is their verbal form of repetitive "acting out." The seemingly playful acting-out person and the obsessive are equally victimized by the straitjacket of stereotyped rigidity; neither has the choice to do otherwise than be stuck in his or her habitual pattern. The range of operation for both is narrowed.

Both types suffer from the misfunctioning of the preconscious, from the lack of full-fledged *true* symbols. The acting-out person's dependence on signs instead of symbols has been discussed at length. In contrast, the obsessive does use symbols to form an orderly cognitive map, where mental representations are neatly distanced from each other and from the self. There is no confusion between inside and outside. What is missing, however, is the experience of the mutual immanence of these two regions, the feeling that the inside imbues the outside and vice versa. There is no joyful experience of life, because in their disconnected state, both the inner and the outer worlds are experienced as arid and affectless. True symbols, remember, both *connect* and separate. In the obsessive, symbols effect only distance, without the "bridging over" that links subjective affects to objective outside reality. The obsessive's symbols are not truly Janus-faced, with one eye looking out, while the other keeps in touch with the emotionally alive id urges. It is because of this one-sided (toward the outside) functioning that the obsessive's symbols begin to resemble signs (labels) in their narrow, one-to-one denotation, lacking in rich emotional connotation. In other words, the obsessive's symbols do not function as chords, reverberating with the "undertones" contained in the manifold "ground" that strives for expression. They are detached notes, isolated from the urges in the id. (That is the reason why these patients' behavior does not exhibit the pressured, heedless action we saw in the driven, acting-out patients, whose sign-"symbols" lacked touch with objective outside reality.)

In contrast to the acting-out patients whose wishes gained immediate access to pictorial presentation, obsessional characters function with a strong repression barrier, which blocks the dangerous id urges from freely entering the preconscious. The dynamic organization fits Freud's model of an organized but bellicose ego in a constant state of vigilance, guarding against any invasion from the id (which would endanger its organization).

At this point the question can be asked: Are the obsessive's id urges indeed more dangerous than those of other people—specifically, than those of the picture-thinking women patients? And, if the answer is "yes," still more questions remain. Is this dangerous quality innate, or is the fierceness of "instinctual impulses" due to the intransigence of the repression barrier, which in turn might have been established in response to a more-than-usual early fearfulness and its corollary—a precociously developed, overstrict superego?

It is important to keep these questions in mind, even though I doubt the existence of a generally valid answer. Theorizing can easily hypothesize cause-and-effect relations for either sequence of these two phenomena. Extreme early fear of "instincts" and precocious superego development might be derived from sadistic impulses, *or* the other way around. The best is to stay with clinical observations and not press the issue of the "true" causal sequence.

Freud's "model" case history for obsessive-compulsive characters was that of the Rat Man (1909). In 1913 he wrote his essay on the predisposition for obsessional neurosis. Sadistic impulses and the anal-erotic phase of libido development were assumed to play the main role in the choice of this form of neurosis. There is no need to repeat here the Rat Man's symptomatology. We all know his compulsively repetitive verbalizations and thought processes. They were concerned with anal-sadistic punishment fantasies and guilt about the possibility of causing people harm or death.

My own work with severely obsessive-compulsive patients bears out the main outline of Freud's description. My patients were exceedingly repetitive in their speech and life patterns. The highly intelligent ones were in intellectual touch with their anal-sadistic impulses and verbalized them repetitively in the fashion I characterized as circular, "verbal acting out." The less intelligent ones were less, or not at all, introspective and displayed more "classically" compulsive symptoms (cryptosymbols). Depressed mood, concern with disabling illness and death, suicide fantasies characterized all of them. Revenge fantasies intermingled with guilt for having caused harm in the past or the likelihood of causing harm in the future. For whatever basic reason, the "instinctual" urges of these patients were sadistic. Loving erotic fantasies were conspicuously absent. They were afraid of the "evil" within themselves, of the danger they could bring to their object world if their controls were loosened. One might call these patients "Thanatos-driven" since their psychic world was saturated with darkness and the feeling of doom (the opposite of the previous group's erotically tinged "pretty pictures").

With their rational cognitive map and strict superego injunctions, these patients did not get themselves into tangible trouble (unlike the picture-thinkers). They performed their tasks well, kept to time schedules strictly, balanced their checkbooks conscientiously. Some produced outstanding intellectual work. The trouble was the total lack of the subjective experience of fulfillment. They functioned and achieved joylessly as if driven by relentlessly repetitive orders, as if forced to do what they did and unable to initiate change. The fear was that once off the track they might become destructive to others and to themselves—and they might have been right.

The superego transformation of obsessional characters needs much time, much work on their stunted libidinal impulses, for a sudden loosening of controls indeed might result in destructive acts. The forces of Eros need kindling (or liberating, or developing, or "infusion"—whatever the proper term may be) and fusion with those of Thanatos, before the obsessive-compulsive personality can create enjoyable changes in his or her life. Amalgamation of the antithetical instinctual drives lightens the intrapsychic atmosphere, in contrast to the fierceness of urges under the condition of instinctual defusion. The darkly and chronically depressed obsessive character need the strong repression barrier as long as their impulses are *experienced* as fierce and destructive. Exceedingly intense "countercathexes" are needed to keep up the order within the preconscious ego. Primary repression as well as "after-repression" are at work, interfering with activities which could be fulfilling for all psychic "systems," for the *whole* person. The lack of synergic cooperation between the unconscious and the preconscious-conscious "systems" precludes the fulfillment that accompanies the "multiple function" of actions (Waelder, 1936).

"Lack of synergic cooperation" means lack of an isomorphic match between unconscious id content and its preconscious expressive form. The trouble is that the preconscious form is not truly expressive of the "deep content" that strives for formed expression. This "mismatch" may result in cryptosymbols or in an ordered preconscious "territory" lacking meaningful contact with its unconscious instinctual-emotional "ground." This intrapsychic split-segmentation lends a detached, ritualized quality to the manifest behavior of obsessively defended persons. They give the feeling of a certain emotional flatness and inauthenticity, not because of "affectations" but because of the lack of some unevenness which goes with emotional spontaneity. The split intrapsychic organization of the obsessive-compulsive becomes more marked with time because the repressed content's striving "upward" necessitates more and more intense countercathexes. Occasional, seemingly unprovoked, angry emotional outbursts indicate the periodic breakdown of the repression barrier. In between these outbursts, the rigid repetitiveness of behavior increases.

Let us take a glimpse back at the dynamics of repression, desymbolization, and the "return of the repressed." This will clarify the genesis and function of repetitiveness as a primary indicator of symbolization deficiency.

Briefly: The delineated form of a preconscious, perceptible symbol disintegrates in consequence of repression. It becomes *desymbolized.*[8] In loosening form, repression acts to "unbind" energy. This lends pressuring, primary-process mobility to repressed content. This pressure contributes to the "upwardly mobile" tendency of the repressed, the "urge" to reenter the preconscious in some perceptible form. The "striving" of the unformed toward expression in a formed gestalt is a universal principle (Portmann, 1956). Formed gestalts bind energy and thus lend stability to any system. The desymbolized content's "urge" toward resymbolization works in this direction of creating a better-equilibrated psychic system; it works toward closure, in this case, "reclosure."

Zeigarnik's (1927) experiments are relevant to this point. Subjects were allowed to finish some tasks but interrupted before finishing others. Although a considerably longer time was spent on the finished tasks, later, when subjects were

[8] Recall that my view on repression and desymbolization counters Freud's idea that repressed material stays unchanged by time in the unconscious and that, when repression is lifted, the person simply perceives what has been hidden from consciousness but kept in the *same form* it had before repression. These differing perspectives imply different beliefs about the function of psychoanalytic treatment.

asked to list *all* the tasks they could remember, unfinished tasks were recalled ninety percent more often than finished ones. In other words, the unfinished openness of gestalts impelled memory with particular strength to return to tasks that were interrupted. Zeigarnik interprets the results in terms of the incomplete gestalt's inherent "striving" or dynamic pressure, toward closure. The repressed, desymbolized material's striving to reappear in delineated symbolized form in the preconscious suggests the same push of incomplete mental content toward closure, toward forming a complete gestalt.

The repression barrier, however, prevents the "returning content" from reconstructing a "good" gestalt. The countercathectic forces interrupt the isomorphic matching between the upward-striving unconscious content and its meaningfully fitting preconscious form. The highly energized repressed content might "manage to work its way" back into the organized preconscious, but only under the condition of blending into the form of a *not*-adequately-expressive preconscious symbol. Had this form adequately expressed the sense of the repressed content, it would not have been "allowed" its perceptible form. Some modicum of representation in the preconscious-conscious system is permissible precisely because the cryptosymbol does not reveal its real meaning.

However, because of its delineated gestalt, the cryptosymbol *formally* fits into the preconscious and can be perceived and supposedly understood by the symbolizer, although its real meaning eludes him or her. Symptoms "fit" into the "style" of the preconscious. Because of this organized quality of symptoms, neurotic behavior does not exhibit the unthought-about drivenness of acting out. But within the area shaped by their symptoms, neurotics think about the wrong thing. The information given by the cryptosymbols (symptoms) is misleading. Consequently, the actions they lead to cannot have satisfactory results. The task dictated by the symptom is never finished since its goal-setting is wrong; it is not a goal conducive to reducing the tension of the original unconscious urge striving for symbolized expression. Thus, like Zeigarnik's subjects, neurotics have to return over and over again to their unfinished task, since the basic motivational tension is never reduced by their cryptosymbol-directed action. Symptomatic actions therefore cannot result in subjective satisfaction. Missymbolization drives its "carrier" into futile, compulsively repetitive behavior.

The case of Sarah, presented below, clearly illustrates the effects of a strong repression barrier in a compulsively defended personality. The stereotyped rigidity and chronic low-grade depression of this patient bear out my theoretical statements with regard to obsessive-compulsive character organization.

The Case of Sarah

Sarah, a Midwestern woman from a puritanical, religious family, complained of periodic intense rheumatic pains in her right shoulder and right arm. She visited many physicians, received injections, took medications, but nothing helped. To Sarah, her pain conveyed the message that she *had* to visit a physician, and if one medication did not work, she had to try another. Since I believed her pain was a cryptosymbol, hiding its real meaning, I encouraged her to talk more about it and to describe the circumstances when it became bad. Usually very "obedient" and respectful of authority (rigid reaction formation), Sarah strongly objected to my suggestion. Rheumatic pain had nothing to do with analysis; it belonged in the realm of medicine. She had not come to me to cure her rheumatism but to help lift her generally depressed mood.

Her pain was none of my business; the doctor would give her the proper injections and medication. When I reminded her that the injections didn't seem to help much, she replied, "Yes, they do help." By now she was shouting—something totally uncharacteristic for her, with her rigid good manners. Before the shots, she explained, she had had pains all the time; now she was free of them for weeks. They returned only when she visited her parents (a monthly event for this woman in her forties). It was the sudden difference in climate between New York and the Midwest that brought out her pain. "Maybe you can change the climatic conditions?" she asked very sarcastically, again in a tone totally uncharacteristic of her.

I knew we were in good, hot territory, but I also knew that the work would be long and arduous because her repression barrier was extremely intransigent. Strict principles of right and wrong defined what she was able (willing) to perceive, blocking out anything that didn't fit. The result was an extremely impoverished dialogue between herself and the world, as well as within herself. She believed, as her parents had taught her, that "we don't hate anybody." Fantasizing was "bad." Instead of fantasizing, reading fiction, or going to the movies, she should read the Bible, something her family did daily.

All this did not augur well for free association. When her previous analyst asked her to free-associate, she would utter rows of single words, meaninglessly strung together, as if she were reading a dictionary. On being asked by her previous analyst for imagery, for pictures, she reacted by reciting "triangle, square, circle, red, blue, white," and so on. This went on for three years. (If she only could have borrowed some pages from my other patients' colorful mental picturebooks!) Sarah's preconscious was a sterile catalogue of objects, a "dependable" cognitive map to guide her along the straight and narrow path. Just how "righteous" this path was could be seen in her habit of repeatedly recalculating all the previous years' taxes to make sure there was no mistake. Once she found that five years before she had unwittingly cheated Uncle Sam of five dollars. She asked an expert how to rectify this error and learned that there is an office to which one can send checks to make up for previous tax evasions, no explanations needed. She immediately dispatched the five dollars to "right" her "lawless" behavior.

Sarah's ideal was to be principled and virtuous, which she felt she was. This gave her some satisfaction, in "principle" at least, but it was not enough to lift her chronically joyless, depressed mood. Actually Sarah never admitted feeling depressed. Before analysis, depression, as a mood, was not symbolized in her mind; it was not a "figure" but only the drab, gray atmosphere of an unshaped background. Sarah rigidly plodded along her path, carrying out her duties; she hardly expected life to be a "bowl of cherries." (Her speech was filled with virtuous clichés.) In fact, if it hadn't been for the advice of a minister, God's servant, she would never have thought of psychoanalysis. Sarah had a church-connected job in a progressive church community, where several of her coworkers and some ministers had been psychoanalyzed. They noticed this woman's extreme rigidity, her compulsive work habits, and her generally depressed mood. She followed up on the minister's advice because it came from the right, "superego"-approved source. I assume she also felt unhappy, but on her own Sarah would never have undertaken such a "selfish" project. Indeed, she voiced the hope that her work (which was already very good) would improve with analysis. Interestingly, her only circumscribed symptom, the rheumatic arm and shoulder pains, developed just after the long talk with the minister who referred her for analysis. (This was three years before I met her.) That made the beginning of her visits to rheumatism specialists and to an analyst coincide.

This coincidence made no impression on Sarah. For her, there was no "meaning" in a physical symptom, except as a sign of physical disorder. The pain indicated the presence of rheumatism, which "meant" one should go to a doctor. To me, however, the timing of the symptom, coincident with the minister's psychologically oriented talk (the first such occasion in Sarah's life), suggested that in the course of that conversation some part of her ironclad repression barrier had been loosened enough to let her unacceptable, denied anger leak through. Now, if these feelings had not been stopped, they might have pushed their way into the preconscious and found the matching words: "I am angry." Then the secret would be out. The sudden formation of a physical symptom can hide such feelings by binding them in the physical pain (see Deutsch, 1959). Of course I did not communicate my hypothesis directly to Sarah.

The thought also crossed my mind that Sarah's physical pain might be a disguised expression of an unconscious wish to communicate the intensity of her emotional pain (about which she could not speak openly), and that the emotional pain might be connected with anger and hate. That the first sign of angry irritation and sarcasm appeared when I "mixed into" this topic lent support to this hypothesis. Perhaps unconsciously she wanted to draw my attention to her symptom. She could easily have avoided my "interference" by remaining silent on this subject. Yet she regularly reported on her trips to physicians, detailing what they said and did to her and what medications they prescribed. On some level, she seemed to want me to translate her cryptosymbol into language she could understand. In other words, there seemed to be two contradictory "unconscious wishes": one to hide and one to communicate.

Some Thoughts on What Should Be Interpreted

The concept of "unconscious wish" is extremely complex and problematic. We don't know at what point nonconscious causation turns into unconscious psychological motivation. At what point do vague, nonconscious urges acquire enough formed constellation to be called an "unconscious wish"? At what point do organismic phenomena change into psychological ones? When and where do energy processes change into meaning processes? Although I cannot answer these basic questions of psychosomatic medicine, I know that as analysts we need to be aware of their existence. In itself this awareness should guard against our glib use of the concept of "unconscious wish" as *the* causal interpretation. A patient may be put off, and rightly so, if the analyst "interprets" that his or her "unconscious wish" produced asthma, acne, or, in Sarah's case, rheumatic pain. In the course of analytic work patients' free associations may come close to formulating in words a wish they did not recognize before, and perhaps never experienced in the form of a wish. In such cases, specific interpretations are not necessary. The patients' own verbalizations can transform vaguely formed (and therefore harmfully intrusive) unconscious urges into formed preconscious-conscious mental structures. In other words, their verbalizations can promote isomorphic symbolization of what has previously remained unsymbolized or been missymbolized. The disturbing symptom may then disappear as a result of the patient's own verbalizations, without the analyst's interpreting its meaning in terms of "unconscious wishes." As we shall see, this was the case with regard to the dissolution of Sarah's rheumatic pain.

In other instances, it might be said that the *analyst's* verbalizations, with the patient's cooperation, *create* the "meaning" of unconsciously active urges. In the case of true repression, the aim of interpretation is reconstitution of the meaning that has once been there, but just as often good "interpretations" *create* the meaning for the very first time. Something like the "story" of an "infantile neurosis" is probably "created" in the course of analysis—out of a multitude of chaotic memories and contradictory, disturbing feelings.

This emphasis on the "creating new meaning" aspect of interpretations follows from my view of symbolization as moving along a continuum of increasingly (or decreasingly, with repression) delineated gestalts. It contrasts with Freud's propositions regarding the nature and effect of repression and consequently the nature of unconscious content. My model implies *progressive* change from an unbound to a bound state of energy, from purely dynamic-energic processes to symbolized, meaningful thought processes. Symbolization (in its true generic sense) is a meaning-creating thought process, carving out, or delineating, one meaning out of the less structured multi-meaning contained in the "raw material" to be symbolized. Interpretations imply creating new symbolic forms, creating new meaning, and thereby ordering the more confused raw material offered by the patient. Whether the raw material has never been symbolized or underwent desymbolization as a consequence of repression, interpretation is always a form-creating act, not simply a *finding* of what has been there after successful removal of repression. This is where my view on the function and nature of symbolization leads to views different from Freud's on the essential nature of analytic work. In my theoretical framework, unconscious content cannot be assumed to have kept its shape and meaning intact after repression.

Freud's oft-cited analogy between the analyst excavating unconscious content, buried there in its original form, and the archaeologist digging up ancient artifacts, preserved in their original shape in the subterranean regions, does not hold up. Although in fact there is a similarity, it lies more in the archaeologist's imaginative, "interpretive" attempts to reconstitute a visible, gestalted "whole," such as a temple or entire city, from fragments that are practically meaningless in themselves (this is analogous to constituting the "story" of infantile neurosis from hazy, disparate fragments). In this *building* of a whole, there is no absolute proof of historical correctness, either for the analyst or for the archaeologist. Yet the self-consistent meaningfulness of the final pattern suggests its own justification. (For photographic and textual illustrations of reconstitutive archaeological work, see Hanfmann, 1972).

As we have seen, memories that do emerge intact in the course of analysis were not previously repressed into "the unconscious," but kept in an "unlit-up" (uncathected) part of the preconscious. They were somehow laterally pushed aside (if we conceptualize "lit up" as central), a process more akin to denial than to the definition of repression.

All this is not theoretical nit-picking but a difference that determines *how* we talk to our patients, which words we use. If something has been repressed and desymbolized, then the formulations must be very tentative, with full awareness that the analyst's "interpretation" actively contributes to the building of a new meaning-structure. The very wording of the interpretation should reflect this fact. On the other hand, if certain resistances are removed and the patient reports a "new" memory in full detail (as in my picture-thinking patients' sudden mention of pleasant memories), then one would assume that these memories have been in the preconscious all the time. They were not desymbolized and repressed, but *denied*.[9] Only the willingness to "light them up" and voice

[9] Denial means not seeing perceivable material which is there, and actually, in a way, still seeing it too. For the difference between repression and denial, see Freud (1915b, 1924a, 1924b, 1927a, 1938) and Jacobson (1957).

them aloud is *new*. In this case, one must recognize that it is the willingness to introduce new material into an old schema that is the consequence of fruitful analytic work, not the recovery of the memory per se. My picture-thinking patient who suddenly described her mother in the kitchen (a contrast to previous images) had not totally forgotten (repressed) this view. It just did not fit into the general picture of an "uncaring slob," which she preferred to frame for display.

Such preconscious material can sometimes be brought to light without laborious interpretation of free associations. In the case of my acting-out patient Jim, with his frozen portrait of his mother, one might simply ask: "What did your mother do when she wasn't in bed, eating crackers with cottage cheese and reading mystery novels?" Often one receives immediate, clear answers, obviously never forgotten, just not fitting into the patient's fixed schema. Once the missing pieces are obtained, one works, not on removing repression, but on using the material to demonstrate how memories are selected and framed for repetitious display and how that restricted picture contributes to the patient's continual self-traumatization. Here the analytic work offers a new angle on one's past, but does not "dig up" or reconstruct the form of repressed material. What happens is that preconscious material that has been "pushed aside" comes into more central focus and in this way modifies structured meaning. Lopsided missymbolization shifts to more isomorphic representation. The patient becomes able to tolerate contradictory parts within the same symbol-picture, even if it means letting parents partly "off the hook."

My point is that much analytic work involves *working with and on the preconscious*, not "excavating" the unconscious. I think this is an important difference which might shorten some analyses. Pathology in the preconscious, as well as its treatment, is a stepchild of psychoanalytic theory. Focusing on the generic process of symbolization lights up the concept of the preconscious in the center of the analyst's own preconscious. This leads us to epistemological considerations of the relation between implicit or explicit theoretical assumptions and perceptions, the influence of the preexisting "mental set" on the very choice of phenomena we consider facts. All these processes take place below the level of consciousness, in the preconscious.

The Bias of All Theory and Interpretation

The conceptual symbols that dominate the analyst's theoretical framework will directly determine the goals, interventions, and style of his or her clinical work. Clinical judgments and activities flow organically from conscious or preconscious theoretical premises, rather than the other way around. In this sense, an interweaving of clinical material with its underlying theoretical orientation is desirable in any presentation. True, clinical observations can change one's theoretical outlook. Yet in the very gathering of data there are implicit theoretical assumptions, "values," that affect what one perceives. I would argue that all scientific theorizing begins with the deductive method, however inductive the later steps in theory-building may be. Psychoanalysts often fail to acknowledge the deductive underpinnings of their theories. The worship of "total objectivity" prevents recognition of the subjectively chosen theoretical symbols that organize the perceptual field in the first place. I cannot emphasize enough that we see the world through the template of our preconscious storehouse of symbols (as the Rorschach test so clearly demonstrates). What the psychoanalyst "sees" in clinical case material invariably intertwines with the preexisting theoretical view. A major advantage of a generic theory of symbolization as the theoretical framework for looking at and thinking about psychological phenomena is that the theory itself "objectively" includes the inevitable subjective component on which any theoretical or clinical contention rests.

A certain group of psychoanalytic theoreticians would exclude any concept that is not directly observable from psychoanalytic theorizing. The idea of "psychic energy" in particular has come under attack (see Chapter 6). In their opinion, all we need to do is listen to our patients' descriptions of their life experiences to arrive at an adequate clinical theory and to interpret correctly. Vague metapsychological concepts, such as bound or unbound energy, supposedly do not facilitate our listening or talking to the patient. To this, I would reply that choosing which aspects or "data" to interpret *already* implies a "primary" organization of the "raw material" offered by the patient. *What* the analyst considers significant is determined by his or her preexisting preconscious symbols. A preconscious organizing "interpretation" always precedes the conscious act of psychoanalytic interpretation. We are not presented with self-evident, "given" facts. We create them by superimposing our preconscious symbols, which serve as a selective filter, upon the mass of infinitely complex "givens" delivered by the patient. The analyst's conscious interpretation of latent "meaning" is based on innumerable nonconscious psychic events in the analyst. This is not "countertransference" but just the way human perception works, and it affects the analyst's judgment of what and how to interpret.

Polanyi (1958, 1966, 1969) has directly questioned the "scientific" nature of science. With Wigner (1969), he discusses "unformalizable" knowledge that underlies human perception of "facts." In his opinion, science is based on such "tacit" intuitive knowledge. There can be no certainty as to the "real" nature and existence of facts science deals with. The method of dealing with them, the way of relating them to each other, the "picture" the scientist forms with the help of his or her "intuitive vision" is what constitutes what we call science. Indeed, Polanyi's writings should be required reading for all psychoanalysts and psychologists. The analytic emphasis on "cure" through interpretation demands a keen awareness of the numerous unknowns and uncertainties implied in an "interpretation." Such an awareness affects the analyst's style in giving interpretations. A stance of "certainty" can be harmful to the patient, for it may perpetuate or enhance the patient's wish for omniscience, through identification with the "all-knowing" analyst. "Interminable analyses" can be the result, due to the "omniscience hunger," particularly of obsessive intellectualizers. Interpretations given in the key of uncertain, subjective hypotheses, on the other hand, may help the patient to accept reality, which is fraught with uncertainties of causation, perception, and prediction.

A "purely" clinical theory is quite simply a misnomer, for any theory arises from "subsidiary," "tacit" assumptions about the nature of reality, which shape what is observed. Clinicians may claim to have excluded *a priori* theoretical constructs from their analytic perceptions, but one must question this assertion. Even if the analyst imagines that he or she relies on observation alone, "interpretations" will still rely nonconsciously on unexplicated theoretical assumptions. Schafer's (1976) emphasis on "concrete action language," for example, reveals a certain preconscious bias about what "in reality" is important.

I have no rules about the use of nouns or verbs in talking to a patient. What seems most important is to enable the patient to understand the context of meaning presented in the interpretation. Let me make my "meaning" clear with an example of a patient whose preconscious was so disorganized that it seemed overcrowded with images. This woman was not able to follow one line of thought, to complete a planned course of action, because everything else in her mind, however unrelated, impinged upon her consciousness with equal and simultaneous urgency. This way of operating caused considerable frustration. Theoretically, I thought of her "mental apparatus" as lacking boundaries or filtering screens between the systems unconscious, preconscious, and conscious. Nor were there gradations of cathexis within her preconscious. Everything was equally important, equally "lit up." In confronting her with this state of affairs, I used the metaphor of a chest of drawers (a noun) in which the drawers themselves had no bottoms. Whatever she put in, through whichever drawer, fell into the same heap. If she then wanted a summer blouse, she had to plow through all the winter sweaters, stockings, etc. Although she had a wealth of clothing (she was a mentally rich person), she could not enjoy this because she wore herself out just in trying to sort out what she needed from the confused mess. Often there was no time to conclude the search, so she remained stuck with something inappropriate. This, too, caused anger and frustration. My patient understood this image, and it "felt" right. Later she used the same image herself. I think it helped her to order her mental drawers. This metaphor proved effective because it vividly conveyed my way of perceiving her material and thus offered her a tool.

The theory of hierarchical levels of energy transformation resulting in meaning-giving processes is intrinsically part of how I perceive and talk to patients. My stance leads me to assume that whatever upsets patients enough to make them seek psychoanalysis involves some misfunctioning of their symbolizing processes. This hypothesis in turn focuses my attention on the functioning and quality of my patients' preconscious, and it influences my choice of significant "data."

My first therapeutic intervention, then, tends to zero in on the patients' communication problems. Patients' painful struggles to express themselves, or to understand what I mean; their repeatedly picking up my words in a context different from the one in which I send them out; the rhythm, syntax, speed, or dynamic intensity of their ways of speaking (including whispering that is barely audible)—all these communication phenomena are selected as data for analysis, before any genetic interpretations of "content." Certainly this communication-centered approach resonates with my generic theory of symbolization, the framework or beacon that directs my perception. But I would not use this approach if I did not believe it to be therapeutically useful. Indeed, it facilitates later reconstitution of repressed or unsymbolized psychic material.

Right now, however, my point is to show why throwing out "metapsychology" and leaving the "clinical" theory to stand on its own seems untenable. One is left with a working hypothesis that has no leg to stand on, no clear, articulated ground underlying psychoanalytic practice. To use the concepts of my generic theory of symbolization, in leaving out energy concepts, one splits *one* cycle into two incomplete halves. This severing takes the meaning out of both halves. Meaning comes from the fact that symbol formation is the *juncture* where pressuring energy processes change into human, meaning-directed acts. In symbol formation energy merges with perception into thought-directed action. I hope I was able to convey the clinical relevance of an "abstract" theoretical model in which "binding of energy" takes central significance.

Return to Sarah

Let us now turn back to the case of Sarah. We left Sarah dangling in the midst of her rheumatic pain. What, we wondered, might the meaning of this pain be? For various reasons, I assumed Sarah's rheumatic pain was a symptom serving to contain unacceptable feelings of hate. I am using the word "symptom" in the sense of a cryptosymbol, which delivers a specific message in a distorted way. A different use would be to think of a symptom as the somatic consequence of "high tension level," of undue stress on the organism. In that case, one might assume that a surplus of unbound energy from intense feelings led to the high tension level, if the feelings had not yet constituted themselves into a recognizable structure one could name "hate." But, whether a cryptosymbol or a stress symptom, I expected Sarah's rheumatic pain to be connected with destructive feelings, kept out of consciousness by repression.

This constellation increases the intensity of pressing urges. If the repressing forces are weak, then the pressure of unbound energy floods the whole psychic "apparatus" and the observable effect is acting out. Sarah, however, was not an acting-out character, at least not in the accepted sense of the term. Her behavior followed a rigid, in some ways mechanized pattern; the label "compulsive character" would fit her better. Flexibility was what she lacked, in body as well as in mind.

Sarah spoke in a clearly audible monotone, with carefully perfect grammar. No sentence was ever sloppy or unfinished. Yet the context of her speech, as well as the mode of expression, was completely unimaginative. Clichés abounded. Fantasizing as a mode of thinking was simply outside her realm of possibility. Dreams were mostly forgotten; she did not even remember that she had dreamt. No interests were mentioned aside from her work, church activities, and contact with her family.

In terms of our theoretical model, we can say that the functioning ego of this patient was supplied with tightly bound psychic energy, which ruled within an impoverished preconscious. Sarah's preconscious storehouse of symbols, her "internal world," was arid, like a sparsely furnished room with only the most essential fixtures. Her mental symbols denoted clearly definable things. Although they provided a cognitive map with which she could navigate securely in her limited world, they lacked connection to affective roots. Her symbols were not Janus-faced structures. They did not "bridge" between the unconscious id and the preconscious-conscious system. Or, to put it another way, they did not connect primary-process with secondary-process functioning. Her colorless speech, her use of clichés instead of her own metaphors, her lack of interest or responsiveness to any form of art—all reflected this one-sidedness. But Sarah did know what was what. She knew that "a spade is a spade." Her mental symbols did not really function as signs in the sense of compelling her to immediate action. But neither were they full-fledged symbols, which carry an aura of multidimensional connotations.

In other words, Sarah suffered from a deficiency in her symbolizing capacity. Her "symbols," although not exactly "signs," were similarly limited, simply designating this is that, like labels in a catalogue. They had lost their connection to the source of energy in the id. Indeed, that Sarah's behavior did not exhibit the obviously pressured, uncontrolled action characteristic of acting-out patients was precisely because her "symbol-signs" lacked energy. They were the products of centripetal, i.e., perceptual, symbolization. They were simply verbal copies, transcribing the relevant section of the outer world with almost no subjective contribution. In Sarah's ordered word catalogue, representations were neatly distanced from each other, and set apart from her own self. Although there was no confusion between inside and outside, there was no experience of the mutual immanence of the two, a lack reflected in her joyless, matter-of-fact tone.

Yet I did not believe Sarah was a naturally low-keyed person. Underneath her constricted manners and lifestyle, I suspected that there was a powder-keg of unbound, unshaped emotion. The large quantity of unbound energy was being strictly kept out of the tightly ordered area of preconscious representations by a strong repression barrier. A lid had to be clamped down on the caldron of unsymbolized urges.

Sarah had no particular "talent" to help her channel her intense id urges into gratifying and socially positive preconscious symbol-structures. Her family background offered no models for identification in the cultural arena, nor had she been encouraged to learn a particular discipline (except for studying the Bible). She was simply expected to do her obligatory homework for school and help out around the house and farm.

Still, other individuals from similar backgrounds do find their way to cultural interests. I think there was a fierceness to Sarah's instinctual urges, a sadistic trend unmitigated by libido or Eros, which made forming and molding these urges into the good gestalts of preconscious symbols highly problematic. This quality of fierceness probably also accounted for the emphatically denotative character of the perceptual symbols that did populate her preconscious. Without an admixture of Eros, her urges may have been too monolithic for any *blending* into percepts originating from the outside. If Sarah's overly sadistic urges had been allowed to blend into percepts, her intentions toward outside objects might have become dangerously aggressive.

But what am I basing these speculations on? Although Sarah never cried out, "I hate you," and indeed, most of the time behaved respectfully toward me, occasionally seemingly neutral things or remarks elicited her rage against me. For instance, I have many plants in my waiting room. Sarah asked me for their Latin names, which I did not know. She became enraged. Why do I have plants, if I don't even know their official names? That one could enjoy plants without knowing their names had not crossed her mind. Obviously the scientific label mattered more than the plant. Here we have a good example of the catalogue quality of Sarah's preconscious symbols. The lack of a scientific label makes, or *should* make, the whole thing disappear. Without neat labels, there is the danger of chaos. But beyond this, I think my not worrying about the name and still enjoying the thing made *me* dangerous. My attitude threatened her neatly labeled world. These feelings were evident from her raging "free associations." It is hard to describe the hate-filled atmosphere she created. She stayed with the topic the entire hour.

Another time a Picasso color print, *Portrait of Jacqueline*, appeared on my waiting room wall. Sarah's reaction was again intense rage. Her sarcasm was cutting. To put such a picture on the wall! No woman looks like that. How can a woman have a yellow and red face? And those crazy eyes! She concluded that I must hate the picture too. I only spent several thousand dollars on it to show off my ability to buy an original Picasso! (Obviously she was not very up to date with prices of original Picassos.) Sarah was so full of rage that even her usually perfect syntax became incoherent.

Why the frenzy over the Picasso? The situation is analogous to the one with the plants. The portrait was a symbol of a woman and, according to Sarah, a symbol should copy exactly what it represents. That was the way her preconscious was constituted. The painter should not mix his own inside into a depiction of the outside. The attack of rage was provoked by the discrepancy between Sarah's perception of a real woman and this "portrait." A portrait should be a portrait, a photographic likeness. If symbols don't unambiguously denote what they represent, then dangerous disorder threatens. In addition, I believe that the fierce emotions suggested by the red and yellow face and strange eyes contributed to Sarah's attack of rage. These features probably scared her, for they threatened the impenetrability of her own repression barrier.

I have already mentioned Sarah's scrupulousness about paying her income tax. When I wondered out loud about the necessity of rectifying a five-dollar error five years after it had been made, Sarah became righteously indignant. Her disparagement of my "low moral" character knew no end. My comment showed how foreigners just don't understand *American* morality.

What these incidents indicated to me was the tremendous pressure of unbound hate boiling underneath Sarah's "overbound" preconscious. Communication was inevitably difficult under these conditions. Usually my words were heard as "labels" so they did not reach her emotionally. Sarah then remained polite but distant. On other occasions, however, as in the above incidents, Sarah became so embroiled in her rage that there was not enough distance between her perception and her anger for her to really hear my words fully, with both cognitive and emotional impact. I thus said very little for a long time. I was busy making mental notes for the future. Although I wanted to focus on anger, it was either too remote or too close for meaningful verbal dialogue.

The first break in Sarah's repression barrier took place by way of a slip of the tongue. It was one of those occasions when the patient's own spontaneous verbalization takes care of interpretation. There was no need for me to add anything. We were talking about her behavior during her previous analysis, which had ended with the therapist's dismissing her because he felt that nothing had happened in three years. I asked how she felt about having wasted three years. Wasn't she angry at the analyst for not having stopped the treatment sooner? She answered that she felt nothing; she had done what she was told to do. She could not have left before the analyst told her to do so (an example of her stereotyped, repetitive behavior, in which she continued on the same track without thinking about it). She was not angry. After all, everybody tries to do his or her best, and that was what the analyst had done (this was probably objectively true). Well, I wondered, did she perhaps keep on with her "triangle, circle, square" associations because she was angry and wanted to annoy and defeat the analyst? "No." But Sarah started to show signs of irritation with me. Soon she stopped talking in sentences and began to "free-associate" in her old way, with rows of words. I protested that she could not do that here. By this time her annoyance had mounted. Finally she burst out, "If you annoy me like Dr. X did, then I'll do the same that I did with him." I just said, "Oh." This was the first incursion of words into the repressed area, and she *knew* it. She could even *name* her newly found feeling. It must have relieved her because with a sense of humor very uncharacteristic of her she added, "I guess I am angry. I guess I was angry at Dr. X." After this, we were able to do some work on the similarity between her father's and Dr. X's rigidity (a resemblance that may have contributed to her willingness to stick it out so long). In any case, our first fight against repression had been won. A meaningful symbol had been formed in her naming (and claiming) a previously denied emotion. Some quantum of unbound energy must have been transmuted into a bound state, making for a somewhat better equilibrium in her "energy household."

The turning point in Sarah's analysis occurred in a discussion of her rheumatic pain. Again, the crucial insight "happened to slip out" in words and needed no further interpretation from me. I pointed out that the timing of her worst pain and her visits to the family farm seemed to coincide. She replied, "You consider it sick to visit my aging parents. I shouldn't spend the money on the trips. I should give it to you." Her parents were always good to her. Maybe at times they were harsh, but they always "meant well." I reminded her of the time when for ten days she had to start each meal by eating three spoonfuls from the garbage pail in punishment for her dirty mouth. (She had said, "For Pete's sake!"—a swear word in her fundamentalist family.) "But Mother meant well then, too," Sarah countered, betraying her irritation with me for staying with this unpleasant topic. In our subsequent sessions Sarah prefaced her remarks with: "I guess you will insist that I talk about my visits home and my mother." She proceeded to recount other memories of harsh punishment. (These memories had never been truly repressed; they had simply not been verbalized in order to protect her valued cliché that mother "meant well." The garbage-eating episode was perhaps too strong an experience to be shoved into the unverbalized corner of her preconscious.)

Then came a wonderfully revealing remark, one that just "slipped out," that Sarah at first tried to withdraw by calling it "a slip." "What I hate most about her [mother] is the way she can kill chickens," Sarah began. She recalled how, as a child, she had hated to see her mother's bloody hands and "weird smile" when she did the killing. Sarah herself had never been willing to kill a chicken and had been teased about that. On one of her recent visits, her mother had again teased her, and had handed her the knife to see if she would now dare to kill a chicken. And then came the "classic." "I guess you would want me to say that I could have killed her with that knife." (Sarah's covering preface here was typical of her way of presenting feelings in this late phase of her analysis.) It hardly took any work on my part to connect this rich material with the pain in her right arm. Indeed, the pain decreased considerably with the decoding of the cryptosymbol and its translation into a form isomorphic with the urge striving for expression. Sarah was no longer misinformed and "misdirected" by her symptom. She stopped visiting physicians. She also stopped the clockwork regularity of her monthly visits to her parents.

Toward the end of treatment Sarah became less stereotyped and rigid in her behavior. She dared to change tracks and try new routes. She left her church-connected job and took an interesting, more prestigious position out of town. For a few months she came in for sessions twice a week, but then *she* chose to stop coming altogether. She now enjoyed life more and had made friends in her new community (she had none before). Yet the formality of her parting seemed a little forced. She assured me that if it were not for the distance, she would love to continue her analysis. I am not sure this was true. She said she would "keep me posted," but she never did. Sarah had hinted at a satisfying lesbian friendship but never stated this openly. One might conjecture that the voice of her superego was guilt-provoking and she did not trust me enough. I was glad that for the first time in her life she seemed to have a loving friendship (at approximately age fifty) and made no effort to "interpret," to make her verbalize this "secret." I thought it was nice that her new secret had to do with Eros instead of Thanatos.

A Theoretical Review

At this point I would like to rejoin certain theoretical considerations to the clinical material. In comparing Sarah's compulsively organized behavior and the acting out of my picture-thinkers, I would postulate that a quantitative difference in the forces of Eros and Thanatos (sadism) accounted for the divergence in pathology. A rigid, compulsive defense structure is needed to fight the potentially harmful outcome of fierce sadistic urges. In terms of psychosexual development, my picture-thinking patients got stuck at an infantile, pleasure-seeking, oral stage, while Sarah showed all the indications of a rigidly defended anal-sadistic character. The first group was proud of their childlike, "artistic" spontaneity, Sarah of her moral fiber. Sarah kept her hating, sadistic feelings under an ironclad repression barrier. But the feelings were there, and they did influence the pattern of her activities. Her meager store of not-full-fledged preconscious symbols forced her into a stereotyped repetitiveness of action that lead to lack of fulfillment and chronic joylessness. Lack of fulfillment imbued her whole life and manifested itself in her low-grade chronic depression, of which she was not consciously aware until her superior told her so. Her "iron will" kept her on a repetitively monotonous course. It was in this inability to change her stereotyped behavior that Sarah most resembled my acting-out patients. They could not change their "flighty" pleasure-seeking behavior, which also repetitiously ended in frustration.

My main contention is that all these patients lacked well-formed preconscious symbols. The repetition so characteristic of all psychopathology reflects this underlying failure in symbolization. As I indicated earlier, human "free will," the flexibility to make changes and adjustments, depends on the rich and well-structured content of the preconscious.[10] The directive guidance of true symbols enables the person to build traversable pathways to fulfilling goals. Both Sarah and the seemingly opposite type of acting-out patients were victimized by the compulsive driving power of not-truly-symbolized

[10] Kubie (1958) localizes the freedom of the creative process within the preconscious. He relies on the "topographic model" and sees the specific, creative significance of the preconscious. "Preconscious processes are not circumscribed by the more pedestrian and literal restrictions of conscious language" (p. 34). On the other hand, if "unconscious processes predominate, the resultant behavior will be rigid, stereotyped and insatiable, unmodifiable" (p. 29).

or missymbolized psychic tendencies.[11] Only full-fledged symbols lead to both realistic adaptation *and* enjoyment of the lifespace one has created. Good symbols unite features of primary- and secondary-process functioning, lending them pleasureful as well as reality-oriented qualities.

At this point I should perhaps restate what I mean by relating truly realistic functioning to good symbolization. By "realistic," I am referring to behavior that accommodates both the demands of the external objective world and the characteristics of the acting person's internal subjective world. I have spoken of immanence of the inside in the outside and vice versa. Any separation of the two leads to lopsidedness, whether the weight is put on the demands of the outside or those of the inside. Only a balanced intermingling of the two aspects can lead to a truly realistic attitude and action. My view of the "reality principle," then, differs from Freud's.

Freud's idea of secondary process is obviously closely related to what I have described as true, isomorphic symbol formation and binding of energy. The function of the secondary process is to serve the reality principle, which in Freud's formulation is limited to "adjustment"; it does not include enjoyment. Indeed, *lack* of enjoyment is not cited by Freud as a form of psychopathology, only manifest depression is.

As we have seen, Freud and his followers restricted symbol formation to its pathological variant: the cryptosymbol. Condensation, which plays such an important role in symptom and dream-symbol formation, has been emphasized as the earmark of primitive, primary-process functioning. Yet, if we take symbol formation in its generic sense, it becomes clear

[11]The pathology of symbol formation in these two types of patients, however, represented diametric opposites on the dimension of binding energy within the preconscious. Sarah operated with a rigidly tight preconscious "catalogue" of labels of things, while the picture-thinkers' preconscious was fluid to the extent of being hardly discernible from their unconscious.

that condensation, though an aspect of primary process, participates in the shaping of *all* symbols, whether the cryptosymbols of symptoms or the isomorphic symbols that are the bricks of secondary-process thinking. In my opinion, connecting primary process with secondary process is one of the true symbol's constructive, "bridging-over," Janus-faced functions which joins the functioning of the whole psychic organization and also introduces capacity for joy as an absolutely necessary aspect of whole-some functioning.

Some Final Clinical Considerations

Let us now return once again to Sarah and see what these ideas imply in terms of treatment. Because Sarah's preconscious ego was sitting on top of a powder-keg of unbound Thanatos-type urges, my approach was cautious. If the powder-keg had suddenly exploded, her bulwark of compulsive sanity might well have gone up in flames as well. In contrast, in working with my picture-thinking acting-out patients, I never had such anxious thoughts. For Sarah, the analytic task was to "carve out" and symbolize her unconscious impulses. It was not a matter of "teaching" her to slow down and engage in reflective self-observation to gain some distance from action. Instead, the aim was the classical one of making the unconscious conscious (which does imply *enhanced* self-observation). In Sarah's case, what had to be made conscious was exactly what she was proud not to have, for she functioned under the aegis of repression and reaction formation.

I believe that it is through the creation of true symbols that psychoanalysis works toward integration. This is the case with both compulsive patients and acting-out ones. As I have indicated, with my picture-thinkers, the symbol-forming process differed from the type of work usually called "psychoanalytic." Instead of aiming to lift a repression barrier, the goal was to organize their preconscious so that symbols rather than signs could be formed. It was not so much that these patients needed to recognize unconscious urges, but that they needed to learn to *think about* their urges and desires. The preconscious was the working ground.

Sarah's analysis, however, matched Freud's model. My interventions, including my transference interpretations, were more "classical" in their form and content. The main difference was my explicit verbalization of uncertainty about the "historical truth" of my assumptions in my attempts to reconstruct her childhood feelings toward her parents (feelings which I assumed were never consciously formulated). This difference is important. It expresses the therapeutic value I ascribe to the formation of appropriate preconscious "containers" into which id impulses can blend, and not the hunt for historical truth (see Freud, 1937b). Let us not forget that, due to the ever-present symbolizing function of human perception and memory formation, the degree of subjective transformation of "memories" can never be determined.

The pressure from Sarah's powder-keg of unsymbolized id impulses decreased as the energy was bound through secondary-process language symbolization. "Unnameable" sadistic impulses received verbal expression. I don't know how much of this was *re*construction and how much a first construction of angry, hating feelings, primarily toward her mother. In any case, once Sarah's sadistic feelings were bound into words, the homeostatic balance in her "energy household" improved. Her behavior became less stereotyped and repetitive, for it was now guided by symbols reverberating with emotion instead of mere labels of objects. She experienced more freedom of choice.

In spite of my emphasis on the integration provided by true symbolization, I believe that symbolizing sadistic impulses was not the only factor contributing to better harmony in Sarah's psychic organization. I think the very experience of talking about her feelings, any feeling about herself, to an attentively listening "audience" (the analyst) brought about some articulation *within* the constellation of her id forces. The symbolization function proper helped to bridge over two rigidly separated "regions," between her boiling unconscious and her rigid preconscious-conscious. The very process of verbalizing personal matters she had never talked about before to anybody created new "regions," imbued with new content and colored by nuances of feeling. Another benefit for Sarah of verbal dialogue was a lessening of the seemingly monolithic, and thus overwhelming, power of the driving id forces. In giving shape to unsymbolized id urges, words detach and differentiate them from the mass of driving power experienced as threatening. Lacking definition, id impulses cluster as an amorphous, vast, menacing force. Strong repressive countercathexes are then instituted. Indeed, if we consider what I have said about the destructiveness of Thanatos, rigid repression may not be such an inappropriate reaction. Free ventilation of unformed sadistic impulses may lead to real tragedy, as we know all too well from newspaper and TV accounts. Sarah may have had good reason to keep her sadistic urges imprisoned before "talking therapy" helped her to articulate that monolithic mass into a more differentiated pattern.

Patterns of force, too, can have different degrees of articulation. Talking about them in the form of dialogue may contribute to their differentiation. With differentiating articulation, the nature of the forces themselves may change. Perhaps there is an analogy in theoretical psychics, in the idea that different patterns of particle distribution are assumed to account for the different "behavior" of forces. But I admit to ignorance here. In any case, I believe that, in addition to helping to make the unconscious conscious, and promoting internal symbolization, psychoanalytic dialogue leads to a differentiation of "monolithic" id energy. As the "particles" are redistributed along various threads, or branches, or channels, the structure of the id itself changes, resulting in a much less threatening constellation than the original unformed one. Maybe all this has to do with amalgamation of Eros and Thanatos. The admixture may be more moldable than the fierceness of Thanatos by itself. Dialogue per se may help along fusion of Eros and Thanatos. This admixture in turn might lend itself better to differentiated articulation. As I said before, we know so little about fundamental "energy processes," in psychology as well as in physics. But that should not keep us from thinking about them and occasionally sharing our not-precise thoughts with others. This way we might hope for clarification—in the long run. Sometimes I feel that theoretical physicists will do more with developing the implications of Freud's dual instinct theory than analysts, who often consider it "non-arrivé."

Conclusion

My emphasis in this chapter has been on the role of psychoanalysis in fostering true, isomorphic symbolization. Sarah's case underlined the *connecting* function of symbols in merging previously split-off parts into good gestalts. The other face of symbols, their *distancing* function, came out clearly in the work with picture-thinking acting-out patients. Here the task was to separate and define what had been heedlessly fused. Depending on the type of deficiency, then, psychoanalytic theory aims to symbolize what has never been symbolized, to resymbolize what has become desymbolized, or to transform cryptosymbols into true symbols.

I believe that symbolization works in the direction of producing order; desymbolization results in increasing disorder. The first is a gestalt-creating process; the second, a gestalt-destroying one. The proportion between the forces of Eros and Thanatos was assumed to influence the proportion between good symbolization and desymbolization or inadequate, noncommunicative symbolization (evident in psychotic art). This is not to deny that whole-some psychic functioning demands an optimal balance and an amalgamated state between the forces of Eros and Thanatos.

It is now time to look more closely at the initial development of the symbolizing capacity. What factors in early life promote good symbolization and what factors promote faulty symbolization? In Part III, I shall take an object relations perspective, focusing specifically on the early relationship between mother and child. (The father's role has been left out, but not because I believe it to be unimportant.) The symbolizing cycle, which consists in internalization of the outside and expression of the inside content, will serve as a reference in localizing disruptions in symbol-forming activities. How, for instance, does the quality of the preconscious reflect the mother's handling of her child? The guiding spirit, the *spiritus rector*, throughout the next part is Winnicott. His description of transitional phenomena entails a developmental theory of symbolization.

PART III

CHAPTER 8
Winnicott's Creativity

I began this book by stipulating that the main task of every human being is to create a fitting lifespace (cf. Lewin, 1935; Goldstein, 1939). At the beginning of life the most important influence on the newborn's lifespace is the mother (or primary caregiver). She mediates between the baby's needs and the environment as a potential source of gratification. As the baby grows into a child and adult, the mother's mediating function becomes internalized in what we call ego functions. The final aim of these functions remains the same from birth to death: to make the unit of the "person in his or her environment" as smoothly fitted and unified a gestalt as possible. Obviously, when mediation between the person's needs and the environment fails, the result is a "bad fit," or poor gestalt. Instead of harmonious connectedness, there will be disruption at the interface where the self meets the environment.

At what point, we may ask, did this disruption begin? Why did mediation between inside and outside fail? Did the person perhaps *misperceive* outside reality from early life on, thus making the building of viable bridges to it impossible? Or did the person overestimate his or her own power in fitting outside reality to internal needs, thereby causing all activity to result in less than gratifying experience? Perhaps, as in Sarah's case, it is the person's *inner* creative potential that has been cut off, so that there is adaptation to objective limitations but no feeling of the inner satisfaction that comes from uniting what is inside with the outside. These are but some of the possibilities every analyst must consider.[1]

In explaining the misfunctioning of the human mind, Freud emphasized fixation on infantile fantasies versus proper perception and adjustment to the demands of outer reality. He implied that an acceptance of the disjunction between one's subjective wishes and what life can offer was part of mental health. In other words, clear objective perception and acceptance of limitations forced upon the person by the exigencies of life and culture became *the* therapeutic goal. While there is validity to this theory, it presents a stoically grim view of life (see Freud, 1927b, 1930). What Freud failed to see is that creativity is a basic human propensity, a human *need*, which must also be fulfilled in the shaping of a satisfying lifespace.

With minor modifications, this view of mental health remained unchallenged for years. (Schilder was an exception, but he did not belong to Freud's circle.) Then came Winnicott. Without any fanfare, he introduced what I consider a totally new view of what constitutes healthy mental functioning. He saw the essence of mental health in a unified lifespace (though he didn't use Lewin's concept), in the lack of a disruptive gap between the person and the environment. He believed in our creative capacity to bridge over the potential gap with symbols that truly *unite*, and simultaneously *represent*, the subjectively treasured inside with, and within, the objectively existing outside world.

[1] We should remember, however, that the beliefs the analyst holds regarding what constitutes healthy life will influence his or her method and therapeutic aims. There is no truly value-free basis for any form of therapy. The analyst hears, sees, and chooses "material" on the basis of a preexisting theory and, in the last analysis, the choice of this theory is based on personal values.

Winnicott saw the first signs of human creativity in the infant's capacity to rectify the disruption of his or her lifespace through hallucinatory perception if gratification from the mother was not forthcoming. Remember that Freud postulated this phenomenon but viewed it from the angle of tension discharge. Winnicott, on the other hand, perceived in infants' initial hallucinatory wish fulfillment, as well as in their later ability to soothe themselves by sucking a thumb or investing the edge of a blanket or a teddy bear with gratifying illusions, the core of all subsequent symbolic creativity. Certainly Winnicott did not advocate living by dreams and illusions without respect for concrete reality as it is generally perceived. What he charted was an "intermediate" territory between the world of private dreams and illusions and that of adjustment to the hard facts of concrete outside reality. He called this "the transitional space." It is here that, first, blankets and other treasured possessions and, later, the full-fledged symbols of art, religion, and other "cultural activities" fill in the "gap" between the person and the outside universe.

I want to add that the imaginative use of this "intermediate space" also serves what I have defined as the "reality principle" (in distinction to Freud), for it promotes the enjoyment necessary for mental health. One has only to look at the tortured life of anhedonic patients to justify this addition to Freud's reality principle. As I indicated, Freud limited the reality principle to accurate perception of the characteristics of the outside world and accurate knowledge of the dangerous inner cravings, with the goal of controlling these urges from laying claim on reality (Freud, 1927b, 1930). Primary-process direct tension discharge was to be superseded by reality-adapted, delayed secondary-process functioning (Freud, 1911). The less intermingling between the two, the more mature the mind. Indeed, the capacity for symbol creation was a liability rather than an asset in Freud's evaluation of innate potentials. Artistic creativity could not be adequately treated within this framework.

Winnicott's Filling In of "Gaps"

Let us now look more closely at Winnicott's contributions. Instead of arguing *against* Freud's ideas, in true Winnicottian manner, he unfailingly picked out the *gaps* in Freud's conceptual world and "realized" these *potential spaces* by creating his own conceptual world into them. The gaps corresponded to the lack of certain concepts or categories of experiences in Freud's theories—maybe in his life.

A case in point is Winnicott's exploration of how enjoyment and love of reality come about, a question overlooked in Freud's emphasis on the necessity of accepting and adapting to reality. Winnicott's concept of the "environmental mother" filled another gap in Freudian theory, with its focus on the mother as the object of instinctual cravings. But the most important difference between the two men, and consequently between the two kinds of psychologies they offer, lies in their attitude toward the possibility and desirability of mixing opposites, particularly features of inner and outer reality.[2]

The relationship between inside-subjective and outside-objective reality was of great concern to both Freud and Winnicott. But while Freud's concern centered on the best method of discriminating between the two with certainty,

[2] It might be that a reason for the differences in Freud's and Winnicott's formulations was the difference in their patient populations. Today we might describe Winnicott's patients as borderline personalities. These are the patients with "unthinkable anxieties" who feel lost in the world and do not experience that they have an "inside." Certainly they *seem* different from the patients who led Freud to focus on the role of internal conflict. Yet it is always possible that this seeming difference has a lot to do with these two analysts' very different conceptual symbols, which guided how they perceived their patients and how they defined and organized the "material" to be analyzed.

Winnicott delighted in showing how the two universes can be intermingled within the same perception or act. For Freud, the proper standard for what is "real" comes from what is outside. The act of judgment, he claimed, has to decide whether the thought refers to something "real," i.e., to something out "there," or to something "not real," i.e., fantasy (Freud, 1925). Freud certainly recognized, to a greater extent than anyone before him, the very "real" effects of fantasies (even unconscious ones) on the person's very real life. Yet his dichotomizing Cartesian *Weltanschauung* excluded the possibility of blending two categories into one concept. Fantasy and "reality" were necessarily opposed.

Compare Freud's Cartesian strictness in dividing inside from outside with the following quotation from Winnicott, which postulates a transitional realm:

> In respect of these transitional objects the parents, as it were, conspire not to challenge the origin. They easily see that the thumb is part of the child and that the next toy or teddy bear or doll is a gift, but with regard to the object in question they undertake to refrain from challenging the infant as to its origin. There is a madness here which is permissible. . . . The madness is that this object is created by the infant and *also* it was there in the environment for the infant's use [1954, p. 201].

Indeed, in his original discussion of transitional objects and phenomena, Winnicott concluded that a neat division of seeming opposites may lead to undesirable character features:

> What emerges from these considerations is the . . . idea that paradox accepted can have positive value. The resolution of paradox leads to a defence organization

> which in the adult one can encounter as true and false self organization [1953b, p. 14].

One more quotation and the essence of Winnicott's view should be clear:

> This intermediate area of experience, unchallenged in respect of its belonging to inner or external (shared) reality, constitutes the greater part of the infant's experience, and throughout life is retained in the intense experiencing that belongs to the arts and to religion and to imaginative living and to creative scientific work [1953b, p. 14].

For Winnicott, creativity was not limited to the making of art objects. Rather, he defined it as a "coloring of the whole attitude to external reality." And he remarked: "It is creative appreciation more than anything else that makes the individual feel that life is worth living" (1971a, p. 65). I believe these statements imply new aims for psychoanalysis and a conception of mental health that differs from Freud's.

Freud, according to his own admission, felt unable to experience "aesthetic emotion." He also stated that his main interest in the visual arts was their subject matter (Freud, 1914b). He added that he was "almost incapable of obtaining any pleasure from music." I find this last statement particularly revealing in light of Susanne Langer's (1942) assertion that music is pure form; whatever the content may be, it is totally expressed through the form. Freud's interest, on the other hand, was always in what was *hidden*, and the immediately perceivable was considered "surface" or "disguise" to be disposed of, whether in art or dreams. Music might have escaped him because there is no "surface" to lift, no content without form. In music, manifest and latent, form and meaning are completely merged.

I think the central significance art held for Winnicott might well have been at the subjective root of the development of his theory of transitional phenomena.

Winnicott's Developmental Theory

I intend now to outline the stages implicit in Winnicott's developmental theory and to show how the child's capacity for symbolization and creativity is affected by the mother's management of each phase. Let us not forget, however, that the mother is not the only determinant in the child's development. The child has his or her own constitutional genetic givens. We do not know the relative weight of genetic and environmental factors in development. The two seem so interwoven that it is hard to even separate them as "two." Still, it is safe to assume that the extremes on the continuum, the severely autistic child and the future creative genius, develop principally on the basis of their constitutional givens. Beethoven's or Leonardo's genius cannot be derived from the early mother-child interaction. In the case of autism, the mother can be trained to care for her autistic child so as to balance out some of the constitutional deficiencies. Yet this is not always possible; with autistic children, even the best professional treatment may not be successful. Nevertheless, aspects of the mother's care may facilitate or thwart life-creating activities, particularly in children with "average to talented" endowment.

The Stage of Dual-Union and Holding

In the first phase the infant and the mother are usually described as an undifferentiated unit, although I think the term "dual-union" (Hermann, 1936) is more appropriate (see Chapter 1, fn. 2). The function of the "good-enough" mother at this stage is to protect the sense of unity and continuity of the infant's existence. For this purpose, the mother's empathic ability to handle her baby in harmony with the baby's own biological rhythm is crucial. If hunger, for instance, is allowed to reach a certain point of tension, then the sense of unity of the infant's existence will be disrupted. Chaotic, ragelike discharge reactions seem to go with the experience of fragmentation or panic (it is hard to find words for the earliest life experiences).

Besides the timing of feedings, the tactile-kinesthetic communication is the most important determinant of the infant's well-being, or lack of same. The infant's skin is the first concrete boundary or interface between the infant and the world. The rhythm, intensity, and the undefinable ways of communicating love through touching and holding will determine whether this skin-boundary is felt as good (a source of pleasure) or bad (a source of discomfort). The feeling of not being at home either in one's skin or in the world quite possibly stems from the latter. The "holding mother" is a salient concept in Winnicott's refreshingly concrete terminology. A mother who holds well gives her infant an initial feeling of unity within his or her skin. Loving and secure holding lay the foundation for basic trust; bad holding for distrust and "unthinkable anxieties," such as sensations of falling into a bottomless abyss.

This holding stage may well be decisive for the later capacity for and love of symbolization. A libidinally cathected skin surface pleasantly delineates the inside from the outside. Communication between the two areas lying on either side of the boundary will be felt as desirable, and symbolization, after all, *is* communication across a boundary (Deri, 1974). A comfortingly wrapped-up inside leads to the experience of a good inner space (Erikson, 1950). Later this inner space will be denoted as the mind, corresponding, within the topographic model (the model best-suited for discussing symbolization), to the preconscious. I also believe that the development of a rich or poor preconscious depends on the primordial feeling quality with which the equally primordial inner space is invested. Specifically, the process of internalization is, in all likelihood, influenced by the feeling with which the infant experiences his or her inside. That a pleasurable experience of the outside facilitates the ease and quality of internalization goes without saying. But what is often overlooked is that the feeling-tone in which the inside is experienced is equally crucial for the outcome of internalization. If the inside is a good place, then one will want to fill it up with good things. The internalized "things," which are symbolic representations of outside objects, may also become imbued with the quality of the space in which they are stored. Let me give a case example.

A patient described his inside as one big mass of "shit." His brain was disgusting, too—filled with decaying, rotting cells. He attributed this state of affairs to his drinking of beer, which he continued to do despite the fact that he found the consistency of beer itself "disgusting." This patient's intelligence was quite high, yet he derived no pleasure from it. Objectively, in terms of grades and achievements, he was a good student. But he felt that anything he took in (whether real or mental food) turned "instantly into shit." His written work, for which he had been praised by his teachers, was experienced the same way. His feeling of disgust prevented him from ever rereading his papers. Metaphorically speaking, they were "flushed down the toilet." Actually, they were pushed into a pile of messy pages, far out of reach, as if they had to be hidden and "quarantined" to avoid contagion.

With this attitude to his inside and to the products that

came from his inside, this man was unable to enjoy studying or creating anything. He was unable to enjoy—period. His friends became suspect to him: Something must be wrong with them, too, if they were attracted to such a "piece of shit." He was the living example of Groucho Marx's saying, "I wouldn't belong to a club that would take me as a member."

According to my patient's memories, as an infant he had not been handled by his mother. She was described as "far away," with "vacant eyes," not noticing the world around her, including her children. He claimed to remember being tied down in a baby carriage and put in front of the house for hours at a time. He could not remember being taken for walks, talked to, played with, or read to. Even allowing for the lopsided distortions of memory, it seems safe to assume that his mother was rather schizoid, detached from her child, a not-"well-holding" mother. She did not communicate love and enjoyment of her child through tactile-kinesthetic means and thus failed to communicate to her infant that he was a "good thing," that everything about him—his inside and his outside—was enjoyable. As an adult, he was not able to enjoy his talents and did not have the capacity for sustained loving relationships.

The self's positive relationship to the preconscious—so crucial for well-functioning symbolization—might well be rooted in the earliest tactile experiences offered to the infant by the holding mother. Similarly, the borderline patient's feeling of emptiness, of no inside, of a lack of trust in the smooth functioning of his or her mind, might have roots as far back as the earliest psychosomatic insecurities experienced in the arms of the nonempathic "holding mother."

The Stage of Hallucinatory Wish Fulfillment

With hallucinatory wish fulfillment, we must assume a beginning structuralization of the infant's mind. Freud postulates this situation in the following terms: high need-tension present but need-gratifying object (breast) absent. Through primary-process functioning, the wish cathects the memory image of the breast with hallucinatory intensity. Freud explains this phenomenon by the primary need for tension discharge.

Winnicott (1953a), on the other hand, describes the same phenomenon differently: "The creative potential of the individual arising out of need produces readiness for an hallucination." He emphasizes: "The mother's love and her close identification with her infant make her aware of the infant's needs to the extent that she provides something . . . in the right place at the right time. This . . . starts off the infant's ability to use *illusion*, without which no contact is possible between the psyche and the environment" (p. 223). The empathic mother places the breast just where and when the infant created the illusion. In this manner the mother facilitates the illusion that the infant's need has "created" the breast.

At this point of development the infant presumably has a vague feeling about an inside and an outside. The mother's optimal responsiveness to the infant's needs gives the infant the *illusion* that there is an outside world that corresponds to his or her needs and capacity to create. The mother's synchronized timing in offering her breast at the height of the infant's mounting need-tension allows the infant to feel in magical control over the objects of the world. Winnicott believes that without experiencing this "primary illusion" of omnipotence, the growing child will not be able to enjoy reality. Frustration may teach a child to perceive and adapt to reality, but only the experience of fulfillment, coming from the outside but magically "created" by the infant's wish, will lead to love of reality.

Let us phrase this in yet another way: The good mother's

empathic offering of her breast amounts to her offering the world as a friendly and fulfilling place. The world will then be positively cathected and so will the act of wishing. This is a good beginning for an optimistic, trusting attitude toward the world and a motivated connectedness to its objects. The pleasure of primary illusion is likely to link up with the capacity for symbolic perception that lends rich coloring to seemingly ordinary objects. This primary illusion does not imply a delusional attitude toward the world, for in the subsequent phases the good mother will inevitably include well-dosed lapses in gratification so that reality perception and reality adaptation can develop.

This first self-created image leading to the absent need (love) object could be called the first protosymbol. It is at this point of mental development, at the earliest move toward symbolization, that Winnicott conceives the origin of what he calls the intermediate or transitional space, transitional between dream and reality, between inside and outside, between person and environment. It is par excellence the dimension of connectedness or, even better, of mutual immanence. This is the space for creative symbol formation, since it is the function of symbols to bridge between opposites. This transitional space, this space for connectedness, accounts for an order in the world based on *inner relatedness* instead of the Cartesian principle of dividedness. The processes taking place within this intermediate space eliminate the disruption between the person and his or her environment. The construction of this concept of transitional space and the value attached to it for mental health are Winnicott's unique contributions to psychoanalysis.

Thus, we can see how much the future vicissitudes of symbolization and creativity, activities conceptually localized in the intermediate space, will depend on the manner in which the mother hands over the world to her child. The paradigm of the primary illusion implies that new objects should be introduced into the child's lifespace in a way which allows the child to experience the illusion that his or her wish partly created them. How many times do we hear patients complain, "They never gave me things I wanted *when* I really wanted them. By the time I got it, it didn't matter to me anymore"? These are the children who always feel deprived, while their parents feel unappreciated.

If parental giving is poorly synchronized with the child's wishes, the result is disruption between the child and the surrounding world. Such children may become overly demanding, continually whining. Whatever they *have* is just not right. Even as adults, these people remain eternally demanding or more obviously angry. Or, such children may stop wishing altogether and experience their surroundings as meaningless, filled with useless, dead objects. Nothing lights up with a positive valence to strive for. This is the arid world of the anhedonic borderline character. Without the ability to formulate wishes, there can be no creativity. These eternally unfulfilled children and adults do not know how to fulfill themselves because there was no fulfilling, giving mother to be internalized. They will become angry, unhappy, alienated adults. Even if they are constitutionally endowed with creative talent, it cannot be used with enjoyment. The prevalence of destructive anger over Eros prevents the creative formation of raw material into good gestalts. Instead of containing usable wishes (a category connected to the functioning of the preconscious), these people experience their inside either as empty or as a seething caldron of undefined, destructive cravings. Sadistic dreams and fantasies are common. The mother's mismanagement of this stage can provoke primitive oral rage, which prevents the formation of psychic structure necessary for good symbol formation and creativity. (Winnicott does not integrate his concepts with stages of psychosexual development.)

If frustrations in this stage are very intense, the infant will not have the capacity for "good illusion formation" to enter the next stage—the creation of transitional objects.

The Stage of Transitional Objects

The creation and use of transitional objects assume the existence of a "good-enough mother." The good-enough mother intuitively knows when and for how long she can and should introduce a delay between the child's needs and the fulfillment she offers. An infant who in the previous stage had the experience of "magic creativity," in the form of primary illusion, will find ways to mend the gap in his or her lifespace produced by the absence of the gratifying mother. At this stage the infant has a growing ability to recognize and accept reality. If earlier its hallucinatory wish fulfillment coincided with the appearance of the real breast, then in the following stage, objects available in outside reality can be perceived and felt as receptive for illusory use. At first the thumb or the fist, later a piece of soft material found around the crib, still later a soft stuffed animal, and finally any toy may be used as a good transitional object. Judging from the baby's actions, these objects do not simply belong to the external world of objects, nor are they purely wishful hallucinations; *they are both at the same time*. This is the paradox that Winnicott insists has to be accepted, and *not* resolved. Once resolved, the fatal Cartesian split between inside and outside will take place and reality, even though "dealt with" adaptively, will never feel deeply enjoyable. It will never be experienced as partly created by the self. (This might be the necessary corollary to an excess of ego autonomy and "neutralized" energy.)

Infants holding onto, sucking, stroking themselves with

their good transitional objects do not yet suffer from too much ego autonomy. Yet thanks to their creative semi-hallucinations, these infants reach some measure of autonomy from the physical presence of the mother. The transitional object is imbued with "good-mother stuff" and therefore undoes separation. Although the transitional object is not yet a symbol *representing* mother, if environmental circumstances remain good, it will later lead to the successful use of symbols to bridge over to the desired but physically absent object. Thus, the child of a good-enough mother will have the creative capacity to return equilibrium into his or her lifespace by means of a benevolent illusion: the transitional object.

Early good transitional objects can do more than open up the way to creative symbolic living in transitional space. They can also lead to an appreciation of the qualities of the objectively perceived, real outside world. Let us imagine the child playing with a teddy bear, which, while the mother is absent, is fused with the illusion of mother-qualities. Suppose that the mother returns within the span of time that the teddy bear contains the illusion of her presence. Once the real mother arrives, the toy yields up its semi-hallucinatory illusion of being *also* the mother and becomes a teddy bear in its own right, with its own material features. The child now has the mother for mother and the teddy bear for teddy bear. The child's objectively perceived world has thus been enlarged. Knowledge of the nature of real objects is needed not only for the sake of the reality principle per se but also for creative action, which requires knowledge and respect for the real qualities of the raw material. Indeed, in locating his "transitional space" as lying *between* the space of dreams and the space of "hard" reality, Winnicott is not quite correct. The transitional space is neither contiguous nor continuous with the "Cartesian" or Euclidian space of "real" reality, but is interwoven with it and can only be lifted out for the sake of conceptualization.

Another way in which the good transitional object helps to enlarge the child's objectively perceived world is by serving as a trusty companion to hold onto when entering new territory. The unknown can be frightening to the small child (and to many adults), but, by carrying the trusty transitional object the child establishes a bridge between the old and known and the new and unknown. It helps to establish a feeling of familiarity within the unfamiliar.

An example of this use of a transitional object is provided by a woman patient who remembered how, as a child and up into her teens, she carried a small doll in her pocket whenever she went to a new place. The only child of hard-working parents, she had had to learn to shift for herself at a very young age. Instead of hiring a babysitter, for instance, her parents would send her to other people's houses, where she was expected to act as a poised young lady and behave well. She managed quite well—maybe too well for her own good, for nobody suspected the anxieties she combatted with her own secret devices. The touch, even the mere knowledge of her doll's presence, gave her a sense of continuity with her room at home, and thus a feeling of continuity with her "real" self. She was afraid of losing herself in the midst of all the new things and people around her. Carrying the little doll was her ingenious invention to guard against an uncanny feeling of alienation, a feeling she knew from the past, before she came up with her "portable identity" solution.

We might compare this use of the transitional object to establish a feeling of familiarity within the unfamiliar to Piaget's "assimilative schema," without which accommodation to the new cannot meaningfully occur. The old, subjective "inside" contributors to perception make possible the assimilation of the truly new, so that the new, instead of remaining a "foreign body" of knowledge, can become organically assimilated into the already-existing world of the child (or the adult).

The fate of the transitional object—whether it promotes good symbolization or deteriorates into a rigidly frozen fetish—depends to a large extent on the length of time the mother remains absent. The empathic mother reappears in time to prevent the metamorphosis of the good transitional object into a dead-end fetish. If children cling too long to their objects, they will not be able to let go, to move into the intermediate transitional space where symbolic, creative imagination reigns. Instead, the fetish object is invested with power and begins to "hold" them. The capacity for playful, "magic illusion" moves toward the fixity of delusion.

Actually, we find a kind of continuum between good transitional objects and neurotically defensive fetishistic phenomena. Good-luck talismans, for instance, are somewhere in between the two. More unusual is the case of a woman lawyer who carried a ribbon in her coat pocket or purse wherever she went. She would secretly touch it whenever she became anxious in a professional situation. In this case, one would assume some deep and unresolved infantile separation anxieties (in all likelihood mingled with sadistic impulses). The same woman became completely perplexed and confused if there was the slightest change in my office, waiting room, or schedule, or if I uttered a word that was not the one she expected. She also engaged in various repetitive, ritualistic acts during our sessions, such as playing with her pop-it beads (they were fashionable at the time)—pulling two apart and then pushing them together again. Although this activity lends itself to phallic interpretation, I think the deeper meaning lies in the practicing of separation and joining together again. Her traumatic childhood kept her functioning at the level of defensive, repetitive, self-destructive acts, in spite of her exceptional intellectual and potentially good creative endowment.

The traumatic effects of maternal deprivation can be seen

in institutionalized children, who often lack true transitional objects. Instead, they clutch rigidly to what might be called fetish objects—without play, without enjoyment, without healthy libido investment in them. Some measure of defense against distressing anxiety is the only function of these objects. How much these children come to depend on these objects as essential to survival is illustrated by a memory from my student days. In Budapest, students in the department of therapeutic psychology (or "defectology," as it is now called in the U.S.S.R.) had to do "practicums" in institutions for children with sensory defects. (The practicum consisted of just being around, observing, taking notes, talking to and playing with the children.) I remember often seeing twelve- to fourteen-year-old blind children walking around with one fist tightly clenched. One day one of the attendants (a nun) got into an ugly physical fight with a big, strong blind boy. He would not open his fist, no matter how hard the nun tried to make him do so. She became enraged because she suspected the boy was hiding something "immoral" (I could never figure out what she thought he was hiding). Finally, with the help of a male attendant, she forced the poor child's fist open. And there was the "immoral" object—a pretty glass marble. They took it away from him. The boy cried and shouted with utter despair and rage. (I'll obviously never forget this terrible scene.)

Greenacre (1969, 1970) nicely differentiates the positive developmental potential of the transitional object from the arrested, frozen quality of the infantile fetish. She stresses how early, traumatic body experiences (on the self or witnessed) may lead to early acute castration fear, for which the fetish object then serves as a "patch." Greenacre says that the "fetish . . . contains congealed anger, born of castration panic" (1969, p. 333).

I think the infantile fetish can also be born of early distress due to abandonment. Abandonment of an infant can lead to narcissistic mortification of such intensity that its effect is most probably experienced as mutilation of the incipient body-self. In the beginning the self *is* the body-self. The infant's lifespace is thrown into disequilibrium if the mother is absent at a time when the infant needs something. Failure to satisfy an intense need results in a painful feeling of incompleteness to the body-self. This painful experience of helplessness might well be compared to a feeling of body mutilation since at this early stage of development there is no separation between the self and the need-satisfying object. In the phallic stage, this same feeling might appear as castration fear. Thus, although the infantile fetish has no developmental potential in terms of good symbol formation and creativity, it does undergo changes in meaning with shifts in the prevailing erotogenic zone.

Difficulties in the relationship between the small child and the mother can reduce the transitional object to various compulsive autoerotic activities, such as hair pulling, protracted thumb sucking, or compulsive masturbation. These symptoms need to be cured, for not only do they lead away from creativity, but they actively inhibit the development of enjoyable play, learning, or any form of creative symbolic activity. The energy tied up in these symptoms preempts the freedom needed for creativity. Mental activity is concentrated instead on the repetitive sadomasochistic fantasies that accompany such fetishistic autoerotic symptoms.

The Stage of Play

The stage of the transitional object merges into what could be called the stage of play. If everything has gone well up to this point, then the child will be able to play freely and creatively, with concentrated dedication. The play itself will show a clear pattern, or form, with a beginning, a middle, and a natural end. It will be neither unimaginatively repetitive (reminding one of fetishistic rituals) nor overexcitedly disorganized, indicating the presence of raw instinctual forces. Probably nobody has described the various qualities of children's play more beautifully than Marion Milner (1952).

Observations of children's play tell us much about the course of earlier development. A child who plays well shows that good illusion and reality were introduced beneficially into his or her early life. And we can see if gratification and frustration were well-timed, in appropriate doses, resulting in good amalgamation of libido and aggression. Both are needed for any form of creative activity, from play to artistic creation. Libido is needed for the building of good form, while an aggressive element is required for the capacity to destroy previous gestalts, without which innovative creation cannot take place. For example, if a little boy (or girl) refuses to knock down his block building once he has finished playing with it, he will not be able to start a new creation because all the blocks will be tied up in the old structure. Without the combination of libido and aggression, creation cannot take place. Children must have had the reassuring experience that their rage (when frustrated) will not "destroy" the mother, even with symbolic destruction of her. Only after such reassuring experiences will they be able to freely use objects for creative enjoyment.

In order for the child to play with enjoyment, a good "play space," i.e., the intermediate transitional space at that phase of development, must exist. This space is hospitable to and generates symbol formation. Winnicott calls it the "potential space" between mother and child. The mother must help to turn this potential space into a creativity-bearing intermediate region that both joins and separates mother and the playing child. (Symbolic acts always join and separate simultaneously.) In the previous phases of development, through appropriate handling of the child's needs, the mother facilitated the formation of good illusions and transitional objects. The mother's main task in the play stage is to create a situation in which the child can play and be alone in her presence. These are the "quiet" times, when the child does not feel pressured by instinctual needs or challenged by environmental demands but can quietly "do his or her own thing" with the knowledge that the trustworthy, responsive mother is somewhere near and available if necessary. In this situation, a calm "ego-relatedness" permeates the intermediate space between the child and what Winnicott calls the "environmental mother." The environmental mother is the continuation of the early holding mother and stands in contrast to the mother who is the object of instinctual cravings. The relatedness between the child and the environmental mother is gratifying in a nonparoxysmal and nonclimactic way. It is out of this situation that the capacity for tenderness and affection grows; it is unnecessary to derive these quiet, loving states from aim-inhibited instinctual drives or the neutralization of energy.

The capacity for durable tender love originates in the baby's enjoyment in being held firmly and lovingly during long intervals when instinctual tensions are at an ebb. It is the same instinctually unexcited, tension-free state in which the child enjoys playing alone in the presence of mother. Here the mother "holds" the child safely, not in her arms, but within the securely "holding" intermediate space she created for the playing child. In this space the child can play safely, trusting his or her own creativity, the usability of the objects for symbolic play, and the durable dependability of the mother, even if she must leave for short periods.

Quiet States versus Paroxysmal Cycles in Developmental Progression

At this point it seems fitting to consider the impact of ongoing "quiet" states versus paroxysmal cycles of instinctual need on affective and cognitive development. Freudian theory proposes that the motivating force in affective development, as well as in the development of ideational processes and the organization of reality experiences, comes from instinctual drive tensions and their motivational corollary: the nervous system's inherent tendency to rid itself of excitations (Freud, 1895, 1915a). Hermann (1936), on the other hand, introduced the idea of a nonclimactic, continuously effective "need for clinging" (*sich anklammern*). He believed that this primary but nonsexual, nonaggressive "instinct" leads, in optimal circumstances, directly to affectionate relationships.

This heuristic modification of instinct theory did not find assimilation into the main trend of psychoanalytic thinking, perhaps because Hermann was the only well-known analyst who did not emigrate during the war but stayed in Budapest. (Also, his works have not been translated, with the exception of "Clinging—Going-in-Search" [1936].) Among psychoanalysts, only Winnicott and, to some degree, Bowlby (1969), saw in the child's nonparoxysmal instinctual relatedness to the mother the roots of secure, affectionate connectedness. This connectedness is the necessary matrix for the unfolding of the child's creative capacities.

Among non-Freudian theorists, this area has received recognition within the framework of creativity from Bally (1945) and Schachtel (1959). Peter Wolff, in his comparative study *The Developmental Psychologies of Jean Piaget and Psychoanalysis*, differentiates the vantage points of these two theories: "Piaget . . . selected only those periods when the child performed at his optimum because organic tension was not interfering with his adaptive processes [while instinctual drive-determined behavior was the core of Freud's developmental theory]" (1960, p. 171).

The "ego-related," good "environmental mother" knows how to provide a safe atmosphere without exciting or impinging on the child's immediate world. She knows how to make usable objects available without forcing them on the child. The child will find them when he or she needs them. Finding them will be as much a creative act as the discovery of "objets trouvés" is for the artist, or driftwood for the beachcomber. Later, as the child grows into an adult, he or she will know how to unconsciously invest the world with parts of him- or herself so that when new parts of the world are found, they will not feel totally alien but as familiar places in which one can find one's own self. The world comes to be a safe place for exploration; it is connected to the self. Whether or not this will happen also depends on the early "mirroring function" of the mother's face and eyes.

The Mother's "Mirroring" Function

As important as holding and tactile experiences are for the growing sense of unity-within-one's-skin for the infant, so is visual contact—mother and child looking at each other—for the playing child. Pleasurable skin feelings contribute to the delineation of a good inside space, which is then experienced as a vague feeling *within* the body. This inner space is the predecessor of the "mind," which corresponds more or less to what is called the preconscious, the storehouse of symbolic internal representations. Symbolic forms are the "playthings" within the "play space" of the preconscious.

We can assume that the mother's internalized image is the earliest content of the slowly emerging preconscious. Her form can be viewed from many angles, but eye-to-eye contact is the most significant. The mother's eyes look at the playing child while the child looks up at the mother watching him or her play. The mother's eyes and face function as a mirror reflecting the loved image of the child to the child. The child will internalize the image of the mother's eyes as it contains him or her. This reciprocal or serial mutual internalization will lead in the child's inner space (budding preconscious) to a sturdy self-affirming structure, its composition analogous to that of Russian wooden dolls. The largest doll contains another doll, which contains another, and so on. Just as the empathic mother intuitively knows how and when to offer her breast, and how to offer objects for her child's creative use, she can look "creatively" and nonintrusively at the playing child. The child gets the message that he or she exists in the world, and that his or her existence is good and enjoyed by the mother. All this imbues the child's inner space through introjection of the richness of the mother's mirroring face.

Adult Creativity and the Inner Space

The series of mother-child interactions I have outlined will finally lead to *creativity*, or the lack of it, in adult life. Active creativity is predicated on the experience that one's self contains a rich and fertile inner space. Erikson's (1950) concept of "generativity," I believe, corresponds to this subjective experience.

Describing the future fate of the child's good transitional object, Winnicott says:

> Its fate is to be gradually allowed to be decathected. . . . By this I mean that in health the transitional object does not 'go inside' nor does the feeling about

> it . . . undergo repression. It is not forgotten and it is not mourned. It loses meaning . . . because the transitional phenomena . . . have become spread out over the whole intermediate territory between 'inner psychic reality' and 'the external world as perceived by two persons in common,' that is to say, over the whole cultural field [1953b, p. 5].

What I believe Winnicott means here is that the transitional object does not "go inside" in the sense of becoming a frozen mental representation that the person clings to (i.e., a kind of mental fetish). It does, however, go inside in the form of a pleasant memory image which then fertilizes the preconscious. The preconscious is the internalized heir of the caring mother providing security and creativity—or of the bad mother. Internalization of experiences goes on all the time. Our object world is continually internalized via our perceptions in the preconscious.

As we have seen, the mother's holding and handling of the infant begin to shape the feeling-quality of the primordial inner space on the pleasure-unpleasure dimension. Later, the good mother facilitates for her child a creative, fertile intermediate play space, which also contains the mother's nurturing, mirroring face and eyes. The child perceives this whole situation in his or her syncretic mode of perception and this complex percept will become internalized, thus contributing to the creation of the preconscious as an internal "playground" for symbolic creativity.

Since the preconscious is that part of mental life which contains everything we know and is not repressed, and which consequently can be brought into consciousness without special effort, it does correspond phenomenologically to what we experience as our "mind." The mind can be experienced as rich or poor, empty or filled, dependable or not dependable, in its function. These are the experiential gestalt qualities of "the mind," which will influence creativity in the narrower, artistic sense as well as in the wide, lifespace-creating sense. A trusting or nontrusting relationship toward one's own mind derives to a great extent from internalization of the mother's caretaking. Figuratively, we could say that in the beginning the mother functions as the child's preconscious mind. In the course of mental development the mother's caretaking features and emotional attitudes are internalized by the child and contribute to mental structuralization, including the child's own subjective attitude to his or her own mind. If a person feels his or her mind is rich and functions dependably, reliably producing the right word and the right concept at the right time, then we have reason to assume that in early childhood the mother offered the objects of the world in a predictably benevolent manner.

Erikson's (1962) "Peace comes from the inner space" can be amended: "Peace comes from the *creative* inner space, which is the base for the symbolic function that bridges over the gaps of time and space, thus uniting what has been separated."

Developmental Deviations

If the mother is not "good enough" or is unempathic, the world she hands over to her child will seem equally inhospitable and unyielding. Without the early experience of illusion coinciding with reality, the child's sense of the unity of his or her life processes, the unity between inside and outside, suffers early disruption. The child's inside will feel fragmented and not good. There may be early signs of psychosomatic discomfort. Frustrations and the absense of trust and hope will stunt the child's creativity. He or she will not be able to invest objects with illusion to tide over the periods of mother's absence. Moreover, even when this unempathic mother is physically present, she is not *with* her child. She cannot create for her child a fertile play space, where objects can be half-found, half-created. Under these conditions, the zone at the interface between the child and the outside world will not become an enjoyable, connecting transitional space. This "potential space" can even acquire bad connotations.

The kind of mother I am describing here is basically narcissistic, but her narcissistic unrelatedness may take different forms. From my clinical perceptions, I have distilled several types of unempathic mothering that may damage the child's creative potential.

The Intrusive Mother

The intrusive mother crowds out the child's spontaneous creativity from the "potential space" between herself and the child. She invades this space with her own physical presence, with her self-determined activities, and sometimes with an overdose of inappropriately chosen and inappropriately offered toys. She may use the child as her own transitional object, whose main function is to give security and badly needed reality to the mother's unfulfilled life. The mother wants to realize *her own* magic illusions about herself *through* her child. *Her* lifespace contains an empty gap between herself and the world, and this gap is to be filled by her child. The child may have been brought into the world to fulfill exactly this function. Such a child is not granted the chance to creatively construct his or her own reality (Piaget, 1937).

This type of narcissistic mother alternates between seductively overstimulating (and thus overexciting) her child, and fighting for her own power and autonomy. Of course seductive overstimulation is also a form of narcissistic power-seeking. The seduced child, like a hypnotized puppet, is helplessly drawn into the orbit of the "magician" mother. But this is "black magic," not creative illusion, and in all likelihood the child will be ruined for all later object relationships. This child will know nothing about durable, tender affect toward a constant object, since there was no constant "environmental mother." Such a quiet, unobtrusive role does not offer the exhibitionistic self-gratification these mothers seek. Later, they may be disappointed, injured in their narcissistic pride, when they see their children grow into heedlessly pleasure-seeking and consequently destructive and self-destructive adults. These "children," too, will try to be exhibitionistic magicians in life.

During the anal and phallic stages, this kind of mother presents a special danger. Around the time of toilet training (but spreading to all spheres of activities), the potential space surrounding the child becomes a battlefield for testing wills. In order for the mother to feel real and potent, the child must perform as ordered. Play activities are not assisted but stage-managed by the mother. Often the child's inside is literally invaded by frequent enemas. In thus manipulating the child's body functions, the mother leaves the child with the feeling that what is inside is bad, necessitating mother's intervention to eliminate it. A very unpromising basis for future creativity.

At this point, however, I should add a qualifier: The effect of an overpowering mother will differ, depending on the child's temperament. Some children, for instance, may become convinced of their own lack of creative potential and grow into self-depreciating, ineffectual adults, imitative and always needing approval from mother or, later, from stand-ins for her. In the case of the male, he is likely to choose a highly efficient, powerful, and domineering wife.

On the other hand, constitutionally more aggressive children may try to fight for their autonomy, to repel the intruder from their lifespace. Yet this very fight for autonomy and alertness against "attack" can turn into a lifelong struggle, accompanied by a paranoid tinge of suspiciousness. The potential space surrounding such people rigidifies into a "struggle-field" for power. The eternal aim for "power over" and the fear of having been "sucked in" may result in a paranoid obsessive character who cannot feel comfortably well-fitted into any milieu.

These patients may be outwardly successful, but they lack the capacity to enjoy any situation. Like the addict who cannot be satiated, no degree of success is enough, for mother's phantom always threatens to subjugate and humiliate them. The fight for autonomy must be carried out with a vengeance precisely because the mother was also controlling with seductiveness. The eternal temptation is for the "grown-up child" to give in to an overpowering, seductive "magician." Fulfilling creativity cannot exist since that is predicated on the unworried intermingling of inside and outside. And, despite outward signs to the contrary, these people feel weak, ineffectual, and bad inside. A "bad" inside cannot be allowed to intermingle with the outside; rather, it needs to be hidden. Human closeness is feared lest this inside badness be seen. Witty, charming social manners may well present a "polished" persona, which serves as the communicating and safely separating interface between the "bad" inside and the outside world. But actually these people feel utterly lonely. Neither truly "nourishing" relationships nor truly creative products can be formed under these conditions. True creativity, in relationships and other activities, is predicated on the courage to let the other see one's own inside "as it is," not camouflaged by a "manufactured," well-polished screen. Magicians produce clever performances that entertain the audience, yet after the performance is over, neither side feels spiritually enriched—in contrast to what happens when true deep relationships are formed or when true art creation enriches both the creator and the "audience."

The anal and phallic stages present special dangers for the character development of children of not-dependable, "magician" mothers. Imprints of the harmful mother-child interactions in the phallic phase may be found in inauthentic grandiosity, false charm, and "false creativity." In her paper on "Perversion, Idealization and Sublimation," Chasseguet-Smirgel (1974) clearly links problems in the phallic phase to the development of "false creativity" and a generally inauthentic character. Drawing on case material, she indicates that the mother may convey the idea that she values the child's penis more than her husband's. The child gains the harmful illusion of having a better, bigger penis than the father—although the child knows that in fact this is not so.[3] The mother has created a false situation. According to Chasseguet-Smirgel, there is then a false idealization of pregenital part-objects, mainly of the uncastratable "anal-phallus"—leading to a spurious, precious, aesthetic attitude to surrounding inanimate objects or to the creation of "false" aesthetic products.

I find Chasseguet-Smirgel's hypothesis convincing, given my own experience with patients whose mothers fell into the overpowering and seductive category. Such mothers, for their own pleasure, foster an exhibitionistic, false "creativity" in their children while stunting authentic, inner-motivated creative acts. Creativity, as a treasured idea, may then become linked to these "children's" struggle for superiority. But no matter how many valuable objects they surround themselves with, or attempt to create, the real inside and the outside never come together. These people remain in essence disconnected from their possessions and creations. Their art

[3] The real penis in the boy; fantasy penis in the girl.

objects resemble infantile fetishes used to "patch up" castration panic, rather than serving as good transitional objects. Overemphasis on the quality and style of clothing, for instance, may serve this purpose.

In these cases, mother's eyes functioned as a false mirror, reflecting false adoration and an unreal image of the child. The child by necessity introjects all this, resulting in a split inside and a "false self." Other people come to be used as a "hall of mirrors"; they are expected to reflect adoration. Although these patients (or people) are willing to work for this reflection, the slightest deviation from the expected reaction results in narcissistic mortification and possibly rage. Living in the midst of mirrors, they are totally isolated. Indeed, a deep, hidden depression may be their only authentic experience.

The above telescoped vignette was based on individuals with a "false self" who take an *outward-directed, active* stance in reaction to a narcissistically intrusive mother. Their attempts to create a visibly rich lifespace for themselves remain unfulfilling because they never had a creatively fertile play space to internalize. Although their lives are cluttered with activities, objects, and people, these are "manipulated" (acted *upon*) to gain power and admiring reflection, rather than participated *with* in truly creative activity. No matter what they visibly achieve, they are unable to create an organically unified lifespace for themselves, based on participation of inside with outside.

Avid Introjectors' Inhibited Creativity

Constitutionally more passive children are not likely to go outward to *fight* for their lifespace vis-à-vis the mother. Given good native intelligence, they may become *avid introjectors* of things they like, and will play with and "live on" their nonmaterial (no *mater*!) mental representations, or symbols. These children live in their internal world. They pull in their boundaries, away from the disappointing or threatening mother, instead of fighting for their space of freedom in the outer world. (A rather large number of my women patients but only a few men belonged to this schematized category. I think this gender distribution is psychologically significant.)

The main variable distinguishing this inward-turning group from the previous outward-going one may well be the child's constitutional givens on the activity-passivity dimension. Nevertheless, the mother's character also seems somewhat different. In both cases, the mother is narcissistic and self-involved, but with the avid introjector, she is less actively intrusive and less the exhibitionistic "magician" type. The mother might have managed the infant's early feeding period adequately, or maybe indulgently, judging from these patients' tendency to use oral intake as a model for interaction with the world. (These patients "eat up" the world with their sense-perceptors and their minds. Many of them also struggle with weight problems.) Or, again, it might be that genetically these infants were slated to become more intellectual, physically passive "oral characters," while the previous group might have been constitutionally predisposed to become more aggressive "anal-phallic" characters. (The gender distribution might have to do with this difference.)

Most of my avid introjectors remembered some early favorite toys they took to bed and also to other places. But their mothers were not able to furnish them with the experience of "playing alone" with mother dependably watching. These mothers were unpredictable and away—for necessary or unnecessary reasons—much of the time. The children were physically well kept but felt "not understood" and alone. "Things" were given to them but not the things they wanted when they wanted them.

The mothers of avid introjectors seemed to be vulnerable and in many ways childlike. They acted as if the child could destroy them. Frequently they were physically sick and depressed. The child had to behave as a little adult, protecting mother and fitting into her needs. Otherwise, she might become sick, or maybe even die. The child learned to avoid emotional outbursts by withdrawing into his or her own mind, playing with "thought-toys" and fantasies in an internal "glass menagerie."

The anal period, usually associated with active aggressive behavior, was passed through with seemingly little cathexis. These children were well controlled and learned easily whatever had to be learned, including sphincter control, except they did not learn how to fight. Their chosen defense was and remained to leave the field of potential battle. They had an inside "field" to retreat to and enjoyed their museum-like preconscious. At an early age these children exploited their capacity to have a rich inner life; they accumulated what Greenacre (1957) refers to as "collective alternates" in their preconscious. Their preconscious became cluttered, making it difficult to keep watch over all its full content simultaneously. Actually, this is exactly what these patients try to do because they do not trust the smooth functioning of their preconscious. Often they are afraid of losing their minds. Anything out of sight might have vanished and might not reappear when needed—like mother. Again, the atmosphere of the preconscious inherits the atmosphere the mother created for her child.

People in this group are gifted by nature and specialists in creating their "internal museums" by symbolizing interesting and beautiful things in their minds. They are responsive to beauty and the arts. They can enjoy taking things in but have great difficulty in output. In this group, the bridging-over function of symbolization only works easily in one direction;

from the outside to the inside. True creativity flows smoothly in a continuous circle: Content is taken in from the outside to the inside, where it undergoes transformation before crossing the boundary again, this time from the inside to the outside. Every time content crosses a boundary, it is symbolically transformed (Deri, 1974).

The "inward-symbolizing" patients under discussion did not have good-enough mothers to establish basic trust toward the world. As children, they were left to their own devices very early. They lacked a safe, creative play space with a "mirroring" mother, who could be introjected. Although these children probably showed more creativity in their play than less gifted children would have, when they played alone they were really alone, without a mother to look at them. Thus, their symbolic play did not "bridge over" to mother, but was created by the self to the self, leading to their solipsistic universe of inward-directed symbolization. They became their own mothers, as it were, nourishing themselves on symbols very early.

In studying the function of symbolization and the conditions for creativity, I have found avid introjectors an exceptionally instructive group. They are likely to seek analytic help and are analyzable, since they know how to use and grow on symbols, such as language and transference. They have taught me a great deal about the reasons for their inhibited outward-going creativity. Usually their presenting symptoms are complaints about feeling inhibited in creative work, whether in writing term papers, dissertations, books, or creating visual art or music. Coupled with these complaints is a general unease at not being able to cope with the real world—although for all practical purposes they do seem to cope well and they may even be successful in their chosen studies or profession. They cannot, however, believe in the continuity of their success. For students, every A, every sign of academic recognition, feels like a chance event. While these patients are usually liked by others, they feel that their relationships with people are tenuous and that their *real* life has to be lived in hiding, so to speak. Life in the world with people tires them, and they can hardly wait to be alone in the privacy of their own rooms (and the privacy of their own minds). In contrast to the outward-directed patients, who cluttered their lives with valuable objects and with activities as signs of visible achievement—at the price, however, of losing contact with their "authentic inner core"—these inward-living patients abhor the accumulation of objects. They try to remain independent of material as well as living "objects" and to seek self-sufficiency in their portable internal universe.

Although these patients remain "authentic," in the sense of not "selling out" to a life motivated by the need for reflected admiration, they themselves feel "inauthentic," for they are unable to live up to what they feel is their real potential. They don't trust that the world outside will be interested in what they can produce out of their own inside. Nor do they trust the *active* creative potency of their own inside. And they do not trust *time*, as a dimension along which good things unfold. As I have already indicated, the prototypic situation for the development of this kind of trust was missing. The environmental mother, as a quietly but creatively present "audience," was missing from the child's play space. The child had no chance to internalize an interested, receptive world because the self-affirming reflection from the mother's face was lacking.

When the young child begins to separate out mother and the rest of the world as "not me," *then* is the time (and urge) for symbolic bridge-building as a way of negating total separation while also accommodating the realistic necessity of separateness. Transitional objects and symbolic play in the vicinity of an available mother expressly serve this connecting-separating function. The successful "bridging-over" function of symbolic play might well be needed for later symbolic creativity, which always implies trust in a receptive audience. Symbol formation always takes place in the context of longing, under the pressure of a "force toward." But for creative symbolization to develop, there must be trust and hope that the other is reachable.

The first human longing or experience of a "force toward" takes place in relation to the distant mother. In other words, the space that separates child from mother becomes the cradle of creative symbol formation. But this symbolizing activity unfolds only if there is a trustworthy, constant mother to reach out to. If this is the case, then the child and later the adult will remain organically connected with the outside world. He or she will feel free to translate the content of his or her private inside world into the public external world, with trust that it will be well received and understood, at least by some.

The potential space between child and mother was not so propitious for our avid introjectors. They felt thwarted precisely in their capacity to translate the private inside into the shared outside. Indeed, they did not feel that the outside was *shared* by them. I have already outlined how they created a rich but lonely inner life. Their defense was a precocious, but therefore precarious, ego development. Mother did not lovingly hand over the world to them. For some reason, the consequence of this was not an aggressive wish to conquer or destroy the world, but rather a desire to preserve it intact inside. Due to inadequate mothering, the current of object libido was not set in active motion, nor was a good amalgamation of Eros and Thanatos achieved. These "passively gifted" children threw their votes, so to speak, on the side of Eros and symbol creation. But here the forces of Eros lacked true vitality, for they did not connect strongly to real people in the world.

Such patients often feel closer to characters in books or to unknown authors than to flesh-and-blood people in their environment. "Collective alternates" of this sort may have helped them to avoid clashes with the inadequate mother. Although their inner symbols do not function as true transitional objects, in the sense of leading over to the "other," they do serve, more or less successfully, to preserve a feeling of wholeness, of what Winnicott calls "the continuity of their existence." Perhaps one could designate their valued internal symbols as high-level fetishes that serve as "patches" (Greenacre, 1969) to protect against an otherwise unbearable feeling of emptiness.

These patients' internal symbols do not represent "congealed anger" (Greenacre, 1969), but neither do they lead to uninhibited, active creativity, for that would require a blending of libido and aggression. To reiterate: Aggression is needed to carve out a good gestalt from its embedding context and also for the act of "expulsion." Creative expulsion probably does imply in a sublimated form the original act of anal elimination. Remember that the anal phase was undercathected in these "unfighting" patients. A struggle over anal functions would have endangered both the continuity of the child's precariously held-together inside and the preservation of the mother, whose existence was still needed for the child's physical survival, no matter how inadequate she might have been in fostering the child's creative growth. These patients' mothers displayed their vulnerability almost as blackmail. Leaving the potential battlefield by decathexis, while overcathecting the private inner world, saved these children from attacking the "destructible" mother. This security measure also brought the illusion of magical control over their nonmaterial thought-products. After a while they were no longer able, or even willing, to attempt the transfer of these "thought-products" into the daylight of the outside world.

Not only did they fear a nonreceptive world, but they were wary of facing up to the very process of externalization.

Inner symbolization, i.e., communication between aspects of the self, is a qualitatively different process from symbolic communication from the self to the external world. In their experiments, Werner and Kaplan (1963) have demonstrated how the distance between addressor and addressee influences the form of symbolic communication. With increasing distance, communication becomes more explicit, more articulated, involving more elements. Conversely, with decreasing distance between addressor and addressee (the utmost case of which is communication only within the self), brevity, ellipsis embodying multiple meanings, condensation of elements, and a generally more amorphous syntax predominate. The development of easy and more articulated symbolic communication over a distance assumes the existence of a cathected distant addressee. If children do not find an interested addressee in the mother, they become fixated on the more amorphous, and therefore more "magically omnipotent" form of internal self-to-self communication. This type of inner communication, precisely because of its fast inclusiveness, may lead to creative insights, but also to frustration if in the course of time the person develops the wish to be manifestly creative. The original need for a self-sufficient magical omnipotence then gives way to a feeling of powerless impotence. It is at this point that the isolated "overintrojective" person may decide to look for help in psychoanalysis.

The psychoanalytic method is well suited to these patients' needs, for the psychoanalytic situation approximates that phase of development where these patients' life course went awry, flowing in only a single direction—away from connecting with the outside world. Psychoanalysis provides a new chance for a creative "play space," where the patient can freely play with his or her thoughts and fantasies in the *pres-*

ence of an other who does not intrude but who quietly mirrors the patient's reality as an understandable communicator. The parenthesized "as if" character of the psychoanalytic situation allows for greater freedom in experimenting with self-expression than is possible in everyday life. Due to the highs and lows of the transference involvement, the patient's perception of the analyst alternates between a character half-created by the patient's fantasies and a real outside person who is an interested "watcher" and listener, and thus a good addressee to direct communication to. The "transference space" is analogous to the child's transitional space, for it is neither inside nor outside space but both simultaneously. In this space, these patients, who used to live their "real" life in hiding within themselves, can gradually venture into real communication with an "other."

As the analyst becomes perceived as an interested outside person, the arrested flow of symbolization, from inside to outside, will gradually acquire direction. The patient begins to talk to the analyst. The use of symbolic language communication within analysis may then lead to symbolic communication (if talent permits, artistic creativity included) with the real outside world. The analyst has a second chance in the patient's life to hand over the world as a receptive partner, hospitable to the patient's creations. In addition, by passing the test of indestructibility, the analyst allows for the fusion of aggression and libido in the patient. This fusion energizes these "inert" people, who never dared to actively tackle raw material or to actively engage the outside world.

This group of patients came for help expressly because they suffered from a disruption in the cycle of creative symbolization. While these patients' "intake" was highly developed and they did respond to their surroundings with keen and richly symbolizing perception, this is only half of the "creative cycle." What they lacked was the ability to carry out the other half: the "output" or *externalization* of forms built with the bricks of their rich preconscious. This stunted creative cycle was particularly painful for them because symbolization per se was the most valued function in their lives. Analytic exploration of the origin of this defect led me to a fuller appreciation of the mother's role in fostering or hindering the development of the child's creativity.

Had these patients been creative geniuses, the mother's role would not have stood out as clearly, for the genetic endowment would have prevailed, irrespective of the early mother-child relationship.

CHAPTER 9

The Psychic Structure of the Creating Artist: A Theoretical Construction

This chapter does not deal with the effect of mother-child interaction on the development of the child's creativity. It is more a thumbnail sketch of the metapsychology of the creative state. The theorizing is based on the generic theory of symbolization detailed in Part II and on case material.[1] Biographies, autobiographies, and letters of artists have also influenced my thinking. However, neither the case histories nor the artists' biographical data will be presented individually. This chapter is not on "the artist's psychic structure" in general, but specifically on the "ideal model" of the creative state. This should have wide implications for our therapeutic aims. My goal is to arrive at a metapsychological "model" or metaphor of creativity, as a concise culmination of all the theorizing on symbolization that went on before.

We all know that artistic creativity does not necessarily lead to a happy, smoothly unfolding, harmonious life. All my

[1] My psychoanalytic case material, counting only "officially" recognized artists, consists of three painters, one photographer, two composers, two novelists, one poet, and two choreographers. Besides this professionally "arrivé" group, I have treated a number of patients involved in creative work at more than an "amateur" level.

artist patients had their bouts with depression, anxiety over work-blocks, fears that the flow of creativity had stopped. While their psychodynamics and individual biographical patterns were quite different, a common feature (with one exception) was the complaint that they were unable to establish a long-lasting, committed relationship. The individual differences showed most during the "low" periods, when creative work stopped or was at an ebb. During periods of active creativity (these periods increased in frequency and duration), the picture changed. Individual differences diminished; so did involvement in painful events of the past or of the present, for that matter. The picture was dominated by the experience of fulfillment, specifically by a feeling of organic cohesiveness between inside and outside. The "inside" was experienced as rich, and so was the outside. The "creative cycle" of intake and output was unobstructed (in contrast to the "passively gifted" patients described in Chapter 8).

These periods of creative elation did not necessarily follow analytic resolution of infantile traumas or parent-child vicissitudes. In the long run there was a relation between these two processes, but the appearance of creative periods also had an autonomous rhythm of its own. Creative artists' talent—not to mention genius (not represented in my group)—has the impetus to "come through" on its own strength. Whatever defense mechanisms operate at other times or in other areas of their lives, they seem to be overcome in the periods, and in the area, of creativity. It is possible, and it is my impression, that genuinely creative people resort to repression considerably less than do other patients, or nonpatients, for that matter. Artists' difficulties in life stem more from their highly complex drive configuration. I believe it is exactly the lack of repression that accounts for the "equal rights" demand of opposing drives. More "ordinary" individuals are more likely to deal with opposing drives by repressing one side and accentuating the other. Artists, on the other hand, aim at resolution by unifying opposites within one complex symbolic form, in other words, through their creative art work. The intensity of opposing internal forces might furnish a particular impetus toward the choice of creative art as a profession (this would fit into Szondi's concept of "operotropism").

What other innate givens or very early personality characteristics enable the talent or genius of the artist to "come through"? Greenacre has much to say about this topic. My limited experience with artists and highly gifted "artist-type" individuals in psychoanalysis completely bears out her observations. In her paper on the childhood of the artist, Greenacre (1957) describes how artists' innately greater sensitivity to sensory stimulation, their wide range of empathy and consequently widened "experiential field," promotes a "love affair with the world" and leads them to "collective alternates" early in their object relations. The latter implies less fixation on the early vicissitudes of the relationship with the primary love objects, i.e., the parents. In another paper Greenacre (1958) says that in the artist there is "from early childhood . . . a sense of fusion with the outer world, in a state of mutual permeability" (p. 530). A more beautiful description of the essence of the transitional space could not be given. In the great artist, the existence of this wide transitional space does not depend on the mother, but is given in specific characteristics of his or her innate psychic structure.

Artists have a special openness to their psychic organization, from the perceptual apparatus to the preconscious, and "down" into the energy reservoir of the id. In the creative process these structures are not pitted against each other; one does not exert control *over* the other, or invade it. Creativity is a unitary organismic process. Real artists have a *sui generis* capacity to make unique organizations out of their experiences, whether these experiences originate in the unconscious or in external perceptions. In either case, the truly creative act molds these experiences of different order into one significant, good gestalt. The artist's perception is particularly wide and sharp in both directions—outside and within.

It can be assumed that creative artists are genetically endowed with far more than the usual capacity for symbol formation. Open communication between their psychic systems is part of this phenomenon. Easy access to primary-process thinking and imagery allows them to furnish the preconscious with a wide variety of symbols so that there is a large quantity of forms to choose from for creative expression. Since the propensity for form creation originates in the genes, which are localized in the id, it is safe to assume that creative artists have access, to an exceptional degree and quality, to genetically given formative id tendencies. This is in contrast to the dualistic view that pits the organism's supposedly primary motivation toward tension discharge against superimposed ego forces toward form creation.

As we saw in Chapter 7, it is not the "normal" state of affairs but rather the effect of repression that segments psychic unity and brings about the damming up of energic pressure, to the point where this pressure must be released through form*less* discharge to preserve some measure of homeostatic equilibrium within the psychic organism. It is the repression barrier that splits psychic structure into *antagonistic* sides of id, ego, and superego. Under normal circumstances, the creative-expressive and tension-reducing motivational tendencies coexist in balance. If repression shuts down the passageway and blocks id content from moving "upward" toward the preconscious, *then* the organism changes into a hydraulic machine, seeking tension reduction at all costs. Instead of creative gestalt-forming activity, one has disorganization or splitting defense mechanisms. (Creative symbolization, which *connects*, is the antidote for splitting.)

During the creative process per se, artists' psychic functioning is exceptionally devoid of repression. This partly accounts for their increased capacity to use creative symbol formation for bringing about—at least temporarily—connected order within their inside as well as between themselves and the surrounding environment. In other words, for artists, the creation of the manifest art work represents the organic connectedness between their inside and the outside world. Accumulation of objects is proverbially not the artist's way to build a fitting personal milieu (as it was for the outward-directed patients described in the last chapter).

At this point I would like to distinguish the artist from those patients I called "passively gifted." Although the latter had a rich inner storehouse of symbolic forms, they lacked the stamina for externalization. Their inside preconscious felt cluttered and separated from their environment since symbolic communication operated in only one direction, from outside to inside, but not the other way around. They lacked the capacity for active symbolic creation. This disruption in the cycle of creativity derived from their intolerance for any display of aggression. The forces of Eros and Thanatos remained unamalgamated.

In contrast, artists are free to use the quantum of aggression needed to complete the creative cycle. Their creative activity is highly libidinized, but the derivatives of "anal-aggressive" productivity are not banned from their repertoire. Instinctual fusion, with Eros in the lead, seems to be naturally achieved by artists.

Good fusion, not "neutralization," of energy is the precondition for artistic creativity. The need for neutralization seems to be predicated on a preponderance of aggression versus libido, while good fusion takes place if libido outweighs aggression. The very process of amalgamation of opposites is a function of Eros (Freud, 1920). Neutralized energy might be at work in critically constructed, intellectualized work with an obsessive tinge; in art criticism rather than in art creation. Only a libidinous fusion of opposing energies can lead to the creation of beautiful forms. I very much disagree with Kris (1952), who, while discussing the pleasure derived from gestalt completion (solution of problems) in science and art, says: "The solution of problems—including all areas of creativity—affords pleasure through discharge of neutral energy" (p. 315). I cannot imagine that discharging neutral anything causes pleasure. Gestalt completion causes pleasure for the sheer fact that a formative act came to fruition.

With regard to instinctual fusion, the preponderance of Eros might be the very condition that makes it possible for creating artists not to resort to unity-splitting repression in spite of their extremely complex instinctual understructure. Creative individuals are more aware (have better internal perception), yet more tolerant, of their contradictory inner tendencies. The ever-present biological and psychological human bisexuality is probably more pronounced in artists. But they also have a high capacity to live with this complex sexual structure, without repressing either side. The same holds for the opposites of active/passive. Both are needed for artistic creativity: the "female" receptiveness, the capacity to allow material to "hatch" in the "womb" of the preconscious, and the active "masculine" aspect of shaping raw material by eliminating what is unnecessary; and finally the birth-giving act of delivering the artistic creation into the outside world. Many members of my "passively gifted" group had trouble accepting their psychological tendencies that "officially" belonged to the opposite gender. Creating artists have no such problems. They are on good terms with their psychic hermaphroditism.

In the same way, one might speculate that in the artist there is an overlapping of libidinal phases, which may be energized with close-to-equal intensity. My clinical work with artists offered several examples of this constellation. Greenacre (1957) refers to the artist's "incomplete organization of libidinal structure" (p. 492) which "may carry the whole gamut of mixed libidinal phase pressures, genital and pregenital" (p. 499). These pressures act with *non*neutralized intensity and "struggle for harmony, of which the creative product is the outcome" (p. 501). At least for the duration of the creative act, artists are able to balance their complex psychic structure by the very act of creation.

The self-healing (whole-making) function of symbolization is by nature the artist's gift. The less creative person falls mentally ill under the same pressure of contradictory tendencies that mobilize the artist to create symbolic forms which unite the opposites within the same artistically good gestalt.

The relationship between the unifying function of the symbol and what Nunberg (1931) calls the "synthetic function of the ego" should be obvious. Because of this ever-present synthesizing function, there is always the *attempt* to express divergent but simultaneously experienced content within one gestalt. This attempt to unify may result in a neurotic symptom if the antithetical contents are separated by a rigid repression barrier. Although neurotic symptoms still bind energy and serve some homeostatic function, symptom formation is an "emergency solution" for the sake of the upkeep of some measure of psychic order. Symptoms attempt to protect the psychic apparatus from disintegrating under the pressure of mutually incompatible wishes. But the neurotic symptom does not fit well into the schema of the *total* personality; it acts as a foreign body which stands in the way of adaptive processes.

The intrapsychic topology of creating artists is very different from that of neurotics. In artists, the opposite tendencies are hierarchically of the same order, juxtaposed, as it were, instead of opposing each other and vying for power. During the process of creation at least, there is no ego splitting or restrictive repression barrier. Because of this, and given an exceptional symbolizing capacity, artists are able to form highly inclusive schemata (Piaget, 1945), that is, symbolic structures without total closure, which are able to assimilate into their structure a wide variety of disparate and contradictory content-components. These large and well-organized schemata serve to enlarge and structure the ego, thereby enhancing its mediating function between the person and the environment. This progressive ego enhancement does not imply increasing "autonomy" from the id, in the sense of increasing polarization. What happens is just the opposite: The assimilating function of the inclusive schemata increases the synergic *cooperation* among *all* areas of the psyche. Under these conditions, there is more intrinsic connectedness among the "intersystemic" psychic functions. This connectedness is based on the vertical extension of ordered gestalts, not on formless fusion. Artists' symbolizing, i.e., "schema"-creating proficiency, leads to transforming an exceptionally extensive area of their total "intrapsychic space" into an articulated region, a characteristic usually attributed to the preconscious. Symbolic gestalts contained within this preconscious-like "space" are readily available for further creative recombination and enhance good communication between the inside and the outside world. Easy availability of preconscious symbolic forms leads to ease in building connecting symbol-bridges between the self and the surrounding environment. During creative periods, the artist's lifespace is cohesive; inside and outside are truly connected.

Although the artist's "love affair with the world" implies a strong empathic reactivity to his or her animate and inanimate surrounding, it does not imply constant and dependable object libido in relation to specific persons. Artistic (aesthetic) empathy may occur in an otherwise self-involved, narcissistic individual. Biographies of great artists offer ample evidence of this. Artists start out with greater-than-usual independence from the emotional vicissitudes of parental care (Greenacre, 1957) and turn to "collective alternates" and a "love affair with the world." It is the artist's unusual aesthetic sensitivity that allows for this empathic, even though often narcissistic, participation with his or her environment. Experiences and perceptions are easily assimilated into inclusive inner schemata, but, because of this comprehensiveness, the assimilated components may form a somewhat abstract, impersonal pattern, in which the emphasis is on their formal characteristics more than their interpersonal significance. Aesthetic experience of life as a whole is both the specific forte and the Achilles' heel of the artist, or of the person with a highly artistic temperament. This stance vis-à-vis life implies distance without depersonalization (the "aesthetic distance"). It is not (or at least not always) a defensive stance, nor are the aesthetic aims "substitutes" for something else.

The artist's lifespace is not disrupted by an empty gap separating self from world. Rather, artists experience the world as one vast transitional space; it is there to be "played" with creatively and to be filled with beautiful things. They enjoy the richness of their inner space and trust that the world will want what they have to give. It is probably a lack of fixation on the original mother that allows artists to relate to the world in all its multiplicity instead of unconsciously viewing it as representing mother in a complex symbolic way. An unusual psychic endowment makes it possible for them to "hand over" the world to themselves and themselves to the world. Their capacity to create their own universe guards them against loneliness and isolation. Truly creative people have a "horn of plenty"—a "magic bag" into which they can dip for creative ideas. They also have the strength to materialize these ideas. This "magic bag" is their unusually extended preconscious, which contains well-formed and "ready-to-use" symbolic forms.

The active stance of creativity, then, is a unified and unifying process. It originates in the archaic instinctual tendencies in the id, and drives upward through the increasingly ordered and ordering levels of the preconscious, until it reaches the realm of consciousness and culminates in the manifest art work preceivable by the outer world. This long journey is facilitated by the intensity of primary-process-type energy, which in this context not only does *not* destroy but actually contributes to the establishment of patterned order within the psychic apparatus. The id does not "invade" the ego in this process, nor does one need to hypothesize a qualified form of "regression," such as "regression in the service of the ego" to account for the participation of primary-process-like phenomena in the creative process (Kris, 1952). The intensity and mobility of energic and formal transformations are "primary" in terms of ontogenetic development, but here they function purely as contributors to *progression*. "Regression in the service of . . ." introduces a zigzag break in the unidirectional creative process, the main feature of which is an unbroken movement upward and outward, away from chaos toward articulated order.

Artistic creativity is predicated on ready connectedness between the psychic "institutions" and, by its very functioning, results in even more ordered connectedness. Once again the principle of "rich is getting richer" prevails. Individuals with particularly strong endowment for symbolization are the rich ones getting richer. The "poor ones," on the other hand, are those with particularly low genetic capacity for symbolization, such as "symbiotic" children. "Symbiotic" children are unable to tolerate distance from the mother; therefore, there is no "potential space" to turn into a *connecting* space through symbolic play or language. Lack of symbolization prevents enrichment and structuralization of their "poor" inner "space."

The Centaur Model: A Model for Mental Health Based on the Unifying Function of Symbol-Forming Creativity

The psychic organization hypothesized for artists during their creative periods would be beneficial for any individual. As I indicated at the beginning, creativity, in the wide sense, is part and parcel of our human endowment, and, in an even wider sense, it is inherent in all organic nature. Psychoanalysis, like other forms of therapy or education, aims at fostering the creative potential of the individual. It aims at the smooth functioning of the "creative cycle" of "symbolizing intake" and "symbolizing output."

Psychoanalysis is directed toward stimulating the symbolizing, order-making capacity of the patient's mind. Good interpretations lay the groundwork for the formation of inclusive schemata in the patient's preconscious. The dynamic effect of these mental schemata lies in the fact that they are complex but unclosed gestalts. Once formed, they act as magnetic fields, drawing in "fitting" content that was previously split off or "misfiled." Half-forgotten memories, or misfiled ones, will be drawn into their proper context due to the "pulling-in" (assimilating) force of the appropriate unclosed schema. Reorganization of the components of a previously existing gestalt is itself a creative act (see Wertheimer, 1945). Psychoanalysis performs a creative act by reorganizing the analysand's mental content.

During the psychoanalytic process of creative gestalt formation and transformation, the bad gestalts of symptoms yield up their constituent elements, which are then drawn into new preconscious schemata initiated by the analyst's interventions. Obviously, for this to come about, there must be a shared area of symbolic language communication between the analysand and the analyst. The new schemata, due to their assimilating power, establish further new gestalts by redistributing old elements. Through this reorganization the old elements acquire new meanings. Remember that the meaning of parts depends on their context, i.e., on their position in a complex gestalt.

Neurotic symptoms split the unity, i.e., the whole-some unitary functioning, of the total organism. The newly formed schemata, helped along by analytic work, are "good" gestalts because they eliminate splits in the "whole" of the psyche, i.e., they unify and connect the psychic systems. This unification then enables the emergence of undisrupted creative acts. The final aim of all creative activity is to establish a fitting lifespace, a harmonious connectedness between person and environment. For the artist, this aim entails the creation of an art work in which parts of the artist's "inside" are expressed in a concrete "outside" object. For the nonartist, a variety of acts may fulfill the same function, from gardening to finding the "right" mate or friend. Anything that results in a harmonious lifespace is evidence of creative life processes and of an unsplit, well-ordered psychic organization.

The fitting metaphor to illustrate the synergic functioning of such a well-articulated yet unified mind is not Freud's (1923) "horse and rider" but rather the *centaur*. Here the intense instincts (the id, or horse) blend into the human figure (the ego, or rider) so that instead of two antagonistic gestalts one has a complex *whole*. This metaphor of the centaur is derived from analyses not only of creative artists but also of individuals I refer to as "artist-types," who are not artists by profession but whose main "ego function" is form-giving and connecting rather than defense.

Freud's metaphor points to a struggle between the animalistic instincts and the superimposed rider, controlling with intellect (not wisdom!). This constellation of forces, far from representing the general human condition, holds only for the isolating, obsessive character, who desperately attempts to exert power over forces felt as originating from sources superior to his or her own intellect. In contrast to this typically obsessive power struggle, the creative artist-type naturally accepts and uses instinctual forces as motive power and raw material for creative activity. The obsessive intellectualizer is fearful, suspicious, and antagonistic to forces of undefinable origin, while the artist-type welcomes undefinable inner promptings and tries to use this "found" power in creative acts rather than subdue it. The utilization of instinctual forces in creation lends authentic intensity and emotional communicativeness to the art work. Creative individuals combine the "lower" with the "higher," the "inside" with the "outside," in good symbolic gestalts. The lifespace of the power-seeking "rider on the horse" is likely to turn into an effortful "struggle-space," while that of the artist-type will have more of the characteristics of a creatively usable, transitional "play space."

Still, as mentioned before, we know that the total life pattern of great artists is often far from harmonious. Their particularly complex drive configuration makes organization of life as a totality a special problem. In agreement with Greenacre, I also hypothesized that the inner tension caused by the contradictory psychic tendencies may furnish specific impetus toward conflict resolution through creative symbol formation. This complex psychic constellation leads to the much-debated question of "creativity and insanity."

Kurt Eissler (1963) believes that *mens sana in corpore sano* will never produce great art, that the creative artist has to be a "sick animal." There is partial truth to this statement (with poetic license), if applied to the artist's intensely antithetical psychic tendencies. What it does not express is the fact that it is the *unimpaired* talent or genius for unification by symbols that gives fulfilling cohesion to the artist's lifespace while creating, even if in between there are periods of depression and occasional despair. Yet the meaning of parts always depends on the whole. Thus, we must view the periods of mental struggle and pain within the totality of the creative artist's life. From this perspective, artists are hardly "sick animals." "Sick animals" would collapse under similar inner pressure and struggle, instead of using the inner disequilibrium for the creation of beautifully balanced works. One has only to think of Beethoven's late quartets or Goethe's *Faust*.

At this point a qualification is in order. The unsegmented, unitary functioning of the total psyche is a necessary but *not sufficient* condition for the creative act. A kind of unification of the psychic systems may be seen in certain pathological conditions, such as psychosis or borderline personality disorders. The critical difference here lies in the blended versus the *de*fused state of the antithetical instinctual forces: libido and aggression. It is the fusion versus defusion of the antithetical forces that links up with great capacity versus incapacity for good symbol formation. The libidinous amalgamation of instinctual opposites (with Eros in the lead) greatly facilitates the formation of inclusive, connecting symbolic structures. These are the extended symbol-bridges (schemata) that lend *ordered connectedness* to the psyche of the creative artist, at least during the process of creation.

In contrast, the "unified" inside of the psychotic or borderline person is *dis*ordered. Opposing urges here too coexist on the same hierarchic level and claim "equal rights" for manifestation, without, however, the unifying and formative mediation of good symbol formation. Moreover, due to the defusion of instincts, raw aggression dominates the scene and precludes good—or practically any—symbolization. Intense rage can disrupt even the formation of cohesive *symptom-gestalts*. The result is total lack of articulation within the psychological "field" under the pressure of amorphous, but mainly sadistic, impulses. Without symbol formation, there is no binding of energy; consequently, the unsegmented "inner space" is "unified" in the sense of *one* seething caldron of unformed instinctual pressure, *not* in the sense of *one* preconscious-like, ordered space.

Critics might say that my metaphor of a centaur also fits the acting-out borderline personality. It is true that the mythical centaurs alternated between generous kindness, wisdom of healing, and love of the arts, and tumultuous "acting out" under the influence of wine. But they were not cunningly nasty or consciously (when they were not drunk) harmful for the sake of power, as were many godlike figures of Greek mythology. Nevertheless, the image of a centaur does imply dangers, and that is a limitation of my metaphor.

In any case, as an image of unsegmented creative functioning, the centaur model implies some changes in the goals of psychoanalysis as a form of treatment, with corresponding subtle changes in "technique." No spectacular parameters need to be introduced. The psychoanalytic situation as conceived by Freud is uniquely suited for developing the patient's creative symbolizing potential. I do not mean "inspirational" prodding of the patient toward the creation of art objects.[2] Great artists are rare and are usually not "produced" by psychoanalysis. But the ability to create an undisrupted, fulfilling lifespace can be helped along by psychoanalysis. If innate talent allows, this includes the release of the patient's artistic creativity.

[2] Art therapy is a totally different method and will not be discussed here. For its excellent possibilities, see Kramer (1971).

CHAPTER 10

Impairment in the Capacity for Authentic Dialogue

The metapsychology of symbolization and the developmental aspects of symbolization have been discussed in previous chapters. Stages and types of mother-child interaction were correlated to the development of the child's symbolizing capacity. Condensed vignettes of some character types were presented from the point of view of their problems in symbol formation and consequently in establishing a connected life-space. Finally, an "ideal" model of the psychic structure of unobstructed creativity was derived from the periods of creative functioning of artists and "artist-type" individuals. Now we turn to the other end of the continuum.

The last three chapters of this book again deal with impairment in symbolization, but now under the specific aegis of how it affects the psychoanalytic dialogue and how treatment can help along the unfolding of the patient's stunted communicating capacity. The focus is on difficulties in meaningful verbal communication between patient and analyst (the absolutely necessary precondition for analytic treatment). Again I shall use the method of presenting "types" of patients grouped together on the basis of similar psychodynamics underlying their incapacity for truly meaningful dialogue.

I began this book by taking Kurt Lewin's concept of the lifespace, i.e., "the Person in his Environment," as *one* gestalt, as the basic unit indicating mental health or "unhealth" (Chapters 1 and 2). The aim of psychoanalysis, then, can be described as helping to establish a satisfactory *dialogue* between the two areas lying at either side of the boundary delineating the "person" from his or her environment. What specific interchanges between inside and outside constitute a "satisfactory dialogue" is a highly individual matter, depending on the person's needs and wishes. Whatever form the interchange takes, one feature of satisfying dialogue remains constant: There must be an interpenetration of the two communicating areas. This interpenetration gives coherence to the lifespace; without it, the person is isolated, separated by an empty gap from the world around him or her.

An increasing number of patients come for analytic help because this empty gap deprives them of feeling truly alive. Anhedonia appears to be widespread in our society. The recent emphasis in the literature on narcissistic character disorders testifies to this state of affairs. "Efficient depersonalization" would be another way to describe a great number of seemingly successful individuals. One might also call to mind Thoreau's description of the "quiet desperation" he felt characterized most people's lives.

Whatever label we use, the fact remains that people suffering from this condition are impaired in their capacity to establish good connectedness between adjacent regions—between regions within their internal mental "space," as well as between the inside and the surrounding outside. As was emphasized throughout this book, it is the function of *symbols* to *bridge over* from one area to the other. The existence and use of symbols prove that separation is accepted and also that separation is healed by connectedness. Anhedonic patients are impaired in the use of symbols as connecting bridges. Therefore, their lifespace suffers from disruptions. Because of these disruptions, they cannot find the path to what they want, they do not know what they want, or they are unable to want anything. Psychoanalysis can be helpful for these patients. But psychoanalysis can only work if the patient is able to grow on the symbols offered by treatment. Not only is our primary means of communication symbolic verbal language, but the psychoanalytic sessions themselves are framed, symbolic "as if" situations. They are "framed" analogously to a work of art and thereby lifted out of the everyday stream of life. Like the drama on the stage, the psychoanalytic situation has its *own* reality, which is different from the reality outside its frame. More freedom of experimentation with self-expression is possible within the parenthesized situation of psychoanalytic treatment than what can be allowed in everyday reality-oriented life. And within this already-parenthesized psychoanalytic situation, there is a special area within a second pair of parentheses: the transference. This is our most powerful symbolic tool. Although it arises spontaneously within the dyadic relationship, it is at the same time purposefully created and utilized by psychoanalysis as a treatment method. The limits of the patient's analyzability are set by his or her capacity to function within and utilize this multiply symbolic treatment.

What, then, can psychoanalysis offer in terms of corrective experience to patients who feel their inside is empty? The patient might have introjected the mother's vacant, unreflecting eyes and therefore experiences his or her own inside as filled with nothingness. Under such conditions, there is no motivation for—or trust in—symbolic communication, since the original situation lacked somebody "out there" to whom the child could have built bridges of symbolic dialogue.

These patients may feel either that they have nothing to say, or, if they do have something to say, that the analyst does not understand them, or is bored by them, or that the analyst falls asleep and in this way vanishes into nothingness as did the early mother. "Do you understand what I mean?" "Are you listening?" "I know this all sounds stupid." "I must be boring you." These are frequently repeated comments, sometimes tic-like in their regularity.

Indeed, with their repetitiveness and the low monotone of their speech, some of these patients seem to be trying to put the analyst to sleep. Obviously it is important that the analyst stay awake and somehow convey his or her alertness and interested presence. If the patient's monotone hinders communication, then I address my first verbal interventions to that problem as a symptom. I also give the reason for this priority, explaining that the patient's speech has a soporific effect and that if all my energy has to go into just hearing the words, and staying awake, then no good analytic work can be done. Sometimes the patient falls asleep during or before the session. I prefer to wake them rather than let them sleep through the hour.

I shall now give an extreme example of a communication problem in analysis. Years ago a woman patient (Jane) always came after my lunch break, when the office was empty. She usually came a little early and went straight into the office. By the time I came in (it could be just a few minutes later), she was in deep sleep. When I woke her, she muttered unintelligible words, as if she had been suddenly awakened in the middle of the night. She needed a few minutes to figure out where she was, and the hour started in a dreamy, hazy atmosphere. She muttered in low voice, as if to herself—in other words, as if I didn't exist (indeed, I felt almost annihilated).

Needless to say, Jane was the child of a mother with "vacant eyes." Her father was noncommunicative with his family. As a child, Jane lived a lonely daydream life. Having lived in her private daydream world for so many years, it was hard for her to express her private fantasies in an understandable syntax. She also lacked "basic trust" and wanted to keep her daydreams secret. At her office, however, Jane had no problems, since in that setting verbal communication referred solely to nonpersonal, objective topics. Nor did she fall asleep there. But as soon as she was by herself, she became sleepy and often in fact fell asleep.[1] Her nondescript daydreams merged into regular dreams. As soon as she left her office, she withdrew into an almost autistic, noncommunicable, private world.

Since Jane's transference consisted of annihilating me as a live partner in a dialogue, much analytic "labor" was required before she could accept me as a listener to talk to, and even more "labor" before *she* could listen and take in what I had to say. Often I had to wake her up both literally and figuratively, in the sense of "forcing" on her the acknowledgment of the existence of the real world around her. Like the mother who represents the world for the infant, I had to make my presence actively felt as an immediate representative (both real and symbolic) of the outside world.

As Jane learned to communicate about her "inside" to me, she began a period of dangerous acting out of her fantasies in real life. To differentiate between levels of reality was not an easy task. She confused communicating her fantasies by symbolic means with action in real life. This confusion still indicated shortcomings in the symbolizing process. It was a worrisome period, at least for me. Although this predated *Looking for Mr. Goodbar*, I was seriously concerned that something of that sort might happen to her. Fortunately it didn't. But this case taught me the dangers of working with noncommunicative patients who have, at an early age, withdrawn from the outside world into their dreamy fantasies.

[1] This patient was almost narcoleptic. Once she fell asleep walking up the stairs from the subway and would have fallen had a stranger not held her up.

Such patients differ from the rich "inward symbolizers" described in Chapter 8, for they are more severely schizoid. (The number of schizoid characters usually runs high in their families, as it did in the case of Jane.) They are fixated at a much earlier level of development, where differentiated perception of the "me" from the "not me" has not yet taken place (although they may function well in the nonpersonal sphere of work life). The "creative cycle of symbolization" has not been disrupted so much as *not begun*. These patients have never built perceptual symbol-bridges that allow them to take in interesting and beautiful things from the outside. They live literally and figuratively half-asleep. Once analysis succeeds in instigating them to verbally elaborate and communicate their dreamy fantasy world, the danger of acting out looms large. For a long time they do not recognize the difference between symbolic expression and three-dimensional action. Their hazy, dreamy inside is much too undifferentiated from the outside to permit distinction between fantasizing, talking about fantasies, and taking action. Before real analysis can begin, then, the analyst has to be an "awakener."

I would speculate that as children these patients used sleep as a total denial of everything, since "everything" was not pleasurable. Or they may have worn themselves out with temper tantrums so that they simply dozed off. They may also have used some fetishistic object or autoerotic activity to render themselves insensible by sleep. (Jane used to put herself to sleep by a combination of hair twirling, thumb sucking, and masturbation.)

Lethargic watching of TV may have a negative impact on poorly symbolizing children's lives. Most TV programs are very bad food for the child's inside, and they thwart the development of creative symbolization. They "transit" into a world of confused excitement. The restless motion of the figures on the video screen covers up the child's feeling of abandonment with disjointed "bad magic"—the opposite of the "good illusion" afforded by toys half-created by the child. TV offers passive, unnourishing omnipotence—a turn of the knob and everything changes, but creative cooperation from the child is not elicited. Just as it is beautiful to watch a child's dedicated concentration in play, it is sad to see a child's body slump and eyes glaze in front of the TV. Mothers who relegate their children to the TV set instead of creating a good "transitional play space" are training their children for unimaginative, asymbolic emptiness. I wonder if the increasing number of children suffering from reading disabilities and labeled as "minimally brain-damaged" are not in part the victims of TV-as-babysitter. Such experiences of emptiness and passivity, coupled with exaggerated stimulus-hunger, might drive them later to drugs for artificial excitement. Children absorb into the inside elements of the care, or lack of care, they receive—TV may be absorbed as stimulus-hunger for "bad filling."

Treatment Modalities for Poorly Symbolizing Patients

In their search for therapy, people suffering from stimulus-hunger coupled with "emptiness" are often attracted to the various "new" treatment modalities in which the therapists seem to share the patients' repugnance for or inability to use symbolic communication, with all its emotional and cognitive richness. Mutual acting out, body contact, and uncontrolled emotional discharge (what I would call forced, pseudo-spontaneous emotionality) are supposed to give the patients what they "really" need. I believe much of this is harmful because it is phony, it is neither "real" nor usefully symbolic. The patient is not two years old, the therapist or group members are not parents or siblings; they cannot possibly give in an authentic and original form what the patient missed out on as a child. What remains is some unpredictable hybrid, an untrustworthy form of hectic acting out. It does not lead to the fruitful appreciation of symbols as connecting bridges, or to binding of energy through structured channeling of instinctual forces. Without these trustworthy events, "empty" patients, who alternate between apathy and rage (homeostatic emergency state due to lack of symbolization), will not acquire a substantial, rich feeling inside—necessary for *authentic* dialogue.

I don't mean to imply that verbal therapy is the only viable mode of treatment. I have already expressed my respect for art therapy, for example. Or, in cases of catatonic schizophrenia, the institutional treatment routine may well include active body care (baths, massage) as a way of fostering a delineated, pleasantly cathected body image (Freeman, Cameron, and McGhie, 1958).

Schilder (1935) was the first to discuss the connection between body image and symbolization (see also Reitman's [1951] hypothesis of a link between the psychotic's confused visual perception and a disturbed body image—mentioned in Chapter 7). I have already pointed out (in Chapter 8) the importance for symbolization of the holding mother, who helps the infant to libidinously cathect his or her skin-boundary and thus begin to pleasantly delineate his or her body from the surrounding outside. A libidinously cathected boundary between inside and outside fosters the wish and capacity for communication between the two areas. This explains why active body care can promote good symbolization and readiness for dialogue in psychotics with a confused and fragmented body image.

Real psychosis, however, presents an extreme, for the essential boundary between inside and outside is mostly missing. We cannot really talk about symbolization here, since without differentiation between inside and outside there is no possibility for symbolic reaching-over from one area to the other. For the psychotic, the inner "abstract" is dealt with as if it were concrete, and vice versa. Schizophrenic language, in which words are treated not as symbols but as *things*, is a prime example of this (see Freud, 1915c). There is no distance between symbol and symbolized (Segal, 1957). Given these deficiencies, I do not believe psychoanalysis is the treatment of choice—certainly not on an outpatient basis. The total hospital environment as therapeutic agent is needed for these patients.

Schizoid "empty" patients, on the other hand, are not as severely impaired in their symbolizing capacity as schizophrenics. I believe the psychoanalytic method is useful with these patients. Emphasis needs to be placed on verbal communication, with attention to nonverbal elements such as tone of voice, rhythm of speech, listening attitude, physical appearance, and office furnishings. There is no need for hasty introduction of obvious technical parameters, with the excuse that these patients are not "classical neurotics." Quite to the contrary, these "borderline-type" patients, more than "classical" neurotics, need the stable, firmly "holding" predictability of the "orthodox" situation. What they don't need is unpredictable "magic," which only nourishes their false sense of omnipotence. Trustworthy stability, predictability, and sustained interest were exactly what they did not get from their mothers. Within the framed analytic "play space" of mainly symbolic communication, the analyst can honestly (authentically) provide these qualities. The psychoanalyst offers a "corrective experience" on the metaphoric or symbolic level, not in attempting to act as a good mother to her child.

We analysts also give the primarily not-symbolic "real" things contained in the totality of verbal and nonverbal communication as part of the whole situation. This is an unavoidable and indeed a useful natural mixture of the parenthesized symbolic and the "real." Whether or not patients differentiate between transferential versus nontransferential use of these two sets of "stimuli" is a good indicator of whether or not the "symbolic attitude" is available to them for the transference proper.

The "symbolic attitude" implies a dual stance vis-à-vis experience, in which the person is aware of the two realms (the symbolic and the "real") and enjoys the interpenetration or alternation of the two. Good symbolic play and perception depend on such a dual attitude. The king and queen in chess are defended at all costs, but only a psychotic would guard them after the play is over. Alice's trials and tribulations ended when she exclaimed: "You are nothing but a bunch of cards"—and she woke up from her dream to find not even playing cards, but leaves blowing in the wind.

The psychic structure of asymbolic patients is too homogenized or too rigid to keep up such a dual attitude. In outside life they may function acceptably, even seemingly quite successfully, under the duress of a strict reality principle. But in analysis they may well develop "psychotic transferences," i.e., transferences experienced as total reality perceptions. Or, they may refuse to participate in symbolic relatedness altogether, since words are "not real" and the "whole situation is ridiculous," or "purely a business transaction." They are determined not to "fall for transference feelings" and love or hate their analyst. They will remain independent and objective. Their fear of losing their boundaries, even their sanity, is palpable. As children, they never learned how to enjoy enriching symbolic play, and if they occasionally attempted real communication, they suffered humiliation at the hands of a nonparticipating or sarcastic mother.

As noted above, under the sway of undifferentiated, almost total projection, the transference is experienced as hundred-percent reality perception. The "real," nonverbal ingredients of the analytic situation are also assimilated into the patient's projective framework and take on a highly idiosyncratic meaning. There is no wedge for interpretation since that would require some modicum of the symbolic dual stance within the patient. With one patient, for instance, a change in the arrangement of books in my office was *perceived* (not fantasized) as motivated by my wish to keep the *Standard Edition* out of the patient's sight in order to keep him from being an analytic genius and thereby humiliating me, the analyst. All this was offered as a statement of fact, not in the spirit of free association or fantasy. Similarly, a shift in the analyst's tone of voice or a chance movement is *known* to signify anger or fascination or sarcasm or whatever.

I'm not suggesting that these "knowing" patients have some uncanny perception of the hidden recesses of the analyst's mind. Usually they are factually wrong, for they don't have the capacity for empathic communication, which would imply a fifty-fifty sharing of the symbolic "space" between patient and analyst. These patients' perceptions, under the amorphous pressure of their own "inside," are like form-minus responses to the Rorschach. In the "minus" response the real shape of the inkblot is disregarded, not "played with" creatively until a percept is formed in which both the shape of the blot and the symbolizing imagination of the subject participate equally. Instead, the subject pours inner content into the blot, irrespective of the inkblot's own shape, and calls it a percept. Like these subjects, totally projecting patients don't know how to engage in dialogue between their inside and the outside, between their own perceptual function and the stimulus offered.

With these patients, one might assume that the mother was unable to offer toys in the right key, namely, to give the child the opportunity to "complete" the toy with his or her creative imagination. Thus, the development of the child's imaginative communication with the outside world was thwarted. The mother may have been absent or aggressively invaded the child's "space," not reading and responding sensitively to the clues and gestures emanating from the child, but unilaterally imposing her own needs. This kind of mother does not *see* her child. The child in turn feels nonexistent, alternating between rage and exhibitionistic "acting up" to command attention—anything to be *seen*. As a result, the child grows up unable to see the "other" as a person in his or her own right, with whom, nevertheless, one *can* establish meaningfully shared communication. Another example of how the individual absorbs and repeats the quality of early child-care experienced from mother.

As children, some of these patients did have what might be called transitional objects, except that these objects did not "transit" anywhere. Rather, they were used solely for the comfort they gave as things that could be omnipotently controlled. These "treasured possessions" functioned more as fetish objects, patching up a gnawing feeling of impotence by offering the "bad illusion" of unreal omnipotence. In later life, human beings are likely to be used for the same purpose. These patients may acquire an exhibitionistic charm due to their insatiable "hunger" to be looked at. With this charm, they can attract others, at least for a while. Since they don't know the first thing about reciprocity (in Piaget's sense) and authentically shared communication, however, these relationships don't last (unless the other person has an extremely masochistic bent). The "friend" or "partner" is expected to function as the early "transitional-fetish object" did, as a person with no motivation of his or her own, simply *there* to bolster omnipotence fantasies and play out a prefabricated script. One wrong—i.e., self-initiated—move on the part of the other elicits rage, and the relationship is over. The other's function is solely to be used as "subjective object."

Talented and exhibitionistically charming patients may *seem* more "filled" and self-confident than clearly lethargic, "empty" patients, but in fact they feel just as unfulfilled and unreal. Their talk is empty chatter or a means of seduction—anything but a good symbolic bridge for shared communication. In psychoanalysis they pose greater problems than their openly noncommunicative counterparts. The hours are filled with words, sometimes interesting, but here, too, the analyst is in essence annihilated. The analyst is only allowed to react in accord with the "set" script. If approval, admiration, seduction, silence—or whatever the patient has written into the script—is not forthcoming, treatment may be interrupted, with or without further rationalizations. On the other hand, if the analyst is willing to play out the script, "analysis" may go on ad infinitum, the process itself becoming a cathected fetish object, transiting nowhere but fulfilling narcissistic needs on both sides. Such unreal "analyses" may be stopped after a while with mutual consent, but the benefit to the patient is, at best, minimal. Admiration or omnipotence-hunger, like all addictions, cannot be filled in kind when decades separate the new situation from the originally traumatizing one. Chances are the ex-patient will wear an "I have been analyzed" badge and continue to be on the lookout for more promising potential "subjective objects" to feed on, for power and glory.

Obsessively intellectualizing patients carry around a somewhat different script to be filled. As children, they, too, felt impotent and traumatized in the face of an unempathic mother, but for constitutional and possibly later oedipal-phase reasons, control of threatening situations through intellectual power has become the goal. Their inside feels empty of "good" things but filled with dangerous, unloving and unlovable "bad" things. They may try to overcome and hide these feelings with a superstructure of temporary overkindness and seeming concern for others. But Thanatos far outweighs Eros in their instinctual makeup. Indeed, for this group, neutralization of energy may well be necessary. Intellectualization is a proven method to achieve this. For the same reason, among the therapeutic modalities, Freudian psychoanalysis will be their choice, and not infrequently will become their profession. It offers a promise to control the unknown by following strict rules of behavior and by intellectual understanding. This, of course, is not how psychoanalysis should work, but enough in its theory lends itself to this interpretation and in some training programs this rigid image is perpetrated. Fortunately, although rarely, the opposite picture has also been drawn, namely, the analogy between psychoanalytic work and artistic creativity (Beres, 1957).

As far as the obsessively intellectualizing patient is concerned, the analytic process consists of a safe bundle of predetermined rules. The analyst is expected to behave exactly as prescribed: a blank screen, mainly silent, occasionally uttering interpretations. The patient tells dreams, free-associates to the dream elements, reports on everyday events, and may even bring up "transference material"—while all the time isolating the words from real feelings. If the analyst, in any detail of his or her behavior, does not fit the "model," the patient becomes upset and perplexed, to the point where he or she literally may not understand the analyst's words. It is enough for the analyst to ask a straightforward everyday question, something an analyst isn't "supposed" to do, and the patient is thrown into confusion and unable to give a straight answer. As long as the analyst religiously adheres to the "rules," there is no chance to observe the patient's communication deficiencies. Such patients may "finish" analysis and feel able to write a dissertation on their own psychodynamics, they may be outwardly successful in status and income and yet remain disconnected strangers from themselves and from others, even from their work. Anhedonia comes in many shapes and forms.

But whatever shape and form anhedonia may take, it is linked to impaired dialogue between inside and outside, even between inside and inside (intrapersonal communication). The lack of smooth, authentic communication freezes, or "locks in," the unsatisfactory inner situation; it prevents resolution and growth. Dialogue facilitates these beneficial changes. It gives a chance for old character-gestalts to change their configuration. Dialogue implies more than symbolization per se. It means *exchange* between two open systems whereby "nutrients" or catalysts can enter either system. Without such openness, there is stagnation. The first aim of psychoanalysis is to make authentic dialogue possible. The second aim is to provide growth-promoting "nutrients" and catalysts for the patient's use.

CHAPTER 11

The Significance for Psychoanalysis of the Symbolizing Nature of Verbal Language

If psychoanalytic therapy must be directed toward catalyzing the patient's capacity for authentic communication, then we can talk about the "dialogue model" of mental well-being. Freud's formulation of psychoanalysis followed from an essentially "closed system" model of psychic functioning. The idea of an authentic dialogue between inside and outside was not part of his definition of mental health.

Winnicott (1965) was the first psychoanalyst who explicitly stated that there is no infant without a "facilitating environment." He described the intricacies of the earliest mother-child "dialogue," even if he did not call it by this name. Indeed, his emphasis on the satisfying intermingling of inside and outside in the "transitional space" is essentially a "dialogue model" of mental health. His concepts of the "true" and the "false" self also suggest the crucial role of authentic communication in determining a balanced, fulfilling life.

The dialogue model places the authentic use of language communication at the center of psychoanalytic therapy. The specifically human mode of communication is symbolic—"man is a symbolical animal" (Cassirer, 1944). Language, with its flexible syntax and its tenses conveying time relations, is the only symbolic system that isomorphically represents the basic structure of the experiential world (Wittgenstein, 1958). It needed Freud's genius (actually initiated by Breuer) to conceive of a "talking therapy" for the reorganization of the patient's disconnected (due to repression) psychic "apparatus." Freud's theory is rooted in the effect of verbalization on the patient's intrapsychic structure.

Freud viewed the analyst's speech as well as the patient's free associations solely as facilitators of intrapsychic change. His aim was to make the repressed unconscious conscious by means of the patient's free association, combined with the interpretations offered by the analyst. The basic rule of free association demands that patients relinquish their usual controls and verbalize, without screening, anything that crosses their minds. Through free association, words come to function as a lever, lifting psychological content from the unconscious or from the primary-process image world, into organized, secondary-process conscious functioning. In Freud's model, the analyst's speech concentrates on (1) eliminating unconscious resistance that interferes with the free flow of the patient's associations, and (2) offering interpretations that translate the unconscious meaning of the patient's free associations and unravel the *real* meaning of the patient's disguising symbols and symptoms.

Freud (1915c) mentioned how the schizophrenic treats words as "things" rather than symbols (although he did not use this term for words). His focus, however, was on "analyzable" patients, who were assumed to be ready for verbal communication. It was only unconscious resistance that might prevent free verbal expression or the acceptance of a specific interpretation offered by the analyst. This resistance was correlated to specific *content*, not to a deficiency in communication per se. Communication deficiencies on the analyst's side were not considered at all. In sum, Freud limited the role of language in psychoanalysis to conveying new, previously unconscious mental content to the patient's conscious ego. *It was definitely the content and not the medium of communication that was the "message."*

With a generic theory of symbolization and a dialogue model of mental health, the above emphasis is reversed. The Janus-face of all symbols was elaborated in Part II precisely because it is the Janus-face of verbal language as a symbolic system of communication that poses major problems for the psychoanalytic method. Only the fully *symbolic* use of language truly connects. The purely *intellectual*, purely denotative use of language merely connects from brain cortex to brain cortex, leaving an empty gap between the addressor and the addressee as far as emotional participation is concerned. One would assume that similar gaps also exist in the intrapsychic structure of the speaker. In this neutralized, isolating use of language, words do not function fully symbolically because they do not carry the lingering aura of their primordial sensorimotor-affective context; they are disconnected from the psychosomatic layer where metaphors originate (Sharpe, 1940). Artists and poets have easy access to this layer, hence the particularly intense affective communicative power of their words and images. It is this simultaneous availability and connectedness of all psychic layers that differentiates the affectively colorful "inner world" and mode of expression of the creative person from the grayly neutralized concepts of the philistine. Good psychoanalytic work aims at helping the analysand to approach the former and avoid the latter state.

Analytic work will be effective only if language communication between the analyst and the analysand extends over the full psychosomatic range and thus encompasses all the regions in which true symbol formation originates. If this is the case, then psychoanalysis, which is essentially a language treatment, should be able to effect the analysand's psychosomatic reorganization purely through language dialogue. In other words, I do not believe there is any need for direct body manipulation. Catharsis by itself, even if accompanied by intense psychosomatic expressions, does not facilitate creative intrapsychic and inside-outside communication. Nor do intellectually "correct" interpretations have any authentically mutative effect *unless*, for both participants, verbal language represents *true* symbolization that bridges the entire "inner space," from the instinctual layers to the brain cortex, and with the active participation of the sensorimotor system. (I do not mean that particular motions must accompany speech, but that there must be a general feeling of aliveness in the total psychosoma.) *True* symbolization involves the *whole* self, including the body image. Unless the analyst experiences his or her body image as an alive organism, the analyst's words will sound hollow—no matter how intelligent. (The same holds for written psychoanalytic material.) Only if spoken language functions as a bridge spanning all layers of the psychosomatic "inner" system, only then will it create a connecting "intermediate symbolic space," where the two participants in the psychoanalytic situation can truly communicate in a dialogue that can have mutative effect.

The generic theory of symbolization and the dialogue model lay stress on the function of language as a shared experience in psychoanalytic therapy. Communication defects, far from being the "specialty" of manifest schizophrenics, are widespread, and they are by no means exclusive to patients. An analyst may be able to organize the patient's primary-process material into logical secondary-process interpretations and yet be deficient in communication. Similarly, as we have seen, some patients do not give any obvious signs of language deficiency, yet the full experience of communication eludes them. Consequently, analysis may have only a minimal effect in terms of initiating deep changes in their life processes.

Two particularly deceptive types who lend themselves to "unreal" analyses are the patients I have described as "exhibitionistic charmers" and "obsessive intellectualizers." Both types are likely to furnish an uninterrupted flow of interesting-sounding material, and both may seem to accept interpretations—without, however, involving what Winnicott calls the "true self" in the analytic process. Their language does not come from the psychosomatic layer where metaphors originate. Their language, even if highly educated, is replete with ready-made clichés—not necessarily the popular clichés, but favored patterns of speech previously fabricated by them and used over and over again. On first hearing, these twists of speech may sound quite catchy and clever. But they repeat. If similar language use is duplicated by the analyst, then the analysis will become "interminable" (even though it can end)—and not because of the constitutional intensity of the instincts (Freud, 1937a) but because of the inauthenticity of the dialogue.

Indeed, it was the number of patients who, after years of "correct" analysis, remained essentially unchanged that motivated Freud to write *Analysis Terminable and Interminable* (1937a). This is a pessimistic work. With his characteristic relentless honesty, Freud, after forty years of psychoanalytic practice, expressed doubts about the therapeutic efficacy of his own method. He recognized the flaws in his previous assumption of a basically well-functioning ego in the neurotic patient. He questioned the effectiveness of psychoanalysis when faced with the constitutional strength and immutability of the instincts, particularly if coupled with a constitutional weakness of the ego. He saw the "death instinct" as an "inherent part of the living matter" and therefore as an ever-present force working against psychic healing. Freud concluded: "we must bow to the superiority of the forces against which we see our efforts come to nothing" (p. 243).

This is a tremendous human confession from the originator of psychoanalysis, but the extent of Freud's pessimism may not have been warranted. While I share Freud's respect for constitutional factors, it seems to me that he did not realize the full potential of his own method because he accepted language communication between two intelligent, verbal people as a given and not as itself subtly problematic. A large proportion of Freud's nonresponsive patients might have responded to treatment, despite untoward constitutional factors, *had* the analytic work concentrated on the process and function of communication per se, instead of focusing solely on content. The priority I am giving to the problem of communication holds not just for obviously schizoid patients but as a general principle in the treatment of all patients. Psychoanalytic training, too, mainly in the supervision phase, should concentrate on the exact wording, syntax, and tone of voice of the student-analyst instead of providing guidance primarily in terms of "correct" content interpretations.

Had Freud seen symbolization as a generic function of human perception and communication, his approach to language within the psychoanalytic situation would have been different. As we have seen, only the products of the dream work and of symptom formation were considered symbols. These symbols were seen purely as disguise, as hiding content instead of revealing a message. Even the communicative, creative aspect of the manifest dream was totally disregarded by Freud. On the other hand, verbal language was not viewed as a product of symbolization. It was seen as purely communicative, without consideration for its great potential for hiding and separating. This polarizing "Cartesian" conceptualization was characteristic of Freud's thinking. It excluded any recognition—as far as so-called "normal" mental products were concerned—of unresolvable paradoxes and concepts of mixed categories, of which the multiple Janus-faces of symbols is the prime example. Yet (paradoxically?) Freud was the first to gain insight into patients' psychic reality by unraveling the meaning of their symbolic languages. In other words, the communicative aspect of supposedly "hiding" symbols was utilized, even though it was not "officially" conceptualized.

This disregard for the dual function, for the hiding and revealing aspects of verbal language, has done great harm to psychoanalytic treatment. As has been said, it has probably accounted for many "interminable" and "unreal" analyses, in which the communicative aspects of verbalization were taken for granted. This allowed the patient to hide his or her "true self" behind verbal language, and the analyst to make interpretations without considering the tremendous importance of the quality of his or her speaking manner, of the exact choice of words, the length (or brevity) of sentences, the syntax. Judging from Freud's case histories, it seems likely that his emphatically given dictionary-translation-type interpretations (*a* means *b*) may not have been "usable" by his patients and may well have accounted in some instances for their unresponsiveness to treatment.

Since the genesis of all symbols implies condensation of the "raw material" to be symbolized, a certain degree of "distortion" is unavoidable in any form of symbolic communication. The salient points chosen by the patient in recounting his or her past history always contain an undefinable degree of subjectively "chosen" emphasis. Indeed, this is true of all verbal accounts of past events, for general history as well as for personal history. Changes in the content of history books depending on the ideology of the régime or of the particular historian testify to this fact. History can never be a totally objective "science." (Actually, in the last analysis, this holds for any science [see Polanyi, 1958, 1966; Wigner, 1969; Kuhn, 1962] but particularly for history.) Each of us perceives our past in terms of our personal "mental symbols" that convey meaning to past events. The lesson of the Rashomon story extends to nearly every person's view of his or her own past, as well as to every listener who hears a verbally recalled "autobiography." The more the personal emotional involvement, the more the nonconscious subjective elaboration of past events. These subjective phenomena, necessarily involved in the symbolizing process of perception, memory formation, and verbal presentation of these memories, make hunting for historical *truth* in psychoanalysis an unattainable aim. Equally unattainable, on the analyst's part, is a totally "objective" perception and registration of the material offered by the patient.

As was discussed in Chapter 7, the conceptual framework of psychoanalytic theory itself, plus the individual analyst's personal value system or "ideology," his or her preconscious store of conceptual symbols, determines not only the "official" interpretation but also the selection and organization of material to be interpreted from the totality of verbal and nonverbal phenomena presented by the analysand during the session. There is a preconscious "pre-interpretation" that precedes the "real" interpretation. Various schools of psychotherapy select different "things" for material, and so do various therapists from the same school.

Again, the "fact" that there are no certain "facts" at our disposal is an important "message" in itself. To my mind, acceptance of this is crucially important for "healthy" life processes, which can never be built on certainties. One has to trust one's subjective evaluation and be willing to take risks. It is the earmark of obsessively organized characters to insist on certainties in general. In analysis they concentrate on finding more and more childhood traumas to be guaranteed by the analyst as "historical truth" revealing, with certainty, the parents' fault. There is a paranoid stance here which puts the analyst in the role of a judge who hands out guilty verdicts against the parents. Acceptance of the uncertainty of causation does not necessarily coincide with forgiving, but in some sense it is not so far from that either. What it does imply is a decathexis of the compulsive concern with whose fault it was—a fruitless concern that impedes any creative move forward.

Examples of the unavoidable subjectivity and uncertainties pervading the analytic process could be multiplied ad infinitum, given the all-pervading function of symbolization in human perception, memory, and communication. It is precisely this fact that lends such salient significance to the transference, a symbolic structure created specifically for therapeutic ends within the ongoing analytic situation. It is the emotional attitudes manifested in the transference that lend themselves to useful interpretive interventions, more so than the patient's report of events from the past. The vicissitudes of emotions and affects are more readily observable in the transference than is the factual content of the patient's "self-written" autobiography. If the defensive transformations and swings of emotions shown in the transference are properly analyzed, then more often than not the patient's perception of the past will also change. Different types of memories and different attitudes to important figures of the past emerge with the transformation of the emotional atmosphere within the patient. The capacity for remorse without self-torturing guilt, the capacity for a critical attitude toward others without destructive and self-destructive hatred, the capacity to forgive without denying, these are the most important transformations. They can come about in an analytic situation that allows all sorts of transference reactions to develop freely and where these are tactfully handled by the "not-destroyable" analyst.

Every analyst makes mistakes within the course of an analysis, and this can give the patient the opportunity to practice forgiving—*if* the analyst admits his or her mistakes. The patient then comes to learn that mistakes can be acknowledged and can be survived, on both sides.

Even though there is no factual certainty to the "historical" aspect of psychoanalysis, the authenticity of communication between the two participants can and should represent "truth." The true use of the symbolic system of language communication implies the participation of the "true self" of both partners in the dialogue. This is indispensable for the true termination of treatment. Once patients reach this point, then they are able to "transit" from the parenthesized area of the psychoanalytic situation into the open area of life, where they will be able to carve out a personally satisfying lifespace, with which to carry out an authentic two-way "dialogue." They will not be insulated either from their true self or from their environment. The creative cycle of symbolizing intake and authentically symbolizing output, i.e., communication, will be unimpeded. Repression, isolation, and other distortions of true communication are not needed anymore.

CHAPTER 12

Using the Psychoanalytic Situation to Foster Good Symbolization

In this final chapter I shall draw some specific therapeutic implications from the generic theory of symbolization and from Winnicott's ideas on transitional phenomena. I intend to focus on aspects of therapy not included in the Freudian model, aspects that derive from developmental deficiencies in symbolization. These defects need to be remedied before more traditional content and resistance interpretations can have any effect. The latter can take effect only if the patient is able to participate in meaningful and "true" verbal dialogue with the analyst. Some other relatively new aspects of therapeutic work derive from the value attached to the capacity for enjoyment coupled with the capacity for realistic functioning.

A Definition of Mental Health

Let me briefly review my perspective on mental health. As I indicated in Part I, a healthy life implies the ability to carve out a personally meaningful, fitting lifespace, with connectedness between the person and his or her relevant milieu. In this milieu certain "objects" or "regions" are experienced as positive valences that feel desirable and toward which the person feels motivated to find a path. The person does not feel either omnipotent or impotent in relation to these desired goals; but rather "part-potent" (Silverberg, 1952). He or she will be able to enjoy the desired goal if reached.

Specifically, in terms of symbolization, the healthy person is able to create expressive symbolic forms that connect his or her "inside" with the outside. The coupling of symbolizing perception with symbolic expression gives the person's life-space cohesiveness and a kind of symmetry, a symmetry between the "person" and the "environment" segments of the lifespace. Since symbolization participates in the circular process of intake (perception) and output (expression), it contributes continuously to the restoration of equilibrium between inner and outer reality.

A creatively symbolizing person's life-shaping activities will thus add up to an organically connected good gestalt. Form-building creativity originates in one's deepest instinctual forces and proceeds from there through successive levels of increasing intrapsychic articulation, until it finally crosses the boundary between inside and outside to become a perceivable part of communally shared reality. This kind of creativity leads to true dialogue between the inside and the outside; there is no isolating gap at the interface where self meets not-self. If, however, motivation does not originate in the instinctual layers and does not pass through all the strata of the psyche in an uninterrupted process, then communication will not be authentic, it will not represent the "true self."

Besides representing the "true self," authentic communication must respect the limitations and rules imposed by communally shared reality. Only the welding together of inner motivation with outside reality leads to genuinely communicative creations, which are subjectively true, yet shareable and nonautistic. Without respect for shared reality, the created form remains autistic, or noncommunicative (as in psychotic art). On the other hand, a preponderant reliance on the outside as the motivating source results in subjectively "false" creations and inauthentic communication. These inauthentic symbolic products represent the "false self" and built only pseudo-bridges between the person and his or her environment. They do not lend unity and coherence to the person's lifespace.

The Impact of Psychoanalytic Therapy

After this recapitulation of the characteristics of mental health, let us now see how psychoanalytic therapy can enhance the patient's communicative life processes. In this regard, Winnicott's ideas are particularly helpful. I have described his transitional or intermediate space as the area for creative symbol formation and consequently for true communication. The first aim of psychoanalytic therapy, then, is the full realization of this connecting region. And here we need to reconsider Winnicott's account of how the early mother-child "dialogue" affects the development of a subjectively satisfying intermediate space, filled with creatively symbolizing activities.

If a person has not had the experience of "good-enough" mothering, psychoanalytic treatment later in life can offer a second chance to remedy the deficiencies caused by the unsatisfactory manner in which the unempathic mother handed over the world to her child. Thanks to the multiple function (Waelder, 1936) of symbolization, the psychoanalyst, within the framework of the psychoanalytic situation, can *symbolically* re-create and rectify the original mother-child situation, in which the mother failed her child. In most instances, psychoanalytic treatment, with minor modifications, can foster the unfolding of the creative principle inherent in the human organism. Analysis provides a new opportunity for handing over the world to patients by means of language. The intricate symbolic system of verbal language allows for the isomorphic representation of the experiential world (Wittgenstein, 1958). The analyst's use of language must be as empathically attuned to the patient's needs as is the good mother's handling of her infant. The good mother knows when to offer her breast, how to unobtrusively leave material around for the child to use in creative play, how to look at her child with lovingly mirroring eyes. Just as all these functions of the good mother become internalized as the building blocks of the child's preconscious, so can the analyst's management of the treatment situation beneficially change the content and the quality of the patient's "inner space" or preconscious. A beneficial change in the structure of, and in the patient's attitude to, his or her preconscious will go a long way toward fostering good symbolization.

Let us look more closely at the ways in which the psychoanalytic treatment method can correctively "replay" crucial aspects of the original mother-child situation. In Chapter 8, we saw how the good mother's "holding" promoted the feeling of a pleasant "inside space," the early precursor of the later preconscious. How the feeling-tone of this primordial inner space can affect later attitudes toward symbolization was also discussed.

The stability and predictability of psychoanalytic sessions can symbolically offer the experience of a trustworthy "holding situation." This experience is particularly needed by borderline patients with "unthinkable anxieties," who experience their lifespace as a dangerous "bottomless pit." These patients, whose body image and self-representation have never coalesced into a stable unity, experience themselves as ever-changing, amorphous creatures, hopelessly trying to find their way in an ever-changing, unpredictable world. The regularly recurring analytic sessions with the constant attentiveness of the analyst and the consistent use of symbolic language communication (in contradistinction to new acting-out methods) can do much to stabilize the shifting self-image and the shifting ground in these unrooted patients' lifespace.

Often these patients' mothers were "empty" borderline characters themselves, who could function dutifully but were incapable of "truly" communicating with their children (or with anybody), whether in gestures or in verbal language. Children of such mothers have the greatest difficulty in experiencing their "inside" as alive and as both a source and a dependable receiver of communication.

Patients have taught me that the mother's "emptiness" is mainly expressed in her "vacant eyes." These are not "feeding," not mirroring eyes. When introjected, they fill the child with "nothingness." The lifespace of the child (and later, adult) feels flat and tasteless. These are the patients who cannot form intentions and seem unable to wish for anything definable, except a general sense of wanting to feel better. Often these patients will say again and again that they don't care about being alive. They might as well die, since they already feel dead while alive. Their lifespace is articulated in terms of "absences," things which are *not* there—not in terms of things which *are* there. There is nothing to be invested with either positive or negative valence.

With these patients, symbolic communication is not only stunted but often hated. In the original mother-child situation there was nobody "out there" to whom a connecting symbolic bridge could be built. These unhappy borderline patients show a mixture of boredom, apathy, and rage. They seem bent on destroying their own thinking apparatus (Bion, 1959), as if to prove they do not have a mind (i.e., that their preconscious—the internalized heir of the "nonexistent" mother—does not exist). Such patients may carry their preconscious "minds" in their pockets in the form of endless notes to remind themselves of the simplest daily tasks. Maybe unconsciously they also carry along their mothers in this symbolic act. Any instance of forgetting, losing, or confusing something is angrily displayed, yet almost with glee, as if to say: "See, I told you so, I don't have a mind to depend on." This is a transference manifestation of the eternal reproach to the unresponsive mother, who failed as a model for a dependable preconscious.

The analyst's first and main task with these patients is to convince them of the reality of their "inside" and to establish their four-dimensional existence. "Four-dimensional" because existence along the dimension of time is a *sine qua non* for the experience of the self as real. These "insideless" borderline patients tend to live their lives—and consequently their analyses—as if time proceeded in a circular pattern, with no beginning and no end to any of their life phases and activities. Nothing is ever left behind (they remain fixated); nothing leads to anything new. This attitude toward time and change is certainly opposed to innovative creativity.

In analysis, these patients may occasionally give the impression of real progress—then suddenly, without any clear triggering event, in the next session everything is back to the beginning and the analyst wonders whether everything has been built on shifting sand and washed or blown away without a trace. Yet, however shattering this setback may seem, I refuse to believe—rightly or wrongly—that anything that "was" can disappear without leaving some trace, even if this is not visible. (I know my logic here is not unassailable but it helps me to avoid therapeutic nihilism.) I convey this belief to the patient and search for the unconscious defensive function of the patient's stubborn denial of the progressive dimension of time, where real changes take place. Interestingly, I came to the insight that these seemingly Thanatos-ridden patients, who supposedly welcome death, actually hope to avoid death by viewing time as circular. Since a circle has no end-point, they indulge in the unconscious fantasy that by insisting on a repetitive circular pattern, they will not reach the end-point of death. Their illusion is that "playing dead" while alive, not pursuing any goals, in a sense takes them "out of the running" toward the inevitable end. It also supports their unconscious fantasy that mother might reappear and undo all the harm she caused. Only after this event would they be willing to start to live.

There are two ways in which the analyst can attempt to eradicate these life-destroying fantasies. One can use the traditional method of interpretation, clarifying the hazy fantasies through secondary-process language. When expressed in this form, the evident absurdity of the fantasies may have a mutative effect on the patient. Sometimes I also remind my patients that whatever they fantasize about the circularity of time, the fact remains that as time goes on they will keep on aging and eventually die, whether or not they choose to "live." The other way in which the analyst can attempt to help these patients is by making up for the deficiencies in the early mother-child relationship through *symbolic means*. "Symbolic" does not mean a "mere" substitute, since the unresolved paradox of the symbol implies that it also contains the symbolized.

The metaphoric "holding" function of the psychoanalytic situation has already been pointed out. Now let us see how the analyst can duplicate the empathic mother's mirroring function. The analyst has to find ways to mirror to the patient the patient's real existence. The treatment phase aiming to achieve this goal may take a long time, but it is absolutely necessary for later meaningful, real communication.

There is no strictly definable "method" for constructively reflecting the patient's real existence. Just as the good mother intuitively knows how to look at her child "creatively," so the analyst has to rely on intuition. Actual face-to-face looking may or may not be part of the process. Verbal contact, tone of voice, can achieve the same function. By no means should the analyst always interpret the patient's wish to sit up for an hour, or part of an hour, as resistance. The patient may have a very real need to look and to be looked at. Rigid frustration of this need may hinder rather than facilitate the analytic process. In this regard, I would like to underline that there is no one, absolutely "correct" way of creating a propitious psychoanalytic setting. This statement holds for the "rules" governing the choice of preferred position for different diagnostic categories of patients. Sitting up is supposedly the "borderline position" because of its "reality orientation," while the couch is used for neurotic patients. Yet I have found that the couch can be useful with "empty" borderline patients. The horizontal position on the couch may well promote the transition from nothingness into connected dialogue with the therapist. The very unusualness of this position for communication can help to avoid clichéd use of language or set patterns of interaction.

As with "holding," mirroring can be replicated in analysis on a *metaphoric* plane, in a symbolically transformed manner. The analyst's actual looking can be, but is not necessarily, involved. Through genuine responsiveness to the patient's psychosomatic presence, the analyst "tells" the patient that he or she exists as a self-initiating individual (or else the analyst would have nothing to react to). It is this well-attuned, matching, reflecting reactivity on the analyst's part that parallels the desirable responsiveness of the holding and mirroring mother. If a patient was deprived of a well-attuned mother in infancy, then the analyst's genuine reactivity may help to eradicate the characterological effects of that early deprivation. With such a patient, any semblance of the image of the objectively detached, blank-screen analyst would be detrimental.

In conveying to the patient a sense of his or her real existence, the analyst may occasionally need to repeat the patient's words verbatim, without adding anything. I learned this from a patient who asked me to do just that. Hearing his own words repeated by the analyst gave substance and reality to those words, as well as to the locus of origin of those words—namely, the patient's "inside." This patient's previous analyst had interpreted his demand as a wish to manipulate the analyst. I think this was an incorrect and harmful interpretation. Autistic children's need for a real mirror to convince themselves of their existence does not entail manipulation of the mirror.

Literal mirroring in language may only be needed in cases of extreme schizoid depersonalization. But the analyst should always match the "insideless" patient's language in a rather symmetrical way. It is therapeutically useful if the analyst couches his or her reaction in words or metaphors the patient has just used. When patients hear the analyst take up their own metaphors, and when they recognize their own words in a somewhat altered context, coming from the analyst, then they begin to experience their whole self as more substantial, filled with shareable "things." In other words, the sharing of metaphors, images, and other forms of speech makes patients experience their preconscious as a usable and dependable part of the psyche. They then feel that their own minds and the analyst's mind have features in common, and this experience decreases their sense of isolation. Repeated experiences of this kind enable these patients to move along the path toward meaningfully shared dialogue.

When a patient experiences his or her own "inside" (his

or her words and metaphors) within the analyst's communication, coming from the outside, then the patient's trust in his or her own capacity to create connectedness to other human beings increases. The analyst then has fulfilled the role the mother missed out on: the analyst has picked up the symbolic bridge the patient tossed across the space between them. With connection established, the patient can internalize the analyst as a mirror reflecting the patient's own existence. The analyst's mirroring speech pattern, general responsiveness, and nonverbal expression of the fact that the patient is an enjoyable human being[1] can belatedly lead to the patient's internalization of self-affirming structure, which the mother's lovingly mirroring look should have furnished long ago.

The importance of the child's introjecting the mother's look which contains the reflection of the loved child cannot be emphasized enough. This introjected structure gives the child the feeling that he or she exists within the context of the outside world and is wanted by the outside world. This "layered" introject lends sturdiness and richness to the child's "inner space." Communication between inside and outside then feels desirable because of their "mutual immanence." The lovingly mirroring mother is somebody "out there" to whom the child can confidently build connecting bridges by language and by other forms of symbolic creativity. The physical presence of the good mother, the original prototype of the responsive "audience" or "addressee," will not be needed later, when her internal representation in the grown child's preconscious can take over the function of assuring the child that his or her symbolic communication will be well received in the outer world. Children whose mothers missed out in contributing to this self- and world-affirming inner structure

[1] Obviously, if the analyst cannot authentically feel this, he or she should not work with the patient.

will not trust either their own communicative capacity or that anybody in the outside world is interested in receiving their communications. As we saw in Chapter 8, many talented patients and nonpatients suffer from such painful inhibition of their creativity. They may start writing or composing a work but lose their confidence midway and often cannot even take a look at what they have accomplished already. They don't trust the communicative quality of their work. They can't trust the existence of a receptive audience.

If later on the analyst's mirroring reactivity can trigger off the introjective process the mother was unable to induce, then the success of therapy is practically guaranteed. Patients now both want to and know how to meaningfully communicate with the analyst. They then experience both their minds (the preconscious) and the analyst as dependably working for them in the course of the therapeutic process. Previously abandoned creative projects are often picked up at this point, when trust in an interested and understanding listener has developed.

Whether or not this success story will happen in analysis depends on (1) the analyst's empathic skill, (2) the human equation between the analyst and the patient (i.e., whether they are able to like each other), and (3) the quality and intensity of the patient's rage. Too much destructive rage prevents enough calmness in the patient to tolerate the slow process that finally leads to good communication with the analyst, and after that with the outside world.

It was stated earlier in this book that good symbol formation requires time and libido. The internalization of the analyst as a constructively mirroring and receptive "addressee" is a complex and lengthy symbolizing process, the outcome of which is a beneficial internal representation. Without enough libido to bring about instinctual fusion, the patient will not be able to construct this beneficial internal representation and thus will not be able to engage in authentic dialogue with the analyst. We all know that patients fluctuate in their ability to express what they mean and in their understanding of the analyst's words. Under the sway of fearful hostility, the most intelligent patients can suddenly misunderstand (or "not hear") even the simplest statements uttered by the analyst. They simply leave the common wavelength needed for communication. To keep up this "shared" wavelength, a certain amount of trust (i.e., libido) is needed. With some patients, it seems impossible to "tease out" the libido needed for effective dialogue. I think that as children these patients were not listened to at all, or they trained themselves early to block out threatening adults' verbal communications. Often they come from hereditarily burdened families, and seem closer to psychosis than to schizoid depersonalization. Frequent outbursts of paroxysmal rage are indicators for differential diagnosis and for very guarded prognosis.

But "insideless" schizoid patients, as we saw, are not the only ones who need to learn meaningful verbal communication in psychoanalytic treatment. Their communication deficiency is perhaps the most obvious since they do not talk easily or fluently. But at least they do not use language to hide their "true self." In contrast, two types of patients I have already discussed, the "exhibitionistic charmers" and the "obsessive intellectualizers," do just that—their fluent language hides the true self. Indeed, they are difficult to treat *because* they are experts at using the symbolic tool of language for emotionally inauthentic communication. These patients' communication deficiency derives from a considerably later stage than that of the "empty" schizoid borderlines, and hereditary factors seem less implicated. Also, their mothers seem quite different in personality from the "vacant-eyed," ephemeral, borderline-type mothers who produce—genetically and by traumatization—the schizoid, depersonalized, nonverbal patients.

The exhibitionistic charmers, as we have seen, are usually the children of exhibitionistic, narcissistic mothers. Instead of making room for a quiet play space, such a mother invades her child's private space with seductive magic. She never really *sees* the child as an individual in his or her own right. She looks only at the child's outside, never at the inside. The child is treated as a decorative object, an enhancement of the mother's narcissism. These mothers functioned as "false mirrors," reflecting an unreal picture of the child. True communication was neither initiated or responded to. True, inner-motivated symbolic creativity or communication in their children was thwarted in favor of showy performances. These children then lose touch with their own authentic inside and, as adults, may become addicted to a role of exhibitionistic seductiveness. As children they were looked at the wrong way by their mothers, and later they want the whole world to look at them in the same wrong way. They need this for the upkeep of their basic denial, by way of which they desperately try to maintain their idealized image of mother. In order to keep up the harmful illusion of a good "magic" mother, they have to perceive themselves as "rich" and happy and block out any deeply buried but authentic feelings of anger, despair, or loneliness. Admiration from the outside becomes necessary to sustain this phony self-image. These mothers were effective-enough "hypnotists" to enslave their children into their own (the mothers') orbit.

In analysis these exhibitionistic charmers try to set up a phony dialogue between themselves and the analyst. It is a difficult therapeutic task to break through their word-filled character armor. Their inauthentic verbal communication should warn the analyst against utilizing the usual interpretive method too soon, no matter with how much "analytically interesting content" the sessions might be filled. The "interesting" content serves as a decoy for the analyst, to deflect his or her attention from the patient's inauthentic "inside." If the analyst falls for this decoy and interprets content before the patient is capable of authentic dialogue, then the interpretations will be just more food for the patient's well-articulated but disconnected "false self."

In contrast to "empty" patients, exhibitionistic charmers act *as if* they had a rich inside. But this is only a glossy surface that covers over an inner, hidden isolation and depression. The analyst needs to convey that he or she *sees* the emotionally abandoned, lonely child "inside" the patient. In other words, the analyst serves as an authentic mirror (rather than a magic one), in which the patient can begin to perceive his or her "true self," without phony embellishments. If only communications from the "hidden, lonely" child are acknowledged by the analyst, then the isolating gap surrounding the patient's true self will turn into a connecting space for authentic communication. Thus, the disruption in the patient's lifespace will be healed. The "connecting space" can be truly bridged over by the use of language. By selective reactivity, i.e., reacting only to what is authentic, the analyst avoids admonishing or drawing attention to the patient's phoniness. The latter would only mobilize further defenses. What is important is to make these patients feel that finally, for the first time, they are really understood and accepted for what they are, without the necessity to "perform."

After this point in analysis has been reached, some patients insist that the analyst acknowledge in them a hidden but "terrible something," a dangerous psychotic or sadistic potential. The inner revolving stage has turned; now they want the very worst hidden recesses of the self to be looked at. After years of dissimulating, they passionately need proof that they will be accepted whoever they "*really*" are, no matter how bad. Or else they feel the analyst, too, only looks at them "through a glass darkly" and not as they really are. This wish of the patient's can be fulfilled if the analyst feels comfortable with the notion that some hidden psychotic potential is part and parcel of human endowment. I try to convey this conviction to the patient by pointing out the difference between "potential" and "manifest," and how acknowledgment of the former can guard against the latter. Szondi's (1963) therapeutic principle underlying his method of *Schicksalsanalysis* is based on this premise.

It can also be conveyed to these patients that their frantic need to exhibit their sickest "core," their fear that the analyst (like everybody else) has been "duped" by their positive traits, stems from their previous attempts to do the opposite, to show nothing but a sparkling "persona," while half-knowing all the time that this was "just for show" and not their true self. Actually, this subgroup is not the most difficult one to treat among the "charmers." Usually they are talented and introspective, if circumstances allow it, as the atmosphere of psychoanalysis does allow.

To bring about authentic communication in "charmer" patients who do not become introspective is a more difficult task, even if they have less of a "psychotic potential" than the above subgroup. A particularly difficult aspect of work with these patients is the fierce competition one faces with the seductive magician mother. These patients will use all the perceptual tricks of denial to preserve their false image of her. They are willing to distort their whole personality rather than risk the wrath of the unmasked "magician" mother. These mothers demand total loyalty, or else . . . The analyst becomes their enemy. Still, there is a chance that, given time, the analyst may win. Offering only truth and acknowledging only truth from the patient have a convincing momentum of their own. Role-playing is tiring (as is denial). The patient may come to appreciate the increase in "life energy" gained by giving up effortful denial and the need to "perform." Moreover, new authentic relationships ease the loss of a harmful illusion.

I shall now take a final look at the "obsessive intellectualizers," who also have problems in authentic communication. These patients, too, are usually the offspring of insensitive, narcissistic mothers who interfered with their quiet symbolic play. These mothers, however, were more commanding than seductive magicians. They were fighting for their power over the child. I have already described how, for these children, the play space becomes a struggle-space of opposing wills and subsequently their lives center on struggle for autonomy and fear of submission. If intellectually well-endowed, they will use their intellect as a tool for power rather than enjoyment. Emotional warmth and openness are feared because they could lead to close connectedness to another person. Emotional closeness makes these people feel vulnerable, because it reminds them of the intrusive, overpowering mother. Language becomes a means of defending against both total isolation and true emotional closeness; it is used in its emotionally distancing capacity, purely as a vehicle for expressing intelligent thoughts. These are the patients who truly fit Freud's metaphor of the horse and rider. They are intellectual ego-"riders" in eternal struggle against their "dangerous" emotions and instincts. Their lifespace is disrupted intrapsychically as well as at the interface between self and environment. Their purely intellectual communication leaves them essentially isolated.

As I mentioned before, obsessive intellectualizers are likely "customers" for psychoanalysis, and may even choose it for a profession. The role of analyst lends itself to defense against both manifest isolation and true closeness. If analytic treatment does not concentrate on these patients' communication defects, then they may go through years of "analysis," accumulating intellectual knowledge in the service of power over instincts, emotions, and people.[2] The analyst who is aware of the danger of psychoanalysis fostering split-off intellectualization will hold off content interpretation for a long time. Instead, he or she will concentrate on making the patient aware of the difference between truly connecting versus intellectually isolating communication.

The analyst must produce within the psychoanalytic situation what the mother has failed to produce for her child, namely, a symbolically creative play space. Since these patients' mothers never knew how to play with their children without squelching their authentic playful creativity, the analyst's task is to make up for these early deficiencies by establishing a symbolization-producing "intermediate space" where analyst and patient can creatively play-work together. In his *Therapeutic Consultations in Child Psychiatry* (1971b), Winnicott offers a beautiful and ingenious model for this kind of "play-work"—the "squiggle-game."

Winnicott starts out by drawing some sort of line, which the child then turns into "something." Then the child draws any sort of line and now it is Winnicott's turn to make it into "something." In the course of this playful "interview," a great deal of authentic dialogue, nonverbal and verbal, takes place between Winnicott and the child. By offering a nondescript line to the child and asking him or her to "make something of it," Winnicott sets up a situation similar to the original "creation" of a transitional object. The child must use symbolic perception to *see* the nondescript line in the context of a newly created gestalt. In order to create this gestalt, the child (or Winnicott) has to weld together the externally given with content from his or her own preconscious. This process, although nonverbal, could be described as a "true dialogue" between the outside and the inside. It is likely to be authentic

[2] With training analysts, one has to watch particularly for such unconscious motivation in the professional choice.

precisely because it is nonverbal, and relies solely on the child's available imagery. The newly created visual form then initiates authentic verbal dialogue between Winnicott and the child. The playful setting promotes creative responsiveness. The nonthreatening play setting loosens the habitual defense system which would operate in a "serious verbal exchange."

Obsessive intellectualizers need some experience analogous to Winnicott's squiggle-game. (Actually, I don't see why the game itself could not be used with adult patients, although I have never tried this.) Since my own work with adult patients is based on language communication, I will try to explicate the ways in which verbal interpretations can approximate the emotionally authentic dialogue of the squiggle-game. Obsessive intellectualizers are in particular need of learning how to "play" freely and creatively within and outside of analysis. What they do *not* need is an impersonal, silent analyst who occasionally mutters "knowing" interpretations. This stance plays into their all-too-willing readiness to fill the *role* of "good patient." It may well be helpful for these defended obsessional patients to be surprised by the analyst's doing something that is not in the "rule-book," particularly if the patient is a candidate or a practicing psychoanalyst (which is often the case).

Dictionary-translation-type interpretations are *always* to be avoided. To tell patients that when they say *a, b, c,* they *really* mean *d, e, f* is an insult to their autonomy—besides, it probably isn't quite true. The analyst has to participate *with* the patient and not act "upon" him or her. To offer dictionary-type interpretations is to "act upon." The difference here lies in the content, the choice of words and syntax, as well as in the analyst's tone of voice. The less all-knowing the analyst's formulations and tone of voice, the greater the likelihood that the analytic work will become a truly shared experience involving the patient's authentic "inside," from the deepest emotional and instinctual layers to his or her intellect. It is this kind of full participation in the psychoanalytic dialogue that results in the eradication of splits within the patient and between the patient and his or her environment. Words, under such conditions, will function as true symbol-bridges connecting previously separated "regions." ("Regions" can refer to intrapsychic regions as well as to two individuals within the same lifespace.)

The patient's communicative and form-creative potential should be fostered by every intervention the analyst makes. Informative statements offered in a professional voice will not serve this aim. Only if interpretations are not "given" (in the sense of "pronounced"), but casually tossed into the patient's play space, i.e., into the transitional space between the patient and analyst, only then can the patient pick up the offered material and weld it with his or her own inner content into a newly created gestalt. Put slightly differently: When the analyst's ideas are unobtrusively thrown into the patient's transitional play space, these ideas can lie around until the patient is ready to "find" them and blend them with his or her wishes and fantasies into a new, very personal ("treasured") possession.[3]

For the analytic situation to acquire the meaning of such a growth-producing intermediate play space, the analyst has to function as a good environmental mother. This is a role the analyst really has to *fulfill*; it is not simply a role given by the patient's transference projections. In the analytic situation, the analyst and the patient—like the environmental mother and the playing child—alternate between active two-way "dialogue" and times when the patient "plays" alone in

[3] Piaget's ideas concerning the formation of new schemata, the assimilation of the new into the existing schema, articulate the same process on an abstract level. The transformation by the patient of the analyst's interpretation into a personally possessed insight, as well as the infant's transformation of a piece of cloth into a transitional object, follow the steps of new schema formation described by Piaget.

the presence of the analyst. "Playing alone" in this setting corresponds to free-associating and fantasizing aloud. At such times the analyst—like the empathic mother—does not intrude, does not rush into the patient's "play space" with his or her own "goods," but dependably listens and watches. The analyst is there and available when needed—if necessary, to be symbolically destroyed and survive this destruction. With his or her presence, the analyst creates an atmosphere in which the capacity for affection and mutual respect can grow. These are feelings for real (in contrast to transference) manifestations, which survive after the vicissitudes of the transference have been resolved, even after the treatment has ended.

Without an understanding of the full meaning of Winnicott's conception of "transitional phenomena," the healing effect of psychoanalysis cannot be comprehended. Making the unconscious conscious by way of "correct" interpretations is not a satisfactory explanation of why psychoanalysis as a treatment method "works." The obsessive intellectualizers, more than any other category of patients, teach us that "correct" interpretations may be registered merely as intellectual "addenda," without resulting in any qualitative change in the patient's life processes.

The crux of the matter lies in the function of words. Words can either function in the constricted sense of signs, carrying strictly circumscribed denotations, functioning as labels that point unambiguously to unitary "things." Or, words can function as true *symbols*, with all the "not-to-be-resolved" paradoxes and "multiple functions" this concept implies. Winnicott's transitional phenomena are "true" symbols in the latter sense (even though transitional objects per se are developmentally categorized as "protosymbols")—or at least they are conducive to the creation of true symbols. Psychoanalysis "works" because the psychoanalytic situation can function as a transitional space, conducive to the creation of true symbols. In this setting, words can have *real* therapeutic effect if they function in the full meaning of symbols (and not as restricted, "unidirectional" symbol-signs, as was seen in the case of Sarah).

Although Winnicott does not spell this out, the "positive value" of the unresolved paradox lies in the preservation of the antithetical functions represented by the true symbol. Remember Winnicott's warning that the "resolution of paradox leads to a defence organization which in the adult one can encounter as true and false self organization" (1953b, p. 14). This statement applies particularly to obsessive intellectualizers, who aim at resolving the potential "paradox" implied in the meaning of words by using them in their constricted sign-function rather than in their multifaceted symbol-function. To the extent that these patients succeed in "resolving" the paradox of words, to that extent they will have "succeeded" in splitting their self into an actively functioning "false self" and a more latent "true self." As long as they keep up this split organization, they will also be able to defend themselves against the healing (or whole-making) effect of psychoanalytic treatment.

True symbolic use of language allows the patient and the analyst to communicate fully; it "paradoxically" allows their "insides" to interpenetrate, while at the same time it safeguards the integrity of both participants. Only if this interpenetration of "insides" takes place can the verbal dialogue have a mutative effect on the participants—and that is how the healing effect of words in psychoanalysis comes about. And that is why an understanding of the *paradoxical* function of the symbol is needed in order to comprehend how psychoanalysis works as a healing method. The purely denotative sign-function of words will never heal deep splits in the self. It is words as "paradoxical" symbols that can truly bridge over discontinuities, analogously to the bridging-over function of transitional objects—because as communicative symbols words are imbued with some of the nature of both participants, while they also share in the nature of their symbolized referents. Words can have a real integrating effect because as symbols they unite into one configuration the addressor, the addressee, the symbolized, and the symbol itself. Picard in *Man and Language* expresses this unifying function of symbols beautifully: "Something of the object is taken into the word and therefore when he speaks man is related to the object because something of it is contained in the word" (1963, p. 103).

If the analyst can hand over his or her capacity to use words with such full symbolic meaning, then the analyst will have contributed to the unfolding of the patient's capacity to truly connect to the world, "because something of it is contained in the word." If the patient acquires the capacity to invest words with his or her own inside nature, then there is a good likelihood that the patient will also be able to invest other objects with subjectively significant symbolic meaning. This is the process of richly symbolic perception that lends coherence and pleasurable quality to the person's lifespace. As with the beneficial effects of the "primary illusion" brought about by the good mother's well-timed and well-offered gratifications, the analyst's well-timed and well-offered words and ideas, if appropriate in content and offered when the patient is ready for them, will contribute to the patient's experience that the outside world corresponds to his or her need and capacity to create.

In the context of good analytic work, patients often have the "illusion" that they have "created" the analyst's verbalizations. How many times do we hear a patient say: "You said exactly what I had in mind," as if it were some magic coincidence. The fact is of course that a good interpretation does verbalize what is already close to the surface in the patient's preconscious. Good empathic rapport between analyst and patient is needed for such gratifying experiences to come about. Therefore the patient's illusion, like all "good illusions," will be partly true: he or she did in part create the well-attuned analyst's verbalizations, just as the infant's need did "create" the appearance of the empathically attuned mother's breast.

The patient who in the course of analysis experiences such "good illusions," and who also acquires the capacity to invest words and other "things" with subjectively significant symbolic meaning, will be able to have the "good illusion" that he or she created the beauty in the world, and this "illusion" too will be partly true. As if from a tremendous Rorschach card, we do create our personal world, our personally relevant lifespace, through our symbolizing perception and organization.

If a "good enough" mother was missing, a good analysis can bring out the patient's creative ability and the necessary trust in this ability to shape for him- or herself a fitting lifespace that is both realistic and enjoyable. The "reality principle" includes the capacity to create an enjoyable lifespace. The existence of an enjoyable lifespace is predicated on the experience of a good creative "inside," and the capacity for rich symbolic perception. Therefore these psychic characteristics must find place in a full reality principle.

As we have seen, Freud's formulation of the reality principle focuses on "unemotional objectivity" and the acceptance of limitations imposed by outer reality, as well as the acceptance of the necessary frustrations which follow from "culture" and "civilization." This is not inclusive enough and also partially incorrect. "Culture" potentially offers the highest manifestation of creative symbolization. A deep appreciation of cultural symbols, symbols of art, for example, connects the person to his or her psychic depth and to the world around. Culture is not the cause for "discontent" or frustration. Also, Freud's definition of the reality principle does not include the psychological "reality" of feeling truly alive. Any "reality principle" couched solely in terms of frustration tolerance and adjustment to necessity may go hand in hand with a life of "quiet desperation"—even in the presence of all the accessories supposedly needed for a "good life."

Anhedonia seems to be the number one psychological disease of our society, with its emphasis on technology and visible success. It would be tragic if psychoanalysis, with its emphasis on "neutralized energy" and the ego's autonomy from the instincts, contributed to the spread of depersonalization and anhedonia. That is the reason that this book emphasizes the capacity to enjoy as a salient feature of the reality principle. Living by the "reality principle" should lead to healthy life rather than to life through the "false self," in chronic low-grade depression or in depersonalized anhedonia.

Psychoanalysis cannot produce artists, but it can elicit patients' authentic form-creative potentials and liberate them from functioning under the auspices of a "false self" and from repetitious fixation on the traumatizing aspects of the past. They can learn to look at the world creatively, with rich symbolic perception and find beauties they were not able to see or hear before.

Winnicott wrote: "It is creative appreciation more than anything else that makes the individual feel that life is worth living" (1971a, p. 65). This statement should hang framed in every analyst's office. And it was another Englishman who succinctly expressed what symbolic perception is all about:

> To see a world in a grain of sand,
> And heaven in a wild flower;

Hold infinity in the palm of your hand,
And eternity in an hour.

—William Blake, "Auguries of Innocence."

References

Amacher, P. (1965), *Freud's Neurological Education and Its Influence on Psychoanalytic Theory* [*Psychol. Issues*, Monogr. 16]. New York: International Universities Press.

Angyal, A. (1965), *Neurosis and Treatment*. New York: Wiley.

Arieti, S. (1976), *Creativity: The Magic Synthesis*. New York: Basic Books.

Bally, G. (1945), *Vom Ursprung und von den Grenzen der Freiheit: Eine Deutung des Spiels bei Tier und Mensch*. Basel: Schwabe.

Beres, D. (1957), Communication in psychoanalysis and in the creative process: A parallel. *J. Amer. Psychoanal. Assn.*, 5:408–423.

Bertalanffy, L. von (1952), *Problems of Life*. New York: Wiley.

Binswanger, L. (1958), The existential analysis school of thought. In: *Existence: A New Dimension in Psychiatry and Psychology*, ed. R. May, E. Angel, & H. F. Ellenberger. New York: Basic Books, pp. 191–213.

Bion, W. R. (1956), Development of schizophrenic thought. In: *Second Thoughts*. London: Heinemann, 1967, pp. 36–42.

——— (1957), Differentiation of the psychotic from the non-psychotic personalities. In: *Second Thoughts*. London: Heinemann, 1967, pp. 43–64.

——— (1959), Attacks on linking. *Int. J. Psycho-Anal.*, 40:308–315.

——— (1965), *Transformations*. London: Heinemann.

——— (1967), *Second Thoughts*. London: Heinemann.

Blake, W. (c. 1790), Auguries of innocence. In: *The Pocket Book of Verse*. New York: Pocket Books, 1940, p. 94.

Bolk, L. (1926), *Das Problem der Menschwerdung*. Jena: Fischer.

Bowlby, J. (1969), *Attachment and Loss*, Vol. 1. New York: Basic Books.

Breuer, J., & Freud, S. (1893–1895), Studies on hysteria. *Standard Edition*, 2. London: Hogarth Press, 1955.

Cassirer, E. (1944), *An Essay on Man*. New Haven: Yale University Press.

Chasseguet-Smirgel, J. (1974), Perversion, idealization and sublimation. *Int. J. Psycho-Anal.*, 55:349–357.

Dawkins, R. (1976), *The Selfish Gene*. New York: Oxford University Press, 1978.

Deri, S. K. (1949), *Introduction to the Szondi Test.* New York: Grune & Stratton.

——— (1965), The homeostatic and the representational function of the symbolic process with reference to the Rat Man's obsessive ideation. Presented at the 24th International Psychoanalytic Congress, Amsterdam.

——— (1966), The Szondi Test as an instrument for reflecting degrees of split and integration within personality. *Szondiana,* 6:100–111 [*Beiheft zur Schweitzer Zeitschrift für Psychologie und Ihre Anwendungen*].

——— (1967), Changing concepts of transference in depth-psychology. *Szondiana,* 7:114–125.

——— (1974), Symbolization in psychoanalysis and Schicksalsanalysis: A revised theory of symbolization. *Szondiana,* 9:35–52.

Deutsch, F., Ed. (1959), *On the Mysterious Leap from the Mind to the Body.* New York: International Universities Press.

Dickerson, R. (1978), Chemical evolution and the origin of life. *Sci. Amer.,* Sept., pp. 70–86.

Ehrenzweig, A. (1953), *The Psychoanalysis of Artistic Vision and Hearing.* New York: Julian Press.

——— (1967), *The Hidden Order of Art.* Berkeley & Los Angeles: University of California Press.

Eissler, K. R. (1963), *Goethe: A Psychoanalytic Study.* Detroit: Wayne State University Press.

Ekstein, R., & Wallerstein, J. (1954), Observations on the psychology of borderline and psychotic children. *The Psychoanalytic Study of the Child,* 9:344–369. New York: International Universities Press.

Erikson, E. H. (1950), *Childhood and Society.* New York: Norton.

——— (1962), *Young Man Luther.* New York: Norton.

Freeman, T., Cameron, J. L., & McGhie, A. (1958), *Chronic Schizophrenia.* New York: International Universities Press.

Freud, A. (1936), *The Ego and the Mechanisms of Defense.* New York: International Universities Press, 1946.

Freud, S. (1887–1902), *Origins of Psychoanalysis: Letters to Wilhelm Fliess, Drafts and Notes,* ed. M. Bonaparte, A. Freud, & E. Kris. New York: Basic Books, 1954.

——— (1891), *On Aphasia.* New York: International Universities Press, 1953.

——— (1894), The neuro-psychoses of defence. *Standard Edition,* 3:45–61. London: Hogarth Press, 1962.

——— (1895), Project for a scientific psychology. In: *Origins of Psychoanalysis,* ed. M. Bonaparte, A. Freud, & E. Kris. New York: Basic Books, 1954, pp. 355–445.

——— (1900), The interpretation of dreams. *Standard Edition,* 4 & 5. London: Hogarth Press, 1953.

——— (1905), Fragments of an analysis of a case of hysteria. *Standard Edition,* 7:7–122. London: Hogarth Press, 1953.

——— (1908), Creative writers and day-dreaming. *Standard Edition,* 9:142–153. London: Hogarth Press, 1959.

——— (1909), Notes upon a case of obsessional neurosis. *Standard Edition,* 10:155–318. London: Hogarth Press, 1955.

——— (1910), Five lectures on psycho-analysis. *Standard Edition*, 11:9–55. London: Hogarth Press, 1957.
——— (1911), Formulations on the two principles of mental functioning. *Standard Edition*, 12:218–226. London: Hogarth Press, 1958.
——— (1913), The disposition to obsessional neurosis. *Standard Edition*, 12:317–326. London: Hogarth Press, 1958.
——— (1914a), On the history of the psycho-analytic movement. *Standard Edition*, 14:7–66. London: Hogarth Press, 1957.
——— (1914b), The Moses of Michelangelo. *Standard Edition*, 13:211–238. London: Hogarth Press, 1955.
——— (1915a), Instincts and their vicissitudes. *Standard Edition*, 14:115–140. London: Hogarth Press, 1957.
——— (1915b), Repression. *Standard Edition*, 14:146–158. London: Hogarth Press, 1957.
——— (1915c), The unconscious. *Standard Edition*, 14:166–204. London: Hogarth Press, 1957.
——— (1920), Beyond the pleasure principle. *Standard Edition*, 18:7–64. London: Hogarth Press, 1955.
——— (1921), Group psychology and the analysis of the ego. *Standard Edition*, 18:69–143. London: Hogarth Press, 1955.
——— (1923), The ego and the id. *Standard Edition*, 19:12–66. London: Hogarth Press, 1961.
——— (1924a), The loss of reality in neurosis and psychosis. *Standard Edition*, 19:183–187. London: Hogarth Press, 1961.
——— (1924b), Neurosis and psychosis. *Standard Edition*, 19:145–153. London: Hogarth Press, 1961.
——— (1925), Negation. *Standard Edition*, 19:235–239. London: Hogarth Press, 1961.
——— (1927a), Fetishism. *Standard Edition*, 21:152–157. London: Hogarth Press, 1961.
——— (1927b), The future of an illusion. *Standard Edition*, 21:5–56. London: Hogarth Press, 1961.
——— (1930), Civilization and its discontents. *Standard Edition*, 21:64–145. London: Hogarth Press, 1961.
——— (1937a), Analysis terminable and interminable. *Standard Edition*, 23:216–253. London: Hogarth Press, 1964.
——— (1937b), Constructions in analysis. *Standard Edition*, 23:257–269. London: Hogarth Press, 1964.
——— (1938), Splitting of the ego in the process of defence. *Standard Edition*, 23:275–278. London: Hogarth Press, 1964.
——— (1940), An outline of psycho-analysis. *Standard Edition*, 23:144–207. London: Hogarth Press, 1964.
Gibson, J. J. (1929), The reproduction of visually perceived forms. *J. Exper. Psychol.*, 12:1–39.
Gideon, S. (1962), *The Eternal Present*. London: Oxford University Press.
Gill, M. M., & Holzman, P. S., Eds. (1976), *Psychology versus Metapsychology: Psychoanalytic Essays in Honor of George S. Klein* [*Psychol. Issues*, Monogr. 36]. New York: International Universities Press.

Goethe, J. W. von (1808), *Faust*, trans. W. Kaufmann. Garden City, N.Y.: Doubleday.

Goldstein, K. (1939), *The Organism*. New York: American Book Co.

Gombrich, E. H. (1951), Meditations on a hobby horse, or the roots of artistic form. In: *Meditations on a Hobby Horse and Other Essays*. London: Phaidon, 1963, pp. 1–11.

——— (1960), *Art and Illusion*. New York: Pantheon.

Gottschaldt, K. (1926), Über den Einfluss der Erfahrung auf die Wahrnehmung von Figuren, I. *Psychol. Forsch.*, 8:261–317.

——— (1929), Über den Einfluss der Erfahrung auf die Wahrnehmung von Figuren, II. *Psychol. Forsch.*, 12:1–87.

Greenacre, P. (1957), The childhood of the artist: Libidinal phase development and giftedness. In: *Emotional Growth*, Vol. 2. New York: International Universities Press, 1971, pp. 479–504.

——— (1958), The family romance of the artist. In: *Emotional Growth*, Vol. 2. New York: International Universities Press, 1971, pp. 505–532.

——— (1969), The fetish and the transitional object. In: *Emotional Growth*, Vol. 1. New York: International Universities Press, 1971, pp. 315–334.

——— (1970), The transitional object and the fetish: With special reference to the role of illusion. In: *Emotional Growth*, Vol. 1. New York: International Universities Press, 1971, pp. 335–352.

——— (1971), *Emotional Growth*, Vols. 1 & 2. New York: International Universities Press.

Guntrip, H. (1969), *Schizoid Phenomena, Object Relations and the Self*. New York: International Universities Press.

Hanfmann, G. (1972), *Letters from Sardis*. Cambridge, Mass.: Harvard University Press.

Hermann, I. (1936), Clinging—going-in-search. *Psychoanal. Quart.*, 45:5–36 (1976).

Jacobson, E. (1957), Denial and repression. *J. Amer. Psychoanal. Assn.*, 5:61–92.

Jaensch, E. R. (1930), *Eidetic Imagery and Topological Methods of Investigation*. London: Kegan Paul.

James, W. (1902), *Varieties of Religious Experience*. New York: Mentor, 1958.

Jones, E. (1912), The theory of symbolism. In: *Papers on Psychoanalysis*, 5th Ed. Baltimore: Williams & Wilkins, 1948, pp. 452–484.

Kay, P. (1977), Review of *Creativity: The Magic Synthesis* by S. Arieti. *J. Amer. Psychoanal. Assn.*, 25:740–743.

Klein, G. S. (1970), Two theories or one? Perspectives to change in psychoanalytic theory. *Bull. Menninger Clinic*, 37:102–152 (1973).

Klein, M. (1930), The importance of symbol formation in the development of the ego. In: *Love, Guilt and Reparation and Other Works*. New York: Delta, 1975, pp. 219–232.

——— (1932), *The Psycho-Analysis of Children*. New York: Delacorte, 1975.

——— (1957), Envy and gratitude. In: *Envy and Gratitude and Other Works*. New York: Delacorte, 1975, pp. 176–235.

Koffka, K. (1935), *Principles of Gestalt Psychology*. New York: Harcourt, Brace.

Köhler, W. (1929), *Gestalt Psychology*. New York: Liveright, 1947.

——— (1938), *The Place of Value in a World of Facts.* New York: Liveright, 1952.

——— (1969), *The Task of Gestalt Psychology.* Princeton, N.J.: Princeton University Press.

Kovel, J. (1978), Things and words: Metapsychology and the historical point of view. *Psychoanal. Contemp. Thought,* 1:21–88.

Kramer, E. (1971), *Art as Therapy with Children.* New York: Schocken Books.

Kris, E. (1952), *Psychoanalytic Explorations in Art.* New York: International Universities Press.

——— & Pappenheim, E. (1946), The function of drawings and the meaning of the "creative spell" in a schizophrenic artist. *Psychoanal. Quart.,* 15:6–31.

Kubie, L. S. (1958), *Neurotic Distortions of the Creative Process.* New York: Noonday Press, 1961.

——— (1978), *Symbol and Neurosis* [*Psychol. Issues,* Monogr. 44]. New York: International Universities Press.

Kuhn, T. S. (1962), *The Structure of Scientific Revolutions.* Chicago: University of Chicago Press.

Langer, S. K. (1942), *Philosophy in a New Key.* New York: Mentor, 1951.

——— (1953), *Feeling and Form: A Theory of Art.* New York: Scribner's.

——— (1967), *Mind: An Essay on Human Feeling,* Vol. 1. Baltimore: Johns Hopkins University Press.

——— (1972), *Mind: An Essay on Human Feeling,* Vol. 2. Baltimore: Johns Hopkins University Press.

Lenneberg, E. H. (1967), *Biological Foundations of Language.* New York: Wiley.

Lewin, K. (1935), *A Dynamic Theory of Personality.* New York: McGraw-Hill.

——— (1936), *Principles of Topological Psychology.* New York: McGraw-Hill.

Luria, A. R., & Yudovich, F. I. (1959), *Speech and the Development of Mental Processes in the Child.* London: Staples Press.

Mahler, M. S. (1968), *On Human Symbiosis and the Vicissitudes of Individuation.* New York: International Universities Press.

Matte-Blanco, I. (1975), *The Unconscious as Infinite Sets.* London: Duckworth.

Milner, M. (1952), Aspects of symbolism in comprehension of the not-self. *Int. J. Psycho-Anal.,* 33:181–195.

Nachmansohn, M. (1925), Concerning experimentally produced dreams. In: *Organization and Pathology of Thought,* ed. D. Rapaport. New York: Columbia University Press, 1951, pp. 257–287.

Neumann, E. (1954), *Art and the Creative Unconscious.* Princeton, N.J.: Princeton University Press.

Nunberg, H. (1931), The synthetic function of the ego. In: *Practice and Theory of Psychoanalysis,* Vol. 1. New York: International Universities Press, 1955, pp. 120–136.

——— (1951), Transference and reality. In: *Practice and Theory of Psychoanalysis,* Vol. 2. New York: International Universities Press, 1965, pp. 118–133.

Penfield, W. (1975), *The Mystery of the Mind.* Princeton, N.J.: Princeton University Press.

Piaget, J. (1936), *The Origins of Intelligence in Children.* New York: International Universities Press, 1952.

——— (1937), *The Construction of Reality in the Child.* New York: Basic Books, 1954.

——— (1945), *Play, Dreams and Imitation in Childhood.* New York: Norton, 1962.

Picard, M. (1963), *Man and Language.* Chicago: Regnery.

Plato (n.d.), Symposium. In: *Collected Dialogues*, ed. E. Hamilton & H. Cairns. New York: Pantheon, 1963, pp. 526–574.

Polanyi, M. (1958), *Personal Knowledge: Toward a Post-Critical Philosophy.* Chicago: University of Chicago Press.

——— (1966), *The Tacit Dimension.* Garden City, N.Y.: Doubleday.

——— (1969), The creative imagination. In: *Toward a Unity of Knowledge* [*Psychol. Issues*, Monogr. 22], ed. M. Grene. New York: International Universities Press, pp. 53–91.

Popper, K. (1959), *On the Logic of Scientific Discovery.* New York: Harper.

Portmann, A. (1956), *Biologie und Geist.* Zurich: Rheim.

——— (1960), *Neue Wege der Biologie.* Munich: Piper.

——— (1965), *Vom Ursprung des Menschen.* Basel: Reinhardt.

Pribram, K. H. (1971), *Languages of the Brain: Experimental Paradoxes and Principles in Neuropsychology.* Englewood Cliffs, N.J.: Prentice-Hall.

Prinzhorn, F. (1922), *Bildernei der Geisteskranken.* Berlin: Springer.

Rapaport, D., Ed. (1951), *Organization and Pathology of Thought.* New York: Columbia University Press.

Reitman, F. (1951), *Psychotic Art.* New York: International Universities Press.

Rubin, E. (1915), *Synsoplevede Figurer.* Copenhagen: Kristiana.

Sartre, J.-P. (1943), *Being and Nothingness.* New York: Pocket Books, 1978.

Schachtel, E. G. (1959), *Metamorphosis.* New York: Basic Books.

Schafer, R. (1976), *A New Language for Psychoanalysis.* New Haven: Yale University Press.

Schilder, P. (1920), On the development of thoughts. In: *Organization and Pathology of Thought*, ed. D. Rapaport. New York: Columbia University Press, 1951, pp. 497–578.

——— (1924), *Medical Psychology.* New York: International Universities Press, 1953.

——— (1935), *The Image and Appearance of the Human Body.* New York: International Universities Press, 1950.

Schrödinger, E. (1945), *What Is Life?* Cambridge, Eng.: Cambridge University Press.

Segal, H. (1957), Notes on symbol formation. *Int. J. Psycho-Anal.*, 38:391–397.

——— (1964), *Introduction to Work of Melanie Klein.* New York: Basic Books.

Sharpe, E. F. (1940), Psycho-physical problems revealed in language: An examination of metaphor. In: *Collected Papers on Psycho-Analysis.* London: Hogarth Press, 1950, pp. 155–169.

Silverberg, W. V. (1952), *Childhood Experience and Personal Destiny: A Psychoanalytic Theory of Neuroses.* New York: Springer.

Spitz, R. A. (1957), *No and Yes.* New York: International Universities Press.

Stekel, W. (1924), The polyphony of thought. In: *Organization and Pathology of Thought*, ed. D. Rapaport. New York: Columbia University Press, 1951, pp. 311–314.

Szondi, L. (1947), *Triebpathologie*, Vol. 1. Bern: Huber.
——— (1963), *Schicksalsanalytische Therapie*. Berlin: Huber.
Tinbergen, N. (1951), *The Study of Instinct*. Oxford: Clarendon.
Uexküll, J. von (1921), *Umwelt und Innenwelt der Tiere*. Berlin: Springer.
Waelder, R. (1936), The principle of multiple function. *Psychoanal. Quart.*, 5:45–62.
Werner, H., & Kaplan, B. (1963), *Symbol Formation*. New York: Wiley.
Wertheimer, M. (1923), Untersuchungen zur Lehre von der Gestalt, II. *Psychol. Forsch.*, 4:301–350.
——— (1945), *Productive Thinking*. New York: Harper.
Weyl, S. (1959), Retardation, acceleration and psychoanalysis. *J. Amer. Psychoanal. Assn.*, 7:329–349.
Wigner, E. P. (1969), Epistemology of quantum mechanics—its appraisal and demands. In: *Toward a Unity of Knowledge* [*Psychol. Issues*, Monogr. 22], ed. M. Grene. New York: International Universities Press, pp. 22–49.
Winnicott, D. W. (1953a), Psychoses and child care. In: *Collected Papers: Through Pediatrics to Psychoanalysis*. New York: Basic Books, 1958, pp. 219–228.
——— (1953b), Transitional objects and transitional phenomena. In: *Playing and Reality*. New York: Basic Books, 1971, pp. 1–25.
——— (1954), Preface to "The first treasured possession" by O. Stevenson. *The Psychoanalytic Study of the Child*, 9:199–201. New York: International Universities Press.
——— (1965), *The Maturational Processes and the Facilitating Environment*. New York: International Universities Press.
——— (1971a), *Playing and Reality*. New York: Basic Books.
——— (1971b), *Therapeutic Consultations in Child Psychiatry*. London: Hogarth Press.
Witkin, H. A., Lewis, H. B., Hertzman, M., Machover, K., Meissner, P. B., & Wapner, S. (1954), *Personality through Perception*. New York: Harper.
Wittgenstein, L. (1958), *The Blue and Brown Books*. Oxford: Blackwell.
Wolff, P. H. (1960), *The Developmental Psychologies of Jean Piaget and Psychoanalysis* [*Psychol. Issues*, Monogr. 5]. New York: International Universities Press.
Zeigarnik, B. (1927), Über das Behalten von erledigten und underledigten Handlungen. *Psychol. Forsch.*, 9:1–85.

Index

Accomodation, 74, 192, 256, 341n
Ach, N., 117
Acting out, 97, 159–167
  obsessive vs., 204–205, 230–232
  picture thinking and, 182–203
  psychotic art as, 168–182
  signs in, 162–165
  treatment of, 164–165, 303–304, 307–308
Adualistic stage, 192–193
Aggression, 16, 60, 260, 277, 285, 294–295; *see also* Sadistic impulses, Thanatos
Amacher, P., 86, 349
Ambiguities, 35–36, 144–146, 198
Anal stage, 268, 270, 273, 277
Angyal, A., 194n, 349
Anhedonia, 298–303, 326–330, 346
  treatment for, 303–308
  see also Borderline disorders
Archetypes, 120–125
Arieti, S., 45, 108n, 349
Aristophanes, 51
Art, 169–175
  collective unconscious and, 120–122
  creation of, 120–122, 169–175, 281–291
  Freud on, 100, 246
  matching in, 142–144, 171, 172
  psychotic, 168–169, 176–182
Artist, psychic structure of, 281–291
Assimilation, 74, 192, 256, 288, 341n
Autistic traits, 166–167, 247
Autonomy, fight for, 268–269

Bachofen, J. J., 46
Balint, M., ix
Bally, G., 262, 349
Barkin, L., xi
Beethoven, L. van, 121, 247, 294
Beres, D., 310, 349
Bertalanffy, L. von, 67, 169, 349
Binswanger, L., 65, 349
Bion, W. R, 97, 146n–147n, 158, 327, 349
Bisexuality, 286
Blake, W., 346–347, 349
Blending, 96–97, 124, 129–134, 156, 294
Bolk, L., 91n, 349
Borderline disorders, 58, 66–67, 88–89, 244n, 250, 294, 305, 326–330
Bosch, H., 121
Boundaries, 30–32, 298
  impaired, 155, 178
  psychoanalysis and, 298
  in symbol formation, 62, 75, 77
  see also Symbolization, bridging-over function of
Bowlby, J., 262, 349

Brentano, F., 117
Breuer, J., 77, 83n, 85, 88–92, 145, 314, 349

Cameron, J. L., 304, 350
Cassirer, E., viii, 62, 80, 81, 109, 314, 349
Centaur model, xi, 291–295
Chagall, M., 170
Chasseguet-Smirgel, J., 270, 349
Child development, 10–12
  cognitive, 57–58
  deviations in, 266–280, 302–303, 335
  Kleinian view of, 58–60
  mirroring and, 263–264, 271, 332–333
  play stage in, 259–261
  quiet vs. paroxysmal cycles in, 262–263
  television and, 302–303
  transitional object and, 166, 245, 254–259
  Winnicott on, 247–280
  see also Infant, Mother
Choice, 63–67, 125, 127–128, 139
Clinging, need for, 262
Collective alternates, 273, 277, 283, 289
Collective unconscious, 120–125
Condensation, 69, 149, 232–233
Conflict model, 87–88, 90, 145
Consciousness, 86–87, 134
  energy binding in, 91, 112
  perception and, 94–95, 104–105, 112
Constable, J., 70, 143, 170
Constitutional endowment, 11, 64, 145, 167, 247
  in artist, 284
  Breuer-Janet view of, 88–90, 92, 145
  schizophrenic thinking and, 178–181
  Szondi on, 125–128
Corot, C., 170
Couch, analytic, 330
Creativity, 11, 45, 144
  aggression and, 60, 260, 277, 285, 294–295
  in artistic process, 120–122, 169–175, 281–291
  centaur model of, xi, 291–295
  definition of, 3–5, 9, 150–151, 324
  developmental deviations and, 266–280
  inhibited, 271–280, 333
  inner space and, 264–266
  insanity and, 175, 293–294; *see also* Psychotic
  libido and, 12–17, 60, 260, 285–287, 294, 353
  "regression" and, 199, 290
  Winnicott on, 242–247, 264–266, 346
Cryptosymbolization, 154–155, 158–159, 209–210, 213, 223
  definition of, 74–75

Dawkins, R., 86, 349
Death instinct, 317–318
  Kleinian view of, 59
  see also Thanatos
Denial, 46, 199, 216–217
Deri, P., vii–xii
Deri, S. K., vii–xii, 6, 13, 55n, 65n, 81, 248, 274, 350
Desymbolization, 155–160, 208, 209
  acting out and, 160–167
  in psychotic, 168, 169
Deutsch, F., 213, 350
Development; *see* Child development, Constitutional endowment, Infant
Dialogue, 42, 235–236, 339–340
  with art work, 171, 172
  impairment in, 297–311, 335–336
  model, 313–316, 322
Dickerson, R., 110n, 350
Dreams, 43–44, 119, 122, 318
Dual instinct theory, 12–17, 169, 262, 263, 285–286; *see also* Aggression, Eros, Libido, Thanatos
Dual-union, 6n, 247–250

Ego
  development, 10, 14, 49, 91–92, 109–110
  as gestalt, 13–15
  id and, 82, 84, 99, 109–116, 119, 156–157, 205, 290
  synthetic function of, 14, 145, 146, 287

Ehrenzweig, A., 175n, 350
Eidetic imagery, 179
Eissler, K. R., 293, 350
Ekstein, R., 178, 350
Energy binding, 77, 78, 85
  blending in, 96–97, 129–134, 156
  form and, 96, 118–119, 133–134, 295
  Freud on, 91–97, 99–100, 109, 110–114
  need for concept of, 79–80, 83, 93, 115, 118–119, 222
  neutralization and, 114–115, 261, 285–286
  tension regulation and, 67–68, 92–93
Environmental mother, 260–261, 263, 341
Erikson, E. H., 7, 249, 264, 266, 350
Eros, 12–17, 60, 175n, 186, 202, 203, 230, 236, 276, 285, 286; *see also* Libodo
Exhibitionistic characters, 267–271, 309, 317, 334–338

Fechner, G. T., 71
Fetish, 257–259, 271, 277, 308
Figure-ground structure, 33–34, 36
  psychoanalysis and, 35, 36
  in psychotic art, 170, 180
Fliess, W., 86–88
Form development, 93, 105
  energy binding and, 96, 118–119, 133–134, 295
  gestalt principles and, 14–15, 29, 32–40, 50, 140–144, 208–209
Free association, 314
Freeman, T., 304, 350
Freud, A., 82, 350
Freud, S., viii, 14, 54, 76, 80, 83–117, 141, 150, 162, 175, 181, 201, 234, 285, 295, 304, 317–318, 338, 349–351
  Breuer-Janet view vs., 89–91, 145
  on consciousness, 86–87, 94–96
  dual instinct theory of, 12, 13, 15, 16, 169, 262, 263
  dualistic view of, 82, 83, 92, 96, 99, 101, 107, 110–116, 119, 138, 244–245, 292–293, 318–319
  energy concepts of, 67n, 77, 79, 83, 84, 91–97, 99–100, 109–114, 131, 156–157, 161
  on hallucinatory wish fulfillment, 47–48, 243, 250–251
  Jungian view and, 122–123
  on obsessive-compulsive, 205–206
  on perceptual identity, 49, 103, 130, 142
  on preconscious, 97–107, 133–134, 137, 146n
  reality principle of, 13, 243, 345, 346
  on repression, 44, 137, 155, 208n, 215, 216n
  on stimulus barrier, 71–72
  structural model of, 107–116, 138
  on symbolization, 43, 44, 73, 75, 84–85, 103, 122, 154, 156, 232, 313–315, 318–319
  Szondi vs., 126
  topographic model of, 34, 108, 112n, 139–140, 153
  Winnicott vs., 242–246
Frustration tolerance, 11, 254

Gauguin, P., 183n
Genes, 50n–51n, 81, 125, 127–128
Gestalt
  ambiguity and, 35–36, 144–146
  closure of, 37, 38, 56, 140, 208–209
  ego as, 13–15
  good, 3, 4, 16–17, 29, 32, 38, 324
  libido and, 13, 16
  lifespace as, 32, 40–42
  principles, 14–15, 29, 32–40, 50, 140–144, 208–209
Gestalt psychology, 14–15, 32–40, 69, 140
Gibson, J. J., 38, 351
Gideon, S., 46–48, 351
Gill, M. M., 79, 351
Goethe, J. W. von, 115–116, 128–129, 294, 352
Goldstein, K., 4, 184, 200, 241, 352
Gombrich, E. H., 70, 142–145, 174, 352
Gottschaldt, K., 33, 352
Greenacre, P., 182, 201, 258, 273, 277,

283, 287, 289, 293, 352
Grolnick, S. A., xi
Guntrip, H., 106, 352

Haldane, J. B., 110n
Hallucinatory wish fulfillment, 47–48, 61, 243, 250–254
Hanfmann, G., 216, 352
Health, mental
  definition of, 4–7, 323–325
  dialogue model of 313–316, 322
Helmholtz, H. L. F. von, 48
Hermann, I., ix, 6n, 248, 262, 352
Hertzman, M., 355
Holding function
  of mother, 247–250, 261, 304, 326
  in psychoanalysis, 326–329
Holzman, P. S., 79, 351
Hope, 7, 9–12
  in case example, 19–25
Hypnosis, 122, 123

Icarus, 66
Id, 76, 78, 81, 93, 122
  ego and, 82, 84, 99, 109–116, 119, 156–157, 205, 290
  energy binding and, 77
  unconscious and, 76, 110
Illusion, 38, 40, 254, 257, 268
  primary, 251–254, 344
  in psychoanalysis, 344–345
Infant, 6–7, 10
  in dual-union, 6n, 247–250
  hallucinatory wish fulfillment in, 47–48, 243, 250–254
  transitional object and, 245, 254–259
  see also Mother
Intellectualization, 310
  obsessive, 293, 309–311, 317, 320–321, 334, 338–339, 342, 343
Internalization, 249, 265, 266, 332
Interpretation, 214–218, 314, 316, 319, 340–341
  bias of, 218–222, 242n, 320
Introjectors, avid, 271–280, 285
Isolation of affect, 106–107
Isomorphism, 39–40, 56, 74, 75, 103, 140–141

Jacobson, E., 216n, 352
Jaensch, E. R., 179, 352
James, W., 69, 352
Janet, P., 88–92, 145
Jones, E., 44, 45, 154, 352
Jung, C. G., 119–126, 129

Kant, I., 71
Kaplan, B., 278, 355
Kaufmann, W., 116, 129
Kay, P., 108n, 352
Klein, G. S., 79, 352
Klein, M., 58–59, 352
Koffka, K., 3n, 32–35, 38, 352
Köhler, W., 3n, 32, 33, 38, 39, 103, 140, 352–353
Korosy, G., 188n
Kovel, J., 79–80, 353
Kramer, E., 295n, 353
Kris, E., 168, 169, 199, 286, 290, 353
Kubie, L. S., 87n, 231n, 353
Kuhn, T. S., 320, 353

Laing, R. D., 175
Langer, S. K., viii, 48, 73, 80, 105, 109, 162, 173, 180, 246, 353
Language, 166, 167
  Freud on, 84–85, 94, 106
  isolation and, 106–107
  in obsessive intellectualizer, 338
  in psychoanalysis, 106–107, 165, 234–235, 313–322, 326, 331, 342–344
Lenneberg, E. H., 167, 353
Lévy-Bruhl, L., 192
Lewin, K., viii, 4, 29–31, 42, 47, 62, 130, 196, 241, 242, 298, 353
Lewis, H. B., 355
Libido, 12–17, 60, 260, 285–287, 294, 333; *see also* Eros
Lifespace, 292
  concept of, 4, 29–32, 241, 242
  as gestalt, 32, 40–42
Lorenz, K., 63
Luria, A. R., 166, 353

Machover, K., 355
Mahler, M.S., 6n, 33, 178, 353

Manic-depressive illness, 188
Marc, F., 183n
Marx, G., 250
Matching, 121, 129–130, 139–146
  in animals, 63
  in art, 142–144, 171, 172
  Freud on, 102–103, 140, 141
  perceptual identity in, 49–52
  repression and, 154
Maternal deprivation, 257–258
Matte-Blanco, I., 139n, 353
McGhie, A., 304, 350
Meissner, P. B., 355
Memory, 37, 48–50, 96
  denial of, 198, 199, 216–217
  subjectivity in, 54, 319–320
  "unconscious," 134–136
Milner, M., 260, 353
Mirroring, 147–148, 271
  of mother, 263–264, 271, 332–333
  in psychoanalysis, 329–333
Missymbolization, 42, 153–237
  dialogue capacity and, 297–311
  in obsessive, 202–213, 222–236, 309–311; *see also* Intellectualization
  in perceptual identity, 52–60, 74
  picture thinking and, 182–201
  repetitiveness in, 203–210
  repression and, 146, 154–160, 207–209
  see also Desymbolization, Exhibitionistic characters, Introjectors
Mother, 5–6, 11, 13, 241, 326
  of avid introjector, 271–280
  environmental, 241, 260–261, 263
  hallucinatory wish fulfillment and, 251–254
  holding, 247–250, 261, 304, 326
  intrusive, 267–271, 335, 338
  mirroring function of, 263–264, 271, 332–33
  split view of, 57–59
  transitional object and, 254–259
  see also Child development, Infant, Maternal deprivation
Mozart, W. A., 121
Muensterberger, W., xi
Multiple function, 101, 102, 118, 325
Nachmansohn, M., 119, 353
Narcissistic disorders, 148
  in mother, 267–280, 335, 338
  see also Exhibitionistic characters
Narcissus, 148
Neumann, E., 120–125, 142, 353
Neutralization, 114–115, 261, 285–286
Nonsymbolization, 202
Numinosity, 121, 126
Nunberg, H., 14, 55, 145, 287, 353

Obsessive disorders, 101, 107, 203–210, 291
  case example of, 210–213, 222–236
  intellectualizing, 293, 309–311, 317, 320–321, 334, 338–339, 342, 343
Operotropism, 127, 283
Oral incorporation, 193–194

Pair formation, 37, 50, 52, 103, 141; *see also* Matching
Pappenheim, E., 168, 169, 353
Paradox, 245–246, 254, 286, 343–344; *see also* Symboll(s), Janus-face of
Pathology; *see* Borderline disorders, Desymbolization, Missymbolization, Perception distortions, Psychotic
Penfield, W., 78n, 353
Perception
  desymbolization and, 159
  distortions in, 52–60, 74
  energy binding and, 104–105, 112
  Freud on, 72, 94–95, 104–105, 112
  gestalt principles of, 14–15, 32–40
  internal, 34, 78, 95, 96, 173
  recognition in, 50–52
  as symbolizing activity, 69–73
Perceptual identity, search for, 49–52, 103, 130, 142
  pathology in, 52–60
  see also Matching
Phallic stage, 268, 270
Piaget, J., 58, 74, 154, 188, 192, 256, 262, 267, 288, 341n, 353–354
Picard, M., 344, 354
Picasso, P., 170, 226
Picture thinking

acting out and, 182–203
in psychotic, 179–182
Pirandello, L., 189
Plato, 51, 71, 354
Play, 259–261, 274
psychoanalysis and, 278–279, 305–306, 340–342
Play-acting, 188–190
Pleasure principle, 10, 13, 91
Polanyi, M., 219, 220, 320, 354
Popper, K., 143, 354
Portmann, A., 80, 133, 208, 354
Prägnanz, 37–39
Preconscious, 35, 78, 87, 124, 134–139, 231
in artist, 288, 290
in avid introjector, 273
ego and, 91, 110–112
Freud on, 87–88, 95, 97–107, 110–112, 133–134, 137n
id impulses and, 131–132
mother's image and, 263–266
repression and, 156
psychoanalytic treatment and, 89, 217–218, 234, 331
unconscious and, 97–107, 110–111, 124, 134, 137
Presentational symbol, 105, 173–174
Pribram, K. H., 69, 354
Primary process, 9–10, 48, 67–68, 109, 233, 243, 290
desymbolization and, 156–157, 162
Prinzhorn, F., 168n, 169, 354
Projection, 54–55, 306–307
Prometheus, 101n
Protosymbols, 47, 61, 252, 342
Psychoanalytic theory
bias of, 181, 218–222, 320
dichotomized, 45; *see also* Freud, S., dualistic view of
energy concept in, 79–80, 83, 93, 115, 118–119, 222
symbolization in, 44, 73, 75, 85n; *see also* Freud, S., on symbolization
Psychoanalytic treatment, 30–31, 233–237, 313–347
acting out and, 164–165, 303–304
dialogue and, 298, 311, 313–316, 322
gestalt principles and, 34–40, 149–150, 291–292
holding function in, 326–329
interpretation in, 214–222, 314, 316, 319, 340–341
introjectors and, 278–279
language in, 106–107, 165, 234–235, 313–322, 326, 331, 342–344
mirroring function in, 329–333
play in, 278–279, 305–306, 340–342
preconscious in, 89, 217–218, 234, 331
working through in, 132–133
see also Transference
Psychotic, 304–305
art, 168–169, 176–187
thinking; *see* Schizophrenic thinking

Rapaport, D., 149n, 354
Reality principle, 13, 232, 243, 245, 345–346
Regression in service of ego, 199, 290
Reitman, F., 168n, 169, 179–181, 200, 304, 354
Repetition compulsion, 12, 127, 169
Repetitiveness, 203–210
in psychotic art, 169, 177
Repression, 90, 98, 104, 146, 284
in artist, 282–283, 285
desymbolization and, 156–157, 160
"forgetting" vs., 135–137, 216–217
interpretation and, 214–216
missymbolization and, 146, 154–160, 207–209
in obsessive, 205, 207, 210–213, 222–236
psychoanalytic view of, 44, 73, 75, 85n
Resistance, 137, 314
Retardation, principle of, 91n
Reversibility, mental, 188, 193
Rubin, E., 35–36, 144, 354

Sadistic impulses, 58–60, 202–203, 206, 207, 225, 230–231, 234–235, 253; *see also* Thanatos
Sartre, J.-P., 166, 354
Schactel, E. G., 262, 354

Schafer, R., 79, 220, 354
Schicksalsanalysis, 66n, 119, 125–129, 337
Schilder, P., 117–118, 137, 242, 304, 354
Schizoid characters, 302, 305–308, 334
Schizophrenic thinking, 45, 105–106, 304–305
  art and, 168–169, 176–182
  picture thinking and, 179–182
Schrödinger, E., 81, 354
Secondary process, 10, 48–49, 68, 109, 162–163, 232, 233, 243
Segal, H., 59, 305, 354
Shaffer, P., 175
Sharpe, E. F., 315, 354
Signorelli, L., 121
Signs
  in animals, 63, 164
  symbols vs., 162–165, 183, 186–188, 194–196
Silverberg, W. V., 324, 354
Skin-boundary, 248–249, 304
Spinoza, B., 128
Spitz, R. A., 354
Splitting, 57–59, 284
  in obsessive, 207–208, 343
Squiggle-game, 339–340
Stekel, W., vii, 149, 354
Stimulus barrier, 71–73
Strachey, J., 97, 108, 111
Structural theory, 99, 107–116, 137–138
Sublimation, 3, 108n, 127
Superego, in obsessive, 205, 207
Symbol(s), 29–60
  definition of, 16–17, 45–47, 122
  as gestalt, 37, 39, 68–69
  Janus-face of, 45, 68, 106, 131, 150, 204, 315
  presentational, 105, 173–174
  signs vs., 162–165, 183, 186–188, 194–196
Symbolization, 42–52, 103, 104, 116–119, 129–151, 215
  blending in, 96–97, 124, 129–134, 156
  bridging-over function of, 29–60, 70, 106, 131, 153, 233, 266, 273–276, 298–299, 343–344
  centrifugal (internal), 75–151, 278
  definition of, 4–5
  directedness and, 62–67, 81, 164
  distance in, 97, 165–167, 178, 193, 278
  energy binding in, 68, 96–97, 103–104, 129–134, 295
  gestalt formation in, 34–40, 68, 141, 208
  inner space and, 248–249, 263–266
  isomorphic, 74, 75
  matching in, 129–130, 139–146
  ontogenetic origins of, 47–48
  organizing function of, 61–76, 153
  perception in, 50–60, 69–71, 73, 137
  in psychoanalysis, 106–107, 165, 234–235, 313–347
  reality principle and, 232
  secondary process in, 48–49, 162–163, 232
  similarities in, 44–45
  tension regulation and, 67–69
  thinking about in, 97, 147–150, 173, 183
  transitional space and, 252
  translating function of, 73–75, 105, 155, 172
  see also Desymbolization, Missymbolization
Symmetry, 50–51, 81, 140, 324
Symptoms, 155, 287
  as cryptosymbols, 74, 154, 158, 209–210, 213, 223
Szondi, L., viii, ix, 64, 65n–66n, 80, 119, 125–129, 283, 337, 355
Szondi Test, 65n–66n, 125–126

Television, 302–303
Tension regulation, 67–69, 92–93, 130, 156, 243, 250–251, 262
Thanatos, 12–17, 60, 175n, 202, 230, 236; *see also* Aggression, Sadistic impulses
Thing-presentation, 103–106, 123, 141
Thinking about, 97, 147–150, 173, 183
Thoreau, H. D., 298
Time, 9–12, 58, 91, 162, 178, 196, 329,

333; *see also* Hope
Tinbergen, N., 63, 164, 355
Toilet training, 268
Topographic model, 34, 99, 134–139
structural model vs., 108–109, 112n, 137–138
Transference, 165, 279, 299, 306–307, 321–322
perceptual distortion in, 55, 57
in picture-thinkers, 184, 186, 189
Transitional objects, 61, 166, 245, 254–259, 264–265, 342
fetish-like, 257–259, 308
Transitional space, 243, 245–246, 252, 276
in artist, 283, 289, 293
in play stage, 260–261
in psychoanalysis, 325–326, 339–343; *see also* Transference
Trust, 13, 334
basic, 7, 186, 248, 274, 276
in case example, 19–25
Turner, J. M. W., 143

Uexküll, J. von, 63, 355
Unconscious, 35, 77–78, 119
familial, 125, 126, 128
id and, 76, 110
interpretation and, 214–216
Jungian, 120–125
preconscious and, 97–107, 110–111, 124, 134, 137

Valences, 4, 31, 130, 132, 324
definition of, 30
Van Gogh, V., 70, 183n
Verbalization; *see* Language
Verdi, G., 121
Vinci, L. da, 247

Yudovich, F. I., 166, 353

Waelder, R., 101, 118, 207, 325, 355
Wallerstein, J., 178, 350
Wapner, S., 355
Werner, H., 278, 355
Wertheimer, M., 3n, 14, 32, 36, 37, 39, 140, 291, 355
Weyl, S., 91n, 355
Wigner, F. P., 219, 320, 355
Winnicott, D. W., viii, ix, xi, 5, 47, 166, 237, 241–280, 313, 317, 323, 325, 339–340, 342, 343, 346, 355
Wish fulfillment, hallucinatory, 47–48, 61, 243, 250–254
Witkin, H. A., 33, 355
Wittgenstein, L., 165, 314, 326, 355
Wolff, P. H., 262, 355
Word-presentation, 103–106, 123, 141
Working through, 132–133, 150

Zeigarnik, B., 208–210, 355